EUROPEAN FOOTBALL ANNUAL 1993-94

EDITED BY BRUCE SMITH

HEADLINE

First published in 1993
by HEADLINE BOOK PUBLISHING

10 9 8 7 6 5 4 3 2 1

Cover photograph:
Paul Gascoigne of Lazio takes on the Roma defence during the 1-1
draw of 29 November 1992. (*Bob Thomas Sports Photography*)

ISBN 0 7472 4155 4

Typeset by Bruce Smith Books Ltd.

Printed and bound in Great Britain by BPCC Hazell Books Ltd
A Member of BPCC Ltd

HEADLINE BOOK PUBLISHING
A division of Hodder Headline PLC
Headline House
79 Great Titchfield Street
London
W1P 7FN

CONTENTS

Note

In a book of this type it is inevitable that some errors will creep in. While every effort has been made to ensure that the details given in this annual are correct at the time of going to press, neither the editor nor the publishers can accept any responsibilities for errors within.

Summer of Discontent

A close season of discontent quite aptly sums up the various revelations since Marseille lifted the Champions' Cup in Munich on a hot, humid night in May. Several countries around Europe have been rocked by scandalous allegations of match-fixing, bribes and the odd 'bung' here and there. The implications for all concerned are far-reaching and serious and if proven could, indeed should result in some of European football's biggest names being banned and even expelled from international competition. The wheels of football justice turn somewhat too slowly and it may well be another season before any punishment is handed down.

Marseille face the prospect of being relegated to the French Second Division if an inquiry (both judicial and football) into their 1-0 win at Valenciennes proves match-fixing allegations are founded. The French Football Association have proved in the past that they are not frightened to deal with the biggest names – at the end of the 1990-91 season they relegated three clubs, Bordeaux among them, for financial insolvency.

The game had originally been scheduled for Saturday 22 May, but Marseille – due to face Milan in the Champions' Cup final just four days later, had the game brought forward two days. Two Valenciennes players, Christophe Robert and Jacques Glassman, claim that they were phoned the day before the match by Marseille player Jean-Jacques Eydelie and offered the sum of FF250,000 for Valenciennes to 'take it easy'. This sum of money was later found by police buried in the garden of Robert's mother-in-law. The win for Marseille virtually secured them the championship, while condemning Valenciennes to a relegation play-off place from which they failed to escape .

As this can of worms opened, so did another for Marseille in the form of Gennadi Kostylev. The CSKA coach alleged that his players were offered cash to ease up in their Champions League ties. The teams drew 1-1 in Berlin, but the French champions romped to a 6-0 win in Marseille. UEFA are launching their own inquiry and Marseille face the real possibility of being dethroned as Champions of Europe and barred from future European competition. The story will continue.

The Marseille incident seems to be just the tip of the iceberg, though, as revelations of match-fixing have hit Poland, Germany, Turkey, Spain and Italy. The latter has a common history of so-called arranged matches and anybody who saw Channel 4's coverage of game between Milan and Brescia will be well aware of it. Milan, in need of a point for the championship, and Brescia, in need of a point in their battle against relegation, were happy to play their part in an impotent 0-0 draw. Then – in a rush of blood late in the game – Albertini had effectively the first shot of the game and placed Milan in the lead. The look of disbelief on the visitors' faces was there for all to see and less than two minutes later Baresi seemed to stand to one side to allow Brunetti through to equalise and restore the status quo.

In Poland an exciting championship race was made a mockery of on the last day of the season. Legia Warsaw and LKS Lodz entered their final games level on points. Goal difference looked likely to be the deciding factor, with LKS knowing that they would need to win by at least three goals more than Legia to take the title.

Legia won 6-0 at mid-table Wisla Krakow while LKS won 7-1 at lowly Olimpia Pozan.

The very next day the Polish football authorities imposed £18,000 fines on all four clubs because of the uproar the teams' performances had provoked in the media and among those present at the games. Subsequently, both Legia and LKS were stripped of their first and second places - the championship and Champions' Cup place was awarded to third placed Lech Poznan.

Turkey faced its own last-day-of-the-season scandal. Galatasaray and Besiktas entered their final games level on points with goal difference looking to be the deciding factor in the favour of Galatasaray. Both teams faced mid-table opposition. Besiktas defeated Genclerbirligi 3-1 while Galatasaray made sure of the championship by winning 8-0 at Ankaragucu. The next day a newspaper claimed that Yugoslav 'keeper Rade Zalad had been paid $40,000...

And, of course, in England there has been the High Court revelation by Alan Sugar that some managers demanded a 'bung' to facilitate a transfer.

The Polish FA have acted swiftly to deal with their problem and, in an effort to ensure that there is no repeat in future, declared that in future all teams level on points will play off for the championship outright. How quickly the other authorities, and indeed UEFA, move to deal with their own problems remains to be seen. But, at the time of writing, it looks as though the passage of time may well see the alleged perpetrators easy for this season at least. And the passage of time sometimes dulls the memory.

Around Europe

Milan duly won their 13th Italian title, but in the end they fairly stuttered to the championship after their 58-match unbeaten Serie A league run came to an end. Of their final 11 league games they won only one and, despite their fabulous early season unbeaten form, had Internazionale not lost three of their last four games they might have pulled off one of the greatest come-backs of all time. Just how jaded Milan were was clear for all to see in their Champions' Cup final defeat. With the double-Dutch departure of Gullit and Rijkaard, they face a new season without their foundation stone. Indeed, the movement of Gullit to Sampdoria to team up with the much-travelled David Platt might well provide the spur for the Genoans to re-capture their championship form of 1990-91.

But the city of Milan is still not without great Dutch stars. While Gullit and Rijkaard depart from Milan, their greatest rivals have probably produced the coup of the season by employing the services of Dennis Bergkamp (£6.4 million) and Wim Jonk (£4 million).

Perhaps the surprise of the season was the relegation of Fiorentina – one of only three sides to have played in every post-war Serie A championship and their first relegation since 1938. They are relegated along with Brescia, Pescara and Ancona with Cremonese, Lecce, Piacenza and Reggiana promoted.

Despite the allegations, Marseille continued trading unabated and captured Portuguese forward Paulo Futre from Benfica, along with French internationals

William Prunier and Daniel Dutuel from Auxerre and Fabrice Henry from Sochaux. League runners-up Paris Saint-Germain, who await the outcome of the FFA's investigations into Marseille's match against Valenciennes, had the consolation of a 3-0 Cup final win over FC Nantes – only their third ever success in the competition.

In Germany, there was another dramatic finale to the domestic season with Werder Bremen taking their third title when they won 3-0 at outgoing holders VfB Stuttgart. Bayern Munich – who had led the table after 32 games of the 34-match season had been played were overhauled on goal difference after the penultimate round of matches and then drew 3-3 in their final fixture at Schalke. Werder's triumph is all the more remarkable when you consider that they did so without boasting a single current German international on their books. Eintracht Frankfurt may have played a more active role in the Bundesliga had they not fielded a fourth foreigner – like Stuttgart – in their 5-2 win over Bayer Uerdingen. In a subsequent inquiry, the DFB reversed the result of the match and gave it as a 2-0 win to Bayer.

In the Cup, Bayer Leverkusen beat Herther Berlin. It was Leverkusen's first ever appearance in the final of the 59-year-old competition, but it was the amateurs of Berlin who took the headlines in front of 76,000 fanatical supporters in Berlin's Olympic stadium. The collection of engineers, mechanics, salesmen and students were beaten by a single goal just 13 minutes from time.

If ever there was a case of déjà vu then it would have never been more apparent than in Spain on the last day of the domestic league season as history repeated itself. For the second successive season, Real Madrid surrendered a one-point lead to Barcelona on the last day. For the second successive season, Real lost at Tenerife while Barcelona won at home to take the spoils in dramatic fashion. It was the first time in Barca's long history that they have managed three titles in succession and provided coach Johan Cruyff with his ninth trophy in five years at the Nou Camp. Scant consolation for Real a week later was a 2-0 win over Zaragoza in the Spanish Cup final at Valencia. Butragueno put them into a 29th minute lead but Real had to wait until two minutes from time to make sure of the silverware with Lasa netted.

Another side to achieve a hat-trick of title success was FC Porto, although the talking-point in Portugal was Benfica's financial plight. The Lisbon club are estimated to be more than £4 million in debt. Their Cup final 5-2 win over Boavista went a small way to reducing their deficit.

Having spent the previous four seasons fighting against relegation FC Aarau were the surprise package in Switzerland. It was only their third title triumph, the previous two coming in 1912 and 1914. In Austria, FK won the championship for the 22nd time, despite Salzburg leading the pack for much of the season.

In Denmark, FC Copenhagen celebrated their first championship less than a year after being formed. They won 3-2 at arch-rivals Brondby to clinch the title with one round of games left. The match was watched by 18,270 – a record for a club game in Denmark. The European Championship success by the national side has clearly been a catalyst to heighten interest at home. Whether the national side can maintain it by qualifying for the World Cup finals remains to be seen.

About Your Playfair

Your *Playfair European Football Annual* is designed to be your armchair pocket guide to the 1993-94 European season. It provides you with all the facts and information you will need to get the most from the ever-increasing amount of coverage of European football on television and in the press. With the advent of Satellite TV there is not a day during the football season when you cannot watch a game – and, for the majority of the time, a live one at that!

Club Naming Conventions

The increased coverage of football within Europe has meant that we have become more familiar with the local usage of teams names. Wherever possible the current common-place name of a side is used. This is, of course, a subjective decision on my behalf, but hopefully one that will allow you to locate and follow the progress of a particular team through this book and the European season. No doubt this will throw up areas of contention among readers. I'm open to persuasion for future editions!

Introduction

Apart from an editorial overview of the season around the Continent this section also explains how the UEFA classification system works. If you always wanted to know how countries were allocated clubs in the UEFA Cup, the answer is here. The end of this section also provides you with the draws for the preliminary and first rounds of all the major cup competitions.

At A Glance

This section is exactly that and provides you instant access to information such as last season's European competitions' results and the past winners of the various club tournaments.

European Cups

Each of the three major club competitions is covered. It is introduced by a review of the season and this is followed by the results, scorers, times and attendances for each of the games. A complete round-up of all the finals is then given including scorers and teams.

Second Leg Outcomes

This is listed by first leg scorers for each of the three competitions and provides you with a means of gauging the potential outcome of a second leg. The score of the first leg home side is always shown first of all. For example, if the first leg of a tie in the Champions' Cup was goalless then the most likely outcome of the second leg was a 2-0 win for the home team in the second leg.

The Club Section

This is a complete alphabetical listing of all clubs accepted for entry into all three European competitions. Each entry is headed by the club name – the popular format – the country of origin and the particular cup they will compete in, namely C1 (Champions' Cup), C2 (Cup-Winners' Cup) or C3 (UEFA Cup). In many instances this is followed by a brief history of the club and then its full name, address, phone number, stadium, and capacity.

Next comes the club's record in Europe which consists of a summary of all the games played in each of the three particular cup competitions completed with a total playing record. This is provided in the popular PWDLFA format. Below this, the seasons that the club participated in each of the cups is detailed along with the total number of times. Unfortunately, there are a few gaps due to the unknown nature of many of the new teams appearing from the former Soviet Union states.

Country by Country

This section is a guide to all UEFA member countries plus Israel. This provides association details and where possible, final league tables. This is supplemented with 5-year winners guides to domestic league and cup competitions along with the country's international record for the year and the complete record in the European Championship, World Cup qualifying rounds and World Cup finals.

Towards the end of the *Playfair European Football Annual* are details of other competitions, plus reviews of the final stages of both the European Nations Cup and the World Cup. The annual concludes with the fixture lists for the top divisions in several of the major European nations.

Acknowledgments

Many thanks to all those that helped in the task of producing the *Playfair European Football Annual*. In particular, thanks to Phil Heady for club histories and playing records, Martin Ritchie and Peter Fitzpatrick for setting and proofreading and Sue Thearle for the European Cup reviews. Special thanks also to Ian Marshall, my editor at Headline, for his efforts and patience.

The Champions' League

The 1991 Champions' Cup final in Bari between Red Star Belgrade and Marseille was the 100th European final in total. Apart from reaching a century of finals, it also marked the dawning of a new era of Champions' Cup history. For, with the start of the 1991-92 season, the Champions' Cup underwent fundamental changes 36 years after its creation in 1955, and set the scene for what surely will become the much-vaunted European Football League.

In its desire to satisfy the wishes of the big European clubs – several of whom had even threatened to form their own breakaway European League – but also with the objective of adding a breath of fresh air to the Champions' Cup, UEFA decided that the eight clubs left in the competition after the first two rounds would form two groups of four teams, with matches to be played on a league basis. This new Champions' League would produce a one-off final to be contested between the two sides topping their respective groups. The financial implications from the extra matches and televison rights (all now supervised by UEFA) would be huge – and so they have proved to be. Each team reaching this stage would play a minimum of six games – three at home and three away.

The first two seasons have proved to be a huge hit with all concerned, however more changes are afoot for the start of the 1993-94 season. Now, the two teams finishing at the top of each of the two Champions' Leagues will meet in a single game for the right to play in the Champions' Cup final. The team finishing top of Group A will meet the team finishing second in Group B. The team finishing top of Group B will meet the team finishing second in Group A. The venue of the game will be the home stadium of the group winners. When the draw for the Champions' League takes place, the two teams with the best classification in the list of coefficients at the start of the season will be seeded. These two teams will be drawn into the two Champions' League groups from separate pots.

As for the final itself, extra time will be played if both sides are level after 90 minutes and, in the event of both teams still being level at the end of 120 minutes a penalty shoot-out will take place.

Seeding

Since the 1990-91 season, UEFA has tried to pacify the larger clubs who complained of being drawn against each other early on in the competition by introducing a league table of those clubs taking part in the three competitions. This table is drawn up on the basis of the clubs' performance index (number of points plus bonus points divided by number of games played). These teams are classified from 1 to 32 in the Champions' and Cup-Winners' Cups and from 1 to 64 in the UEFA Cup.

The first 16 ranked teams in each of the three competitions are given seeded status and, as a result, cannot meet in the first two rounds.

For the Champions' Cup and the Cup-Winners' Cup there are simply two hats, one containing the seeded clubs and one containing the rest of the clubs, those classified 17 to 32.

For the UEFA Cup, however, it is somewhat more complicated because of the greater number of clubs at the start – 64. In this case, UEFA decided to manipulate the draw by composing eight groups of eight clubs and placing two seeded teams (1 to 16) and six other teams (17 to 64) in each group.

The same system is carried through until the quarter-final stages, when a conventional draw is made to determine both the distribution of the two four-team groups in the Champions' Cup and the four quarter-final pairings in the Cup-Winners' and UEFA Cups.

UEFA Coefficients

Since the creation in 1972 of the UEFA Cup, a competition which brings together those clubs who have finished just behind their respective national champions, UEFA has classified the competing countries by according them a performance index at the end of each season, using a coefficient calculated on the basis of the performances of each country's clubs and the number of clubs entered. Added together over five seasons, these co-efficients enable UEFA to allocate the 64 UEFA Cup places according to the classification of the 32 countries, as follows:

Countries in positions 1 to 3:	4 clubs
Countries in positions 4 to 8:	3 clubs
Countries in positions 9 to 21:	2 clubs
Countries in positions 22 to 32:	1 club

To calculate the co-efficients, UEFA uses the following formula:

- The total number of points accumulated by a country during the course of the season (2 points for a victory, 1 point for a draw, 0 for a defeat) are added to any bonus points gained. One bonus point is obtained for each team qualifying for the quarter-finals, the semi-finals and the final. A team reaching the Champions' League gains a point and a further point for the semi-final stage (from 1993-94) and a further point for reaching the final. In the event of a penalty shoot-out, the points are shared as if the match were drawn, with one point each for the winner and the loser.

- This total is then divided by the number of clubs who entered the three competitions.

A worked example may make this clearer:

At the start of the season Spain has five clubs accepted into European competition, one in the Champions' Cup, one in the Cup-Winners' Cup and three in the UEFA Cup. Let us assume that these five clubs earn a total of 56 points, plus 8 bonus points, giving a grand total of 64 points.

Spain's performance index for this season is therefore the following:

$$64 \text{ (number of points) } /5 \text{ (number of teams) } = 12.800$$

This index is then added to those of the previous four seasons. A similar index is calculated for each of the UEFA member countries and the five-year totals used to form a league ranking from which UEFA Cup entries are allocated.

As the European Cups are run parallel to national championships (the old Soviet Union and the Scandinavian countries excepted), the UEFA Cup place allocation is made a year ahead of the actual competition. Thus, to make the allocation for the 1993-94 season, the five seasons from 1987-88 to 1991-92 are the ones taken into account.

Note that Israel are not members of UEFA and therefore do not come into the overall classification. For both these reasons they are not eligible to enter the UEFA Cup.

UEFA Overall Classification for 1987/88 – 1991/92

Pos	Country	Points
1	Italy	52.837
2	Germany	42.927
3	Spain	40.266
4	Belgium	37.633
5	France	37.250
6	Holland	27.500
7	Portugal	27.366
8	Russia	25.666
9	Yugoslavia*	25.516
10	Romania	24.550
11	RCS †	20.000
12	Scotland	19.750
13	England	19.250
14	Austria	18.000
15	Denmark	16.665
16	Greece	16.500
17	Turkey	14.998
18	Switzerland	14.750
19	Poland	12.166
20	Sweden	12.100
21	Hungary	11.500
22	Bulgaria	10.416
23	Finland	9.999
24	Wales*	9.000
25	Albania*	7.666
26	Iceland	5.000
27	Norway	4.999
28	Cyprus	4.000
29	Northern Ireland	3.332
30	Republic of Ireland	2.665
31	Malta	1.999
32	Luxembourg	1.665
33	Latvia*	
34	Liechtenstein*	
35	Lithuania*	
36	Estonia*	

Pos	Country	Points
37	Slovenia	
38	Faeroe Islands*	
39	Ukraine	
40	Israel*	

* Did not participate in the 1992-93 UEFA Cup.
† RCS = Representation of Czechs and Slovaks – the former Yugoslavia.

European Cup Draws
1993-94

Key to abbreviations

		Geo	Georgia	Nor	Norway
Alb	Albania	Ger	Germany	Pol	Poland
Aus	Austria	Gre	Greece	Por	Portugal
Bel	Belgium	Hol	Holland	Rep. Ire	Rep. of Ireland
Biel	Bielorussia	Hun	Hungary	Rom	Romania
Bul	Bulgaria	Ice	Iceland	Rus	Russia
Cro	Croatia	Isr	Israel	Sco	Scotland
Cyp	Cyprus	Ita	Italy	Slova	Slovakia
Czech	Czech	Lat	Latvia	Slove	Slovenia
	Republic	Liech	Liechtenstein	Esp	Spain
Den	Denmark	Lit	Lithuania	Swe	Sweden
Eng	England	Lux	Luxembourg	Swi	Switzerland
Est	Estonia	Mal	Malta	Tur	Turkey
Fae	Faeroe Islands	Mold	Moldavia	Ukr	Ukraine
Fin	Finland	N. Ire	Northern	Wal	Wales
Fra	France		Ireland		

Champions' Cup Preliminary Round

To be played over two legs with the first named clubs at home in the first-leg.
Matches to be played on August 17-18 and August 31 or September 1.

Avenir Beggen (Lux)	v	Rosenborg BK (Nor)
Cwmbran Town (Wal)	v	Cork City (Rep. Ire)
Ekranas Panevezys (Lith)	v	Floriana (Mal)
HJK Helsinki (Fin)	v	Norma Tallinn (Est)
Iberya (Dynamo) Tbilisi (Geo)	v	Linfield (N. Ire)
Omonia Nicosia (Cyp)	v	FC Aarau (Swi)
Partizani Tirana (Alb)	v	IA Akranes (Ice)
Skonto Riga (Lat)	v	Olimpija Ljubljana (Slove)
Tofta B68 (Fae)	v	Croatia Zagreb (Cro)
Zimbru Kishinev (Mold)	v	Beitar Jerusalem (Isr)

Champions' Cup 1st Round

To be played over two legs with the first named clubs at home in the first-leg.
Matches to be played on September 14-15 and September 28-29.

AIK Stockholm (Swe)	v	Sparta Prague (Czech)
Avenir Beggen (Lux)		
or Rosenborg BK (Nor)	v	Austria Vienna (Aus)
Dynamo Kiev (Ukr)	v	Barcelona (Esp)
FC Porto (Por)	v	Ekranas Panevezys (Lith)
		or Floriana (Mal)
Galatasaray (Tur)	v	Cwmbran Town (Wal)
		or Cork City (Rep. Ire)
HJK Helsinki (Fin)		
or Norma Tallinn (Est)	v	RSC Anderlecht (Bel)
Honved Kipest (Hun)	v	Manchester United (Eng)
Iberya Tbilisi (Geo)		
or Linfield (N. Ire)	v	FC Copenhagen (Den)
Lech Poznan (Pol)	v	Zimbru Kishinev (Mold)
		or Beitar Jerusalem (Isr)
Marseille (Fra)	v	AEK Athens (Gre)
Omonia Nicosia (Cyp)		
or FC Aarau (Swi)	v	Milan (Ita)
Partizani Tirana (Alb)		
or IA Akranes (Ice)	v	Feyenoord (Hol)
Rangers (Sco)	v	Levski Sofia (Bul)
Skonto Riga (Lat)		
or Olimpija Ljubljana (Slove)	v	Spartak Moscow (Rus)
Steaua Bucharest (Rom)	v	Tofta B68 (Fae)
		or Croatia Zagreb (Cro)
Werder Bremen (Ger)	v	Dinamo Minsk (Biel)

Cup-Winners' Cup Preliminary Round

To be played over two legs with the first named clubs at home in the first-leg.
Matches to be played on August 17-18 and August 31 or September 1.

Bangor (N. Ire)	v	Apoel Nicosia (Cyp)
Belzers (Liech)	v	Albpetrol (Alb)
FC Lugano (Swi)	v	Neman Grodno (Biel)

Karpaty Lvov (Ukr)	v	Shelbourne (Rep. Ire)
Maccabi Haifa (Isr)	v	Dudelange (Lux)
Nikol Tallinn (Est)	v	Lillestrom SK (Nor)
OB Odense (Den)	v	Publikum Celje (Slova)
RAF Jelgava (Lat)	v	Havnar HB (Fae)
Sliema Wanderers (Mal)	v	Degerfors IF (Swe)
Valur (Ice)	v	MyPa (Fin)
VSZ Kosice (Slove)	v	Zhalgiris Vilnius (Lith)

Cup-Winners' Cup 1st Round

To be played over two legs with the first named clubs at home in the first-leg. Matches to be played on September 14-15 and September 28-29.

Bangor (N. Ire)		
or Apoel Nicosia (Cyp)	v	Paris Saint-Germain (Fra)
Bayer Leverkusen (Ger)	v	Zbrojovka Brno (Czech)
Benfica (Por)	v	GKS Katowice (Pol)
Besiktas (Tur)	v	VSZ Kosice (Slove)
		or Zhalgiris Vilnius (Lith)
CSKA Sofia (Bul)	v	Belzers (Liech)
		or Albpetrol (Alb)
FC Tirol-Innsbruck (Aus)	v	Ferencvaros (Hun)
Hajduk Split (Cro)	v	Ajax (Hol)
Nikol Tallinn (Est)		
or Lillestrom SK (Nor)	v	Torino (Ita)
OB Odense (Den)		
or Publikum Celje (Slova)	v	Arsenal (Eng)
Panathinaikos (Gre)	v	Karpaty Lvov (Ukr)
		or Shelbourne (Rep. Ire)
Real Madrid (Esp)	v	FC Lugano (Swi)
		or Neman Grodno (Biel)
Sliema Wanderers (Mal)		
or Degerfors IF (Swe)	v	Parma (Ita)
Standard Liege (Bel)	v	Cardiff City (Wal)
Torpedo Moscow (Rus)	v	Dudelange (Lux)
		or Maccabi Haifa (Isr)
Universitatea Craiova (Rom)	v	RAF Jelgava (Lat)
		or Havnar HB (Fae)
Valur (Ice)		
or MyPa (Fin)	v	Aberdeen (Sco)

UEFA Cup 1st Round

To be played over two legs with the first named clubs at home in the first-leg.
Matches to be played on September 14-15 and September 28-29.

AaB Aalborg (Den)	v	Deportivo La Coruna (Esp)
Admira Wacker (Aus)	v	Dnepr Dnepropetrovsk (Ukr)
Bohemians (Rep. Ire)	v	Bordeaux (Fra)
Borussia Dortmund (Ger)	v	Spartak Vladikavkaz (Rus)
Botev Plovdiv (Bul)	v	Olympiakos (Gre)
Brondby (Den)	v	Dundee United (Sco)
Crusaders (N. Ire)	v	Servette (Swi)
Dinamo Bucharest (Rom)	v	Cagliari (Ita)
Dinamo Moscow (Rus)	v	Eintracht Frankfurt (Ger)
FC Nantes (Fra)	v	Valencia (Esp)
FC Twente (Hol)	v	Bayern Munich (Ger)
Gloria Bistrita (Rom)	v	Maribor Branik (Slova)
Heart of Midlothian (Sco)	v	Atletico Madrid (Esp)
IFK Norrkoping (Swe)	v	KV Mechelen (Bel)
Internazionale (Ita)	v	Rapid Bucharest (Rom)
Juventus (Ita)	v	Lokomotiv Moscow (Rus)
Karlsruhe SC (Ger)	v	PSV Eindhoven (Hol)
Kocaelispor Kulubu (Tur)	v	Sporting Lisbon (Por)
KR Reykjavik (Ice)	v	MTK Budapest (Hun)
Kuusysi Lahti (Fin)	v	KSV Waregem (Bel)
Lazio (Ita)	v	Lokomotiv Plovdiv (Bul)
Norwich City (Eng)	v	Vitesse Arnhem (Hol)
Osters IF (Swe)	v	Kongsvinger IL (Nor)
Royal Antwerp (Bel)	v	Maritimo (Por)
Slavia Prague (Czech)	v	OFI Crete (Gre)
Slovan Bratislava (Slova)	v	Aston Villa (Eng)
SV Casino Salzburg (Aus)	v	Dac Dunjaska Streda (Slova)
Tenerife (Esp)	v	Monaco (Fra)
Trabzonspor (Tur)	v	Valletta (Mal)
US Luxembourg (Lux)	v	Boavista FC (Por)
Vac FC Samsung (Hun)	v	Apollon Limassol (Cyp)
Young Boys Berne (Swit)	v	Celtic (Sco)

The Champions' Cup
1992-93 Results at a Glance

Rd	Team One	Team Two	1L	2L	Agg
PR	Kl Kalksvikar	Skonto Riga	1-3	0-3	1-6
PR	Olimpija Ljubljana	Norma Tallinn	3-0	2-0	5-0
PR	Shelbourne	Tavria Simferopol	0-0	1-2	1-2
PR	Valetta	Maccabi Tel Aviv	0-2	0-1	0-3
1R	AEK Athens †	Apoel	1-1	2-2	3-3
1R	Barcelona	Viking Stavanger	1-0	0-0	1-0
1R	FK Austria	CSKA Sofia	3-1	2-3	5-4
1R	Glentoran	Marseille	0-5	0-3	8-0
1R	IFK Gothenburg	Besiktas	2-0	1-2	3-2
1R	Kuusysi Lahti	Dinamo Bucharest	1-0	0-2	1-2
1R	Lech Poznan	Skonto Riga	2-0	0-0	2-0
1R	Maccabi Tel Aviv	Club Bruges	0-1	0-3	0-4
1R	Milan	Olimpija Ljubljana	4-0	3-0	7-0
1R	PSV Eindhoven	Zhalgiris Vilnius	6-0	2-0	8-0
1R	Rangers	Lyngby	2-0	1-0	3-0
1R	Sion	Tavria Simferopol	4-1	3-1	7-2
1R	Slovan Bratislava	Ferencvaros	4-1	0-0	4-1
1R	Stuttgart †	Leeds United	3-0	1-4	4-4
	Replay ordered as Stuttgart fielded an ineligible player.				
	Leeds United	Stuttgart	2-1		6-5
1R	US Luxembourg	FC Porto	1-4	0-5	9-1
1R	Vikingur Reykjavik	CSKA Moscow	0-1	0-4	0-5
2R	AEK Athens †	PSV Eindhoven	1-0	0-3	1-3
2R	Club Bruges †	FK Austria	2-0	1-3	3-3
2R	CSKA Moscow	Barcelona	1-1	3-2	4-3
2R	Dinamo Bucharest	Marseille	0-0	0-2	0-2
2R	IFK Gothenburg	Lech Poznan	1-0	3-0	4-0
2R	Rangers	Leeds United	2-1	2-1	4-2
2R	Sion	FC Porto	2-2	0-4	6-2
2R	Slovan Bratislava	Milan	0-1	0-4	5-0

Champions League – Pool A

Club Bruges	CSKA Moscow	1-0	2-1
Rangers	Marseille	2-2	1-1
CSKA Moscow	Rangers	0-1	0-0
Marseille	Club Bruges	3-0	1-0
Club Bruges	Rangers	1-1	1-2
CSKA Moscow	Marseille	1-1	0-6

Final Table		Cty	P	W	D	L	F	A	Pts
1.	Marseille	Fra	6	3	3	0	14	4	9
2.	Rangers	Sco	6	2	4	0	7	5	8
3.	Club Bruges	Bel	6	2	1	3	5	8	5
4.	CSKA Moscow	CIS	6	0	2	4	2	11	2

Champions League – Pool B

Milan	IFK Gothenburg	4-0	1-0
FC Porto	PSV Eindhoven	2-2	1-0
IFK Gothenburg	FC Porto	1-0	0-2
PSV Eindhoven	Milan	1-2	0-2
PSV Eindhoven	IFK Gothenburg	1-3	0-3
FC Porto	Milan	0-1	0-1

Final Table		Cty	P	W	D	L	F	A	Pts
1.	Milan	Ita	6	6	0	0	11	1	12
2.	IFK Gothenburg	Swe	6	3	0	3	7	8	6
3.	FC Porto	Por	6	2	1	3	5	5	5
4.	PSV Eindhoven	Hol	6	0	1	5	4	13	1

Final

| Marseille | Milan | 1-0 |

† Win on away goals rule: * after extra time

The Champions' Cup Finals 1956-93 at a Glance

Year	Date	Winners	Finalists	Score	Att.
1956	13/6/56	Real Madrid	Stade de Reims	4-3	38,000
1957	30/5/57	Real Madrid	Fiorentina	2-0	124,000
1958	28/6/58	Real Madrid	Milan	3-2*	67,000
1959	03/6/59	Real Madrid	Stade de Reims	2-0	80,000
1960	18/5/60	Real Madrid	Eintracht Frankfurt	7-3	135,000
1961	31/5/61	Benfica	Barcelona	3-2	27,000
1962	02/5/62	Benfica	Real Madrid	5-3	65,000
1963	22/5/63	Milan	Benfica	2-1	45,000
1964	27/5/64	Internazionale	Real Madrid	3-1	72,000
1965	27/5/65	Internazionale	Benfica	1-0	85,000
1966	11/5/66	Real Madrid	Partizan Belgrade	2-1	55,000
1967	25/5/67	Celtic	Internazionale	2-1	54,000
1968	29/5/68	Manchester United	Benfica	4-1*	100,000
1969	28/5/69	Milan	Ajax	4-1	31,000
1970	06/5/70	Feyenoord	Celtic	2-1*	53,000
1971	02/6/71	Ajax	Panathinaikos	2-0	83,000
1972	31/5/72	Ajax	Internazionale	2-0	61,000
1973	30/5/73	Ajax	Juventus	1-0	89,000
1974	15/5/74	Bayern Munich	Atletico Madrid	1-1*	49,000
	17/5/74	Bayern Munich	Atletico Madrid	4-0†	23,000
1975	28/5/75	Bayern Munich	Leeds United	2-0	48,000
1976	12/5/76	Bayern Munich	Saint-Etienne	1-0	63,000
1977	25/5/77	Liverpool	B. Monchengladbach	3-1	52,000
1978	10/5/78	Liverpool	Club Bruges	1-0	92,000
1979	30/5/79	Nottingham Forest	Malmo FF	1-0	57,000
1980	28/5/80	Nottingham Forest	SV Hamburg	1-0	50,000
1981	27/5/81	Liverpool	Real Madrid	1-0	48,000
1982	26/5/82	Aston Villa	Bayern Munich	1-0	46,000
1983	25/5/83	SV Hamburg	Juventus	1-0	75,000
1984	30/5/84	Liverpool	Roma	1-1	69,000
1985	29/5/85	Juventus	Liverpool	1-0	58,000
1986	07/5/86	Steaua Bucharest	Barcelona	0-0	70,000
		Steaua won 2-0 on penalties			
1987	27/5/87	FC Porto	Bayern Munich	2-1	56,000

1988	25/5/88	PSV Eindhoven	Benfica	0-0	55,000
		PSV Eindhoven won 6-5 on penalties			
1989	24/5/89	Milan	Steaua Bucharest	4-0	97,000
1990	23/5/90	Milan	Benfica	1-0	57,000
1991	29/5/91	Red Star Belgrade	Marseille	0-0	50,000
		Red Star Belgrade won 5-3 on penalties			
1992	20/5/92	Barcelona	Sampdoria	1-0	71,000
1993	26/5/93	Marseille	Milan	1-0	73,300

*† Replay * After extra time.*

The Cup-Winners' Cup
1992-93 Results at a Glance

Rd	Team One	Team Two	1L	2L	Agg
PR	Avenir Beggen	B36 Thorshavn	1-0	1-1	2-1
PR	Maribor Branik	Hamrun Spartans	4-0	1-2	5-2
PR	Stromsgodset	Hapoel Tel Aviv	0-2	0-2	0-4
PR	Vaduz (Liechtenstein)	Chernomorets	0-5	1-7	1-12
1R	AIK Stockholm	AGF Aarhus †	3-3	1-1	4-4
1R	Airdrieonians	Sparta Prague	0-1	1-2	1-3
1R	Glenavon	Royal Antwerp	1-1	1-1	2-2
	Antwerp win 3-1 on penalties after extra time				
1R	Werder Bremen	Hannover	3-1	1-2	4-3
1R	Bohemians (Dublin)	Steaua Bucharest	0-0	0-4	0-4
1R	Maribor Branik	Atletico Madrid	0-3	1-6	1-9
1R	Cardiff City	Admira Wacker	1-1	0-2	1-3
1R	Feyenoord †	Hapoel Tel Aviv	1-0	1-2	2-2
1R	Levski Sofia	Lucerne †	2-1	0-1	2-2
1R	Liverpool	Apollon	6-1	2-1	8-2
1R	Miedz Legnica	Monaco	0-1	0-0	0-1
1R	Spartak Moscow	Avenir Beggen	0-0	5-1	5-1
1R	Parma	Ujpest Dozsa	1-0	1-1	2-1
1R	Trabzonspor	TPs Turun	2-0	2-2	4-2
1R	Olympiakos	Chernomorets	0-1	3-0	3-1
1R	Valur	Boavista	0-0	0-3	0-3
2R	AGF Aarhus	Steaua Bucharest †	3-2	1-2	4-4
2R	Admira Wacker	Royal Antwerp *	2-4	4-3	6-7
2R	Lucerne	Feyenoord	1-0	1-4	2-4
2R	Monaco	Olympiakos	0-1	0-0	0-1
2R	Parma	Boavista	0-0	2-0	2-0
2R	Spartak Moscow	Liverpool	4-2	2-0	6-2
2R	Trabzonspor	Atletico Madrid	0-2	0-0	0-2
2R	Werder Bremen	Sparta Prague	2-3	0-1	2-4
QF	Royal Antwerp †	Steaua Bucharest	0-0	1-1	1-1
QF	Feyenoord	Spartak Moscow	0-1	1-3	1-4

QF	Olympiakos	Atletico Madrid	1-1	1-3	2-4
QF	Sparta Prague	Parma	0-0	0-2	0-2
SF	Atletico Madrid	Parma †	1-2	1-0	2-2
SF	Spartak Moscow	Royal Antwerp	1-0	1-3	2-3
F	Parma	Royal Antwerp	3-1		

*† Win on away goals rule. * After extra time*

Cup-Winners' Cup Finals 1961-93 at a Glance

Year	Date			Score	Att.
1961	17/5/61	Rangers	Fiorentina	0-2	80,000
	27/5/61	Fiorentina	Rangers	2-1	50,000
	Fiorentina win 4-1 on aggregate				
1962	10/5/62	Atletico Madrid	Fiorentina	1-1	27,000
	05/9/62	Atletico Madrid	Fiorentina	3-0†	38,000
1963	15/5/63	Tottenham Hotspur	Atletico Madrid	5-1	49,000
1964	13/5/64	Sporting Lisbon	MTK Budapest	3-3	3,000
	15/5/64	Sporting Lisbon	MTK Budapest	1-0†	19,000
1965	19/5/65	West Ham United	1860 Munich	2-0	100,000
1966	05/5/66	Borussia Dortmund	Liverpool	2-1	41,000
1967	31/5/67	Bayern Munich	Rangers	1-0	69,000
1968	23/5/68	Milan	SV Hamburg	2-0	53,000
1969	21/5/69	Slovan Bratislava	Barcelona	3-2	19,000
1970	29/4/70	Manchester City	Gornik Zabrze	2-1	8,000
1971	19/5/71	Chelsea	Real Madrid	1-1	42,000
	21/5/71	Chelsea	Real Madrid	2-1†	35,000
1972	24/5/72	Rangers	Dinamo Moscow	3-2	24,000
1973	16/5/73	Milan	Leeds United	1-0	45,000
1974	08/5/74	Magdeburg	Milan	2-0	4,000
1975	14/5/75	Dinamo Kiev	Fenencvaros	3-0	10,000
1976	05/5/76	RCS Anderlecht	West Ham Utd	4-2	58,000
1977	11/5/77	SV Hamburg	RSC Anderlecht	2-0	66,000
1978	03/5/78	RSC Anderlecht	Austria Vienna	4-0	48,000
1979	16/5/79	Barcelona	Fortuna D'dorf	4-3	58,000
1980	15/5/80	Valencia	Arsenal	0-0	36,000
	Valencia won 5-4 on penalties				
1981	13/5/81	Dinamo Tbilisi	Carl Zeiss Jena	2-1	9,000
1982	12/5/82	Barcelona	Standard Liege	2-1	100,000
1983	11/5/83	Aberdeen	Real Madrid	2-1	17,000
1984	16/5/84	Juventus	FC Porto	2-1	60,000
1985	15/5/85	Everton	Rapid Vienna	3-1	50,000
1986	02/5/86	Dinamo Kiev	Atletico Madrid	3-0	39,000
1987	13/5/87	Ajax	L'tive Leipzig	1-0	35,000
1988	11/5/88	KV Mechelen	Ajax	1-0	40,000

1989	10/5/89	Barcelona	Sampdoria	2-0	45,000
1989	09/5/90	Sampdoria	RSC Anderlecht	2-0	20,000
1991	15/5/91	Manchester United	Barcelona	2-1	42,000
1992	06/5/92	Werder Bremen	Monaco	2-0	15,000
1993	12/5/93	Parma	Royal Antwerp	3-1	37,393

The UEFA Cup
1992-93 Results at a Glance

Rd	Team One	Team Two	1L	2L	Agg
1R	Admira Wacker	Roma	1-4	0-1	1-5
1R	Austria Salzburg	Ajax	0-3	1-3	1-6
1R	Benfica	Belvedur Izola	3-0	5-0	8-0
1R	Caen	Real Zaragoza	3-2	0-2	3-4
1R	Cologne	Celtic	2-0	0-3	2-3
1R	Dinamo Kiev †	Rapid Vienna	1-0	2-3	3-3
1R	Dinamo Moscow	Rosenborg	5-1	0-2	5-3
1R	Electroputere Craiova	Panathinaikos	0-6	0-4	0-10
1R	FC Copenhagen	MP Mikkeli	5-0	5-1	10-1
1R	Fenerbahce	Botev Plovdiv	3-1	2-2	5-3
1R	Floriana	Borussia Dortmund	0-1	2-7	2-8
1R	Fram Reykjavik	Kaiserslautern	0-3	0-4	0-7
1R	GKS Katowice	Galatasaray	0-0	1-2	1-2
1R	Grasshoppers Zurich*	Sporting Lisbon	1-2	3-1	4-3
1R	Hibernian	RCS Anderlecht †	2-2	1-1	3-3
1R	IFK Norrkoping	Torino	1-0	0-3	1-3
1R	Juventus	Anorthosis	6-1	4-0	10-1
1R	KV Mechelen	Orebro	2-1	0-0	2-1
1R	Lokomotiv Plovdiv	Auxerre	2-2	1-7	3-9
1R	Manchester United	Torpedo Moscow	0-0	0-0	0-0
	Torpedo win 4-3 on penalties after extra time				
1R	Paris Saint-Germain	PAOK Salonika	1-0	2-0	3-0
1R	Politehnica Timisoara	Real Madrid	1-1	0-4	1-5
1R	Sheffield Wednesday	Spora Luxembourg	8-1	2-1	10-2
1R	Sigma Olomouc	Uniuversitatae Craiova	1-0	2-1	3-1
1R	Slavia Prague	Heart of Midlothian	1-0	2-4	3-4
1R	Standard Liege	Portadown	5-0	0-0	5-0
1R	Vaci Izzo	Groningen	1-0	1-1	2-1
1R	Valencia	Napoli	1-5	0-1	1-6
1R	Vitesse Arnhem	Derry City	3-0	2-1	5-1
1R	Vitoria Guimaraes	Real Sociedad	3-0	0-2	3-2
1R	Widzew Lodz	Eintracht Frankfurt	2-2	0-9	2-11
1R	Xamax Neuchatel	Frem Copenhagen	2-2	1-4	3-6

2R	RCS Anderlecht	Dinamo Kiev	4-2	3-0	7-2
2R	Auxerre	FC Copenhagen	5-0	2-0	7-0
2R	Benfica	Vaci Izzo	5-1	1-0	6-1
2R	Borussia Dortmund	Celtic	1-0	2-1	3-1
2R	Eintracht Frankfurt	Galatasaray	0-0	0-1	0-1
2R	Fenerbahce	Sigma Olomouc	1-0	1-7	2-7
2R	Frem Copenhagen	Real Zaragoza	0-1	1-5	1-6
2R	Heart of Midlothian	Standard Liege	0-1	0-1	0-2
2R	Kaiserslautern	Sheffield Wednesday	3-1	2-2	5-3
2R	Napoli	Paris Saint-Germain	0-2	0-0	0-2
2R	Panathinaikos	Juventus	0-1	0-0	0-1
2R	Real Madrid	Torpedo Moscow	5-2	2-3	7-5
2R	Roma	Grasshoppers Zurich	3-0	3-4	6-4
2R	Torino	Dinamo Moscow	1-2	0-0	1-2
2R	Vitoria Guimaraes	Ajax	0-3	1-2	1-5
2R	Vitesse Arnhem	KV Mechelen	1-0	1-0	2-0
3R	Ajax	Kaiserslautern	2-0	1-0	3-0
3R	Borussia Dortmund	Real Zaragoza	3-1	1-2	4-3
3R	Dinamo Moscow	Benfica	2-2	0-2	2-4
3R	Paris Saint-Germain †	RSC Anderlecht	0-0	1-1	1-1
3R	Roma	Galatasaray	3-1	2-3	5-4
3R	Sigma Olomouc	Juventus	1-2	0-5	1-7
3R	Standard Liege	Auxerre	2-2	1-2	3-4
3R	Vitesse Arnhem	Real Madrid	0-1	0-1	0-2
QF	Auxerre	Ajax	4-2	0-1	4-3
QF	Benfica	Juventus	2-1	0-3	2-4
QF	Real Madrid	Paris Saint-Germain	3-1	1-4	4-5
QF	Roma	Borussia Dortmund	1-0	0-2	1-2
SF	Borussia Dortmund	Auxerre	2-0	0-2	2-2
	Borussia Dortmund win 6-5 on penalties.				
SF	Juventus	Paris Saint-Germain	2-1	1-0	3-1
F	Borussia Dortmund	Juventus	1-3	0-3	1-6

† *Win on away goals rule* * *After extra time*

UEFA Cup Finals
1958-93 at a Glance

Year	Team One	Team Two	1L	2L	Agg
1958	London Select XI	Barcelona	2-2	0-6	2-8
1960	Birmingham City	Barcelona	0-0	1-4	1-4
1961	Birmingham City	Roma	2-2	0-2	2-4
1962	Valencia	Barcelona	6-2	1-1	7-3
1963	Dinamo Zagreb	Valencia	1-2	0-2	1-4
1964	Real Zaragoza	Valencia	2-1		
1965	Ferencvaros	Juventus	1-0		
1966	Barcelona	Real Zaragoza	0-1	4-2	4-3
1967	Dinamo Zagreb	Leeds United	2-0	0-0	2-0
1968	Leeds United	Ferencvaros	1-0	0-0	1-0
1969	Newcastle United	Ujpest Dozsa	3-0	3-2	6-2
1970	RSC Anderlecht	Arsenal	3-1	0-3	3-4
1971	Juventus	Leeds United †	2-2	1-1	3-3
1972	Wolverhampton W.	Tottenham Hotspur	1-2	1-1	2-3
1973	Liverpool	B. Monchengladbach	3-0	0-2	3-2
1974	Tottenham Hotspur	Feyenoord	2-2	0-2	2-4
1975	Bor. Monchengladbach	FC Twente	0-0	5-1	5-1
1976	Liverpool	Club Bruges	3-2	1-1	4-3
1977	Juventus†	Athletic Bilbao	1-0	1-2	2-2
1978	Sec Bastia	PSV Eindhoven	0-0	0-3	0-3
1979	Red Star Belgrade	B.Monchengladbach	1-1	0-1	1-2
1980	Bor. Monchengladbach	Eintracht Frankfurt†	3-2	0-1	3-3
1981	Ipswich Town	AZ 67 Alkmaar	3-0	2-4	5-4
1982	IFK Gotenburg	SV Hamburg	1-0	3-0	4-0
1983	RSC Anderlecht	Benfica	1-0	1-1	2-1
1984	RSC Anderlecht	Tottenham Hotspur	1-1	1-1	2-2
	Tottenham won 4-3 on penalties				
1985	Videoton SC	Real Madrid	0-3	1-0	1-3
1986	Real Madrid	Cologne	5-1	0-2	5-3
1987	IFK Gothenburg	Dundee United	1-0	1-1	2-1
1988	Espanol	Bayer Leverkusen	3-0	0-3	3-3
	Bayer win 3-2 on penalties				
1989	Napoli	VfB Stuttgart	2-1	3-3	5-4
1990	Juventus	Fiorentina	3-1	0-0	3-1
1991	Internazionale	Roma	2-0	0-1	2-1
1992	Torino	Ajax†	2-2	0-0	2-2
1993	Borussia Dortmund	Juventus	1-3	0-3	1-6

European Footballer of the Year 1956-1992

From France Football

1956	Stanley Mathews	Blackpool	Eng	47
	Alfredo Di Stefano	Real Madrid	Esp	44
1957	Alfredo Di Stefano	Real Madrid	Esp	72
	Billy Wright	Wolverhampton Wdrs	Eng	19
1958	Raymond Kopa	Real Madrid	Fra	71
	Helmut Rahn	Rot-Weiss Essen	Frg	40
1959	Alfredo Di Stefano	Real Madrid	Esp	80
	Raymond Kopa	Stade de Reims	Fra	42
1960	Luis Suarez	Barcelona	Esp	54
	Ferenc Puskas	Real Madrid	Hun	37
1961	Omar Sivori	Juventus	Ita	46
	Luis Suarez	Internazionale	Esp	40
1962	Josef Masopust	Dukla Prague	Tch	65
	Eusebio	Benfica	Por	–
1963	Lev Yashin	Dinamo Moscow	Urs	73
	Gianni Rivera	Milan	Ita	56
1964	Denis Law	Manchester United	Sco	61
	Luis Suarez	Internazionale	Esp	43
1965	Eusebio	Benfica	Por	–
	Giacinto Facchetti	Internazionale	Ita	–
1966	Bobby Charlton	Manchester United	Eng	81
	Eusebio	Benfica	Por	80
1967	Florian Albert	Ferencvaros	Hun	68
	Bobby Charton	Manchester United	Eng	40
1968	George Best	Manchester United	N.Ire	61
	Bobby Charlton	Manchester United	Eng	53
1969	Gianni Rivera	Milan	Ita	83
	Gigi Riva	Cagliari	Ita	79
1970	Gerd Muller	Bayern Munich	Frg	77
	Bobby Moore	West Ham United	Eng	69
1971	Johan Cruyff	Ajax	Hol	116
	Sandro Mazzola	Internazionale	Ita	57
1972	Franz Beckenbauer	Bayern Munich	Frg	81
	Gerd Muller	Bayern Munich	Frg	79

29

1973	Johan Cruyff	Barcelona	Hol	96
	Dino Zoff	Juventus	Ita	47
1974	Johan Cruyff	Barcelona	Hol	116
	Franz Beckenbauer	Bayern Munich	Frg	105
1975	Oleg Blokhin	Dynamo Kiev	Urs	122
	Franz Beckenbauer	Bayern Munich	Frg	42
1976	Franz Beckenbauer	Bayern Munich	Frg	91
	Robby Rensenbrink	RSC Anderlecht	Hol	75
1977	Allan Simonsen	Bor.Monchengladbach	Den	74
	Kevin Keegan	Liverpool	Eng	71
1978	Kevin Keegan	SV Hamburg	Eng	87
	Hans Krankl	Rapid Vienna	Aut	81
1979	Kevin Keegan	SV Hamburg	Eng	118
	Karl-Heinz Rummenigge	Bayern Munich	Frg	52
1980	Karl-Heinz Rummenigge	Bayern Munich	Frg	122
	Bernd Schuster	Barcelona	Frg	34
1981	Karl-Heinz Rummenigge	Bayern Munich	Frg	106
	Paul Breitner	Bayern Munich	Frg	64
1982	Paolo Rossi	Juventus	Ita	115
	Alain Giresse	Bordeaux	Fra	64
1983	Michel Platini	Juventus	Fra	110
	Kenny Dalglish	Liverpool	Sco	26
1984	Michel Platini	Juventus	Fra	128
	Jean Tigana	Bordeaux	Fra	57
1985	Michel Platini	Juventus	Fra	127
	Preben Elkjaer-Larsen	Hellas Verona	Den	48
1986	Igor Belanov	Dynamo Kiev	Urs	84
	Gary Lineker	Barcelona	Eng	62
1987	Ruud Gullit	Milan	Hol	106
	Paolo Rutre	Atletico Madrid	Por	91
1988	Marco Van Basten	Milan	Hol	129
	Ruud Gullit	Milan	Hol	88
1989	Marco Van Basten	Milan	Hol	119
	Franco Baresi	Milan	Ita	80
1990	Lothar Matthaus	Internazionale	Frg	137
	Salvatore Schillaci	Juventus	Ita	84
1991	Jean-Pierre Papin	Marseile	Fra	141
	Darko Pancev	Red Star Belgrade	Yug	42
1992	Marco Van Basten	Milan	Hol	98
	Hristo Stoichkov	Barcelona	Bul	80

Champions' Cup 1992-93

Olympique Boli!

Bernard Tapie finally achieved his life-long ambition when Marseille were crowned Champions of Europe on a humid evening in Munich. Basile Boli's glanced nearpost header from Abedi Pele's corner two minutes from half time still separated the teams 47 minutes later and provided an historic first Champions' Cup success for French football proving once and for all that Milan's policy of spend, spend, spend could not guarantee them outright success. That the French champions' victory would subsequently become tarnished by allegations of match-rigging, brought disgrace and dishonour to a club who had successfully perpetrated one of the greatest upsets of the competition.

Milan, orchestrated by the charismatic media mogul Silvio Berlusconi, who had invested some £35 million on a so-called 'dream team' last summer, started the final as hot favourites despite having their invincible tag dented. Their undefeated league run came to an end after 58 games – almost two years of Serie A competition. Milan, it should be remembered had also won the Champions' Cup twice in the previous four years.

But Marseille could look to the two clubs' last meeting in the competition in 1991, when Marseille clinched an unexpected quarter-final victory over the then champions and so incensed the Italians that Milan incurred a 12-month ban from the competition for trying to get the contest abandoned.

Despite losing the likes of Waddle, Papin and Mozer, all of whom had contributed so much to Marseille's disappointing excursion to the final of 1991, the French had blossomed thanks to the devastating form of German international Rudi Voller, basking in the twilight of his career, and the contribution of Ghanaian Abedi Pele and Croatian striker Alen Boksic.

Problems Mount

Despite their position as favourites, Milan went into the match with selection problems of their own. Dutch striker Marco Van Basten had just returned from a troublesome ankle injury and was still finding his way back to full fitness. Fellow-countryman Frank Rijkaard chose the eve of the final to announce that he would be leaving Milan at the end of the season and Ruud Gullit wasn't even selected for the squad. And, just to emphasise the power of the Italian champions' squad, French striker Jean-Pierre Papin was left on the substitutes' bench.

His replacement on this occasion was Daniele Massaro, whose early profligacy was destined to cost Milan dear. Massaro had four clear chances to give his side the lead in the first half, but each was spurned or wasted.

Marseille had offered efforts from Voller and Boksic to trouble the Italian defence in the first half, and two minutes before the interval the French side forced a corner. Pele stepped up to take it and planted an inch-perfect centre onto the head of defender Boli, who forced his way through a crowd of players to glance his header past Rossi.

Milan brought on Papin less than 10 minutes into the second half, but the diminutive striker could do little to galvanise his side into life, missing his only clearcut opportunity to score with 15 minutes left.

At the final whistle the French fans were sent into a paroxysms of ecstasy, as 72-year-old coach Raymond Goethals celebrated a shrewd tactical victory, and the Italians were left to ponder the wisdom in investing so much money in a team that had failed them.

Foreign Fields

The 1992-93 competition will doubtless be remembered as much for what happened off the field as on it. With the French bribery scandal set to run and run long after the final itself has receded into distant memory, the progress of the British teams was to be much admired.

Without doubt the tie of the first round was Leeds United's epic against Stuttgart. Making their first appearance in European competition for 17 years, Leeds lost the first leg in Germany 3-0 and looked certain to exit the competition despite a valiant 4-1 fightback in the second leg at Elland Road.

But, remarkably, the Germans were found to have fielded an illegal foreign player and UEFA ordered the match to be replayed in Barcelona on a Friday night, after Leeds had been awarded a 3-0 home result. Happily for English football, justice was seen to be done when substitute Carl Shutt gave his side a well-deserved victory with a late winner, after the irrepressible Gordon Strachan had put Leeds in front.

However, the Yorkshire side's joy was short-lived. The second round draw threw up the intriguing prospect of a Championship of Britain, the English champions against Scottish champions Rangers, who eventually ran out relatively easy winners.

Gary McAllister struck the first blow in this epic contest, scoring an unbelievable 25-yard drive after just two minutes of the first leg. But on a wet and windy night at Ibrox, Rangers fought their way back into contention thanks to a goal from poacher extraordinaire Ally McCoist and an own goal from Leeds keeper John Lukic, who inexplicably punched the ball into his own net direct from a corner.

Regrettably Leeds did not fare much better in the second leg. Mark Hateley produced a spectacular 30-yard volley again after just two minutes of the contest, and McCoist added a second before Leeds could reply with a late consolation from Eric Cantona. Rangers continued to produce explosive and resilient football in the Champions' League, only to exit the competition unbeaten courtesy of an impoverished goal difference which handed a final slot to Marseille.

Reigning champions Barcelona almost went out at the first hurdle, scraping a 1-0 victory over Norwegian side Viking Stavanger. But their luck did not last long, being knocked out in round two by CSKA Moscow. The result was made all the more improbable because CSKA were trailing 2-0 after the first leg at the Nou Camp, but somehow rallied themselves sufficiently to produce a 3-0 result in front of their own fans in Moscow.

The two Champions' Leagues, such a successful and progressive innovation, consisted of Rangers, Marseille, CSKA Moscow and Club Bruges in Group A and Milan, IFK Gothenburg, FC Porto and PSV Eindhoven in Group B.

But, despite the battle royal in Group A between Rangers and Marseille for qualification, with Rangers drawing twice with the French champions, 2-2 and 1-1, Milan completely dominated their group, with surprisingly little objection from FC Porto or PSV.

Preliminary Round

Kl Kalksvikar Danielsen (4)	**Skonto Riga** Astatiev (28, 46), Semenov (89)	**1-3**	**1,500**
Skonto Riga Yeliseyev (4), Semyonev (38), Astafiev (52)	**KL Klaksvikar**	**3-0**	**3,000**

Skonto Riga win 6-1 on aggregate

Olimpija Ljubljana Ubavic (50), Topic (52), Vrabac (72)	**Norma Tallin**	**3-0**	**3,000**
Norma Tallinn	**Olimpija Ljubljana** Zulic (27), Djuranovic (89)	**0-2**	**1,000**

Olimpija win 5-0 on aggregate

Shelbourne	**Tavria Simferopol**	**0-0**	**4,000**
Tavria Simferopol Shevchenko (8), Sheikhametov (13)	**Shelbourne** Dally (41)	**2-1**	**16,000**

Tavria win 2-1 on aggregate

Valletta	**Maccabi Tel Aviv** Cohen (83), Nimni (88)	**0-2**	**3,000**
Maccabi Tel Aviv Melika (23)	**Valletta**	**1-0**	**5,000**

Maccabi win 3-0 on aggregate

1st Round

AEK Athens	**Apoel Nicosia**	**1-1**	**28,000**
Alexandris (41)	Hadjilukas (72)		
Apoel Nicosia	**AEK Athens**	**2-2**	**16,000**
Gogic (77), Sasulitis (84)	Sabanadzovic (30), Alexandris (70)		

AEK win 3-3 on away goals rule

Barcelona	**Viking Stavanger**	**1-0**	**36,000**
Amor (86)			
Viking Stavanger	**Barcelona**	**0-0**	**12,041**

Barcelona win 1-0 on aggregate

FK Austria	**CSKA Sofia**	**3-1**	**7,000**
Hasenhuttl (16), Fridrikas (82)	Shiskov (57)		
Kogler (90)			
CSKA Sofia	**FK Austria**	**3-2**	**8,000**
Metkov (4), Andonov (60, 72 pen)	Flogel (26), Ivanauskas (68)		

FK Austria win 5-4 on aggregate

Glentoran	**Marseille**	**0-5**	**8,000**
	Voller (4), Martin Vazquez (22, 29),		
	Sauzee (42), Ferreri (85)		
Marseille	**Glentoran**	**3-0**	**10,000**
Omam Biyrik (6), Pele (13), Boli (72)			

Marseille win 8-0 on aggregate

IFK Gothenburg	**Besiktas**	**2-0**	**5,923**
Eskelinen (72), Ekstrom (82)			
Besiktas	**IFK Gothenburg**	**2-1**	**31,400**
Metin (25), Feyyaz (73)	Eskelinen (11)		

IFK win 3-2 on aggregate

Kuusysi Lahti	**Dinamo Bucharest**	**1-0**	**1,330**
Rinne (17)			
Dinamo Bucharest	**Kuusysi Lahti**	**2-0**	**14,000**
Gerstenmajer (63), Demollanri (116)			

Dinamo win 2-1 on aggregate after extra time

Lech Poznan	**Skonto Riga**	**2-0**	**10,000**
Trzeciak (26), Podbrozny (41)			
Skonto Riga	**Lech Poznan**	**0-0**	**3,500**

Lech win 2-0 on aggregate

Maccabi Tel Aviv	Club Bruges	0-1	17,000
	Staelens (35)		
Club Bruges	Maccabi Tel Aviv	3-0	7,000
Staelens (60), Verheyen (77, 85)			

Bruges win 4-0 on aggregate

Milan	Olimpija Ljubljana	4-0	14,300
Van Basten (5, 49), Albertini (7), Papin (64)			
Olimpija Ljubljana	Milan	0-3	12,000
	Massaro (31), Rijkaard (50), Tassotti (85)		

Milan win 7-0 on aggregate

PSV Eindhoven	Zhalgiris Vilnius	6-0	13,000
E Koeman (24), Elleman (35, 59, 64) Kieft (68), Numan (78)			
Zhalgiris Vilnius	PSV Eindhoven	0-2	4,500
	Numan (26), Romario (39)		

PSV win 8-0 on aggregate

Rangers	Lyngby	2-0	40,036
Hateley (40), Huistra (67)			
Lyngby	Rangers	0-1	4,237
	Durrant (84)		

Rangers win 3-0 on aggregate

Sion	Tavria Simferopol	4-1	8,500
Hottiger (17), Tulio (31, 73), Assis (76)	Shevchenko (84 pen)		
Tavria Simferopol	Sion	1-3	10,000
Shevchenko (69 pen)	Tulio (67), Carlos Luis (77), Domingos (88)		

Sion win 7-2 on aggregate

Slovan Bratislava	Ferencvaros	4-1	25,000
Costic (19), Dubovsky (51, 53), Morvec (83)	Lipcsei (75)		
Ferencvaros	Slovan Bratislava	0-0	25,500

Slovan win 4-1 on aggregate

Stuttgart	Leeds United	3-0	38,000
Walter (62, 68), Buck (82)			
Leeds United	Stuttgart	4-1	20,457
Speed (18), McAllister (38), Cantona (66), Chapman (80)	Buck (33)		

Stuttgart win on away goals but replay ordered as
Stuttgart field an ineligible player

| **Leeds United** | **Stuttgart** | 2-1 | 10,000 |
| Strachan (34), Shutt (76) | Golke (40) | | |

Leeds win 6-5 on aggregate

US Luxembourg	**FC Porto**	1-4	4,000
Deville (63)	Semedo (41), Fernando Couto (47),		
	Toni (51), Domingos (89)		
FC Porto	**US Luxembourg**	5-0	30,000
Kostadinov (16, 32), Toni (26, 61),			
Jose Carlos (67)			

Porto win 9-1 on aggregate

Vikingur Reykjavik	**CSKA Moscow**	0-1	1,000
	Korsakov (75)		
CSKA Moscow	**Vikingur Reykjavik**	4-0	10,000
Sergevey (24), Korsakov (37),			
Grishin (44), Kolesnikov (89)			

CSKA win 5-0 on aggregate

2nd Round

AEK Athens	**PSV Eindhoven**	1-0	27,000
Dimitriadis (53)			
PSV Eindhoven	**AEK Athens**	3-0	21,750
Romario (5, 50, 84)			

PSV win 3-1 on aggregate

Club Bruges	**FK Austria**	2-0	16,000
Verheyen (35), Booy (41)			
FK Austria	**Club Bruges**	3-1	15,500
Zsak (49), Fridrikas (73), Ivanauskas (90)	Van der Heyden (65)		

3-3 aggregate, Club Bruges win on away goals rule

CSKA Moscow	**Barcelona**	1-1	32,500
Grishin (18)	Beguiristain (60)		
Barcelona	**CSKA Moscow**	2-3	63,500
Nadal (12), Beguiristain (31)	Buchmanov (44),		
	Mashkarin (56), Korsakov (60)		

CSKA win 4-3 on aggregate

Dinamo Bucharest	**Marseille**	0-0	28,000
Marseille	**Dinamo Bucharest**	2-0	30,000
Boksic (35, 69)			

Marseille win 2-0 on aggregate

IFK Gothenburg	Lech Poznan	1-0	8,800
Bengtsson (85)			
Lech Poznan	IFK Gothenburg	0-3	28,000
	Ekstrom (27), M Nilsson (47), Mild (83)		

Gothenburg win 4-0 on aggregate

Rangers	Leeds United	2-1	44,000
Lukic (21 o.g.), McCoist (37)	McAllister (1)		
Leeds United	Rangers	1-2	25,118
Cantona (85)	Hateley (3), McCoist (59)		

Rangers win 4-2 on aggregate

Sion	FC Porto	2-2	14,800
Orlando (55), Assis (61)	Semedo (80), Couto (82) `		
FC Porto	Sion	4-0	35,000
Jorge Costa (50), Domingos (55),			
Kostadinov (63), Jaime Magalhaes (87)			

Porto win 6-2 on aggregate

Slovan Bratislava	Milan	0-1	35,000
	Maldini (61)		
Milan	Slovan Bratislava	4-0	27,500
Boban (28), Rijkaard (29), Simone (49),			
Papin (71)			

Milan win 5-0 on aggregate

Champions League – Group A

Club Bruges	CSKA Moscow	1-0	21,500
Amokachi (17)			
Rangers	Marseille	2-2	41,624
McSwegan (76), Hateley (82)	Boksic (31), Voller (55)		
CSKA Moscow	Rangers	0-1	9,000
	Ferguson (13)		
Marseille	Club Bruges	3-0	30,000
Sauzee (4 pen), Boksic (10, 26)			
Club Bruges	Rangers	1-1	19,000
Dziubinski (44)	Huistra (72)		
CSKA Moscow	Marseille	1-1	20,000
Faizulin (55)	Pele (27)		
Marseille	CSKA Moscow	6-0	40,000
Sauzee (4 pen, 34, 48), Pele (42),			
Ferreri (70), Desailly (78)			
Rangers	Club Bruges	2-1	42,731
Durrant (40), Nisbet (71)	Staelens (51)		

| Marseille | Rangers | 1-1 | 40,000 |
Sauzee (18) — Durrant (52)

| CSKA Moscow | Club Bruges | 1-2 | 2,500 |
Sergeyev (18) — Schaessens (43), Verheyen (83)

| Club Bruges | Marseille | 0-1 | 19,000 |
Boksic (2)

| Rangers | CSKA Moscow | 0-0 | 43, 142 |

Final Table

Team	Cty	P	W	D	L	F	A	Pts
Marseille	Fra	6	3	3	0	14	4	9
Rangers	Sco	6	2	4	0	7	5	8
Club Bruges	Bel	6	2	1	3	5	8	5
CSKA Moscow	CIS	6	0	2	4	2	11	2

Champions League – Group B

Milan — **IFK Gothenburg** — 4-0 61,000
Van Basten (33, 53 pen, 61, 62)

FC Porto — **PSV Eindhoven** — 2-2 50,000
Jaime Magalhaes (35), Jose Carlos (75) — Romario (43, 60)

IFK Gothenburg — **FC Porto** — 1-0 22,303
Eriksson (87)

PSV Eindhoven — **Milan** — 1-2 27,000
Romario (66) — Rijkaard (19), Simone (62)

PSV Eindhoven — **IFK Gothenburg** — 1-3 27,500
Numan (7) — Nilsson (19), Ekstrom (34, 44)

FC Porto — **Milan** — 0-1 55,000
Papin (71)

IFK Gothenburg — **PSV Eindhoven** — 3-0 35,250
Nilsson (2), Ekstrom (44), Martinsson (48)

Milan — **FC Porto** — 1-0 67,389
Eranio (31)

IFK Gothenburg — **Milan** — 0-1 40,300
Massaro (70)

PSV Eindhoven — **FC Porto** — 0-1 25,750
Jose Carlos (77 pen)

FC Porto — **IFK Gothenburg** — 2-0 15,000
Ze Carlos (42), Timofte (56)

Milan — **PSV Eindhoven** — 2-0 56,862
Simone (5, 18)

Final Table

Team	Cty	P	W	D	L	F	A	Pts
Milan	Ita	6	6	0	0	11	1	12
IFK Gothenburg	Swe	6	3	0	3	7	8	6
FC Porto	Por	6	2	1	3	5	5	5
PSV Eindhoven	Hol	6	0	1	5	4	13	1

Final

26th May 1993   Olympiastadion, Munich

Marseille   **Milan**   **1-0 64,444**

Boli (43)

Marseille: Barthez, Angloma (Sub: Durand 61 min), Boli, Desailly, Di Meco, Eydelie, Deschamps, Sauzee, Pele, Boksic, Voller (Sub: Thomas 80 min).

Milan: Rossi, Tassotti, Baresi, Costacurta, Maldini, Rijkaard, Albertini, Donadoni (Sub: Papin 55 min), Lentini, van Basten (Sub: Eranio 85 min), Massaro.

Champions' Cup Final Details 1955/56-1992/93

1956

13th June, 1956   *Parc des Princes, Paris*   *38,000*

Real Madrid   **4**   **Stade de Reims**   **3**

Di Stefano (14), Rial (30, 79), Marquitos 67   Leblond (6), Templin (10), Hidalgo (62)

Real Madrid: Alonso, Atienza, Marquitos, Lesmes, Munzo, Zarraga, Joseito, Marchal, Di Stefano, Rial, Gento. Tr: Villalonga
Stade de Reims: Jacuet, Zimny, Jonquet, Giraudo, Leblond, Siatka, Hidalgo, Glovacki, Bilard, Templin. Tr: Batteaux

1957

30th May, 1957   *Bernabeu, Madrid*   *124,000*

Real Madrid   **2**   **Fiorentina**   **0**

Di Stefano (70), Gento (76)

Real Madrid: Alonso, Torres, Marquitos, Lemes, Munoz, Zarraga, Kopa, Mateos, Di Stefano, Rial, Gento. Tr: Villalonga
Fiorentina: Sarti, Magnini, Orzan, Cervato, Scaramucci, Segato, Julinho, Gratton, Virgili, Monturori, Bizzarri. Tr: Bernardini.

1958

28th June, 1958   *Heysel, Brussels*   *67,000*

Real Madrid   **3**   **Milan**   **2**

Di Stefano (74), Rial (79), Gento (107)   Schiaffino (69), Grillo (78)

Real Madrid: Alonso, Atienza, Santamaria, Lesmes, Santisteban, Zarraga, Kopa, Joseito, Di Stefano, Rial, Gento. Tr: Carniglia
Milan: Soldan, Fontana, Maldini, Beraldo, Bergamaschi, Radice, Danova, Liedolm, Schiaffino, Grillo, Cucchiaroni. Tr: Viani

1959

3rd June, 1959   *Neckarstadion, Stuttgart*   *80,000*

Real Madrid   **2**   **Stade de Reims**   **0**

Mateos (2), Di Stefano (47)

Real Madrid: Dominguez, Marquitos, Santamaria Zarraga, Santisteban, Ruiz, Kopa, Mateos, Di Stefano, Rial, Gento. Tr: Carniglia

Stade de Reims: Colonna, Rodzik, Jonquet, Giraudo, Penverne, Leblond, Lamartine, Bilard, Fontaine, Piantoni, Vincent. Tr: Batteux

1960

18th May, 1960   *Hampden Park, Glasgow*   135,000

Real Madrid   **7**   **Eintracht Frankfurt**   **3**

Di Stefano (27, 30, 77), Puskas (45, 56, 60,71)   Kress (10), Stein (64, 72)
Real Madrid: Dominguez, Marquitos, Santamaria, Pachin, Vidal, Zarraga, Canario, Del Sol, Di Stefano, Puskas, Gento. Tr Munoz
Eintracht Frankfurt: Loy, Lutz, Eigenbrodt, Hofer, Weilbacher, Stinka, Kress, Lindner, Stein, Pfaff, N. Meier. Tr: Oswald

1961

31st May 1961   *Wankdorf, Berne*   27,000

Benfica   **3**   **Barcelona**   **2**

Aguas (30) Own Goal (32), Coluna (55)   Kocsis (20), Czibor (75)
Benfica: Costa Pereira, Joao, Germano, Angelo, Netro, Cruz, Augusto, Sontana, Aguas, Coluna, Cavem. Tr: Guttmann
Barcelona: Ramellets, Foncho, Gensana, Gracia, Verges, Garay, Kubala, Kocsis, Evaristo, Suarez, Czibor. Tr: Orizaola

1962

2nd May, 1962   *Olympisch Stadion, Amsterdam*   65,000

Benfica   **5**   **Real Madrid**   **3**

Aguas (25), Cavem (34), Coluna (51),   Puskas (17, 23, 38)
Eusebio (65, 68)
Benfica: Costa Pereira, Joao, Germano, Angelo, Cavem, Cruz, Augusto, Eusebio, Aguas, Coluna, Simoes. Tr: Guttmann
Real Madrid: Araquistain, Casado, Santamaria, Miera, Felo, Pachin, Tejada, Del Sol, Di Stefano, Puskas, Gento. Tr: Munoz

1963

22nd May, 1963   *Wembley, London*   45,000

Milan   **2**   **Benfica**   **1**

Altafini (58, 70)   Eusebio (19)
Milan: Ghezzi, David, Maldini, Trebbi, Benitez, Trapattoni, Pivatelli, Sani, Altafini, Rivera, Mora. Tr: Rocco
Benfica: Costa Pereira, Cavem, Cruz, Humberto, Raul, Coluna, Santana, Augusto, Torres, Eusebio, Simoes. Tr: Riera

1964

27th May, 1964   *Prater, Vienna*   *72,000*
Internazionale   **3**   **Real Madrid**   **1**
Mazzola (43, 76), Milani (61)   Felo (70)
Internazionale: Sarti, Burgnich, Guarneri, Facchetti, Tagnin, Picchi, Jair,
Mazzola, Milani, Suarez, Corso. Tr: Herrera
Real Madrid: Vicente, Isidro, Santamaria, Pachin, Zoco, Muller, Amancio,
Felo, Di Stefano, Puskas, Gento. Tr: Munoz

1965

27th May, 1965   *San Siro, Milan*   *85,000*
Internazionale   **1**   **Benfica**   **0**
Jair (42)
Internazionale: Sarti, Burgnich, Guarneri, Facchetti, Bedin, Picchi, Jair,
Mazzola, Peiro, Suarez, Corso. Tr: Herrera
Benfica: Costa Pereira, Cavem, Cruz, Germano, Raul, Neto, Coluna,
Augusto, Eusebio, Torres, Simoes. Tr: Schwartz

1966

11th May, 1966   *Heysel, Brussels*   *55,000*
Real Madrid   **2**   **Partizan Belgrade**   **1**
Amancio (70), Serena (75)   Vasovic (55)
Real Madrid: Araquistain Pachin, De Felipe, Zoco, Sanchis, Pirri, Velazquez,
Serena, Amancio, Grosso, Gento. Tr: Munoz
Partizan Belgrade: Soskic, Jusufi, Rasovic, Vasovic, Milhailovic, Kovacevic,
Becejac, Bajic, Hasanagic, Galic, Pirmajer. Tr: Gegic

1967

25th May, 1967   *Estadio Nacional, Lisbon*   *54,000*
Celtic   **2**   **Internazionale**   **1**
Gemmell (63), Chalmers (85)   Mazzola (8)
Celtic: Simpson, Craig, McNeill, Gemmell, Murdoch, Clark, Johnstone,
Wallace, Chalmers, Auld, Lennox. Tr: Stein
Internazionale: Sarti, Burgnich, Guarneri, Facchetti, Bedin, Picchi,
Domenghini, Mazzola, Cappellini, Bicicli, Corso. Tr: Herrera

1968

29th May 1968   *Wembley Stadium, London* 100,000
Manchester United   **4**   **Benfica**   **1**
Charlton (53, 99), Best (93), Kidd (94)   Graca (75)
Manchester United: Stepney, Brennan, Stiles, Foulkes, Dunne, Crerand,
Charlton, Sadler, Best, Kidd, Aston. Tr: Busby

Benfica: Henrique, Adolfo, Humberto, Jacinto, Cruz, Graca, Coluna, Augusto, Eusebio, Torres, Simones. Tr: Otto Gloria

1969

28th May, 1969		*Bernabeu, Madrid*	*31,000*
Milan	**4**	**Ajax**	**1**
Prati (7, 40, 75), Sormani (67)		Vasovic (60)	

Milan: Cudicini, Malatrasi, Anquilletti, Schnellinger, Rosato, Trapattoni, Londetti, Rivera, Hamrin, Sormani, Prati. Tr: Rocco
Ajax: Bals, Suurbier (Muller), Hulshoff, Vasovic, Van Duivenbode, Pronk, Groot (Nuninga), Swart, Cruyff, Danielsson, Keizer. Tr: Michels

1970

6th May, 1970		*San Siro, Milan*	*53,000*
Feyenoord	**2**	**Celtic**	**1**
Israel (31), Kindvall (117)		Gemmell (29)	

Feyenoord: Fieters Graafland, Romeijn (Haak), Laseroms, Israel, Van Duivenbode, Hasil, Jansen, Van Hanegem, Wery, Kindvall, Moulijn. Tr: Happel
Celtic: Williams, Hay, Grogan, McNeill, Gemmell, Murdoch, Auld (Connelly), Johnstone, Lennox, Wallace, Hughes. Tr: Stein

1971

2nd June, 1971		*Wembley, London*	*83,000*
Ajax	**2**	**Panathinaikos**	**0**
Van Dijk (5) Own Goal (87)			

Ajax: Stuy, Neeskens, Hulshoff, Vasovic, Suurbier, Rijnders (Blankenburg), Muhren G, Swart (Haan), Cruyff, Van Dijk, Keizer. Tr: Michels
Panathinaikos: Oeconomopoulos, Tomaras, Kapsis, Sourpis, Viahos, Kamaras, Ileferakia, Gammos, Antoniadis, Domazos, Filakouris. Tr: Puskas

1972

31st May, 1972		*Feyenoord, Rotterdam*	*61,000*
Ajax	**2**	**Internazionale**	**0**
Cruyff (47, 78)			

Ajax: Stuy, Suurbier, Blankenburg, Hulshoff, Krol, Neeskens, Haan, Muhren G, Swart, Cruyff, Keizer. Tr: Kovacs
Internazionale: Bordon, Burgnich, Facchetti, Bellugi, Oriali, Giubertoni (Bertini), Bedin, Frustalupi, Jair (Pellizarro), Mazzola, Boninsegna. Tr: Invernizzi

1973

30th May, 1973   *Red Star, Belgrade*   *89,000*
Ajax   **1**   **Juventus**   **0**
Rep (4)
Ajax: Stuy, Suurbier, Hulshoff, Blankenburg, Krol, Neeskens, Muhren G,
Haan, Rep, Cruyff, Keizer. Tr: Kovacs
Juventus: Zoff, Salvadore, Marchetti, Morini, Longobucco, Causio
(Cuccureddu), Furino, Capello, Altafini, Anastasi, Bettega (Haller).
Tr: Vycpalek

1974

15th May, 1974   *Heysel, Brussels*   *49,000*
Bayern Munich   **1**   **Atletico Madrid**   **1**
Schwarzenbeck (119)   Luis (114)
Bayern Munich: Maier, Hansen, Breitner, Schwarzenbeck, Beckenbauer, Roth,
Zobel, Hoeness, Torstensson (Durnberger), Muller, Kapellmann. Tr: Lattek
Atletico Madrid: Reina, Melo, Capon, Adelardo, Heredia, Luis, Eusebio,
Irureta, Ufarte (Becerra), Garate, Salcedo (Alberto). Tr: Lorenzo

Replay – 17th May, 1974   *Heysel, Brussels*   *23,000*
Bayern Munich   **4**   **Atletico Madrid**   **0**
Hoeness (28, 83), Muller (58, 71)
Bayern Munich: Maier, Hansen, Breitner, Schwarzenbeck, Beckenbauer,
Roth, Zobel, Hoeness, Torstensson, Muller, Kapellmann. Tr: Lattek
Atletico Madrid: Reina, Melo, Capon, Adelardo (Benegas), Heredia, Luis,
Eusebio, Alberto (Ufarte), Garate, Salcedo, Becerra. Tr: Lorenzo

1975

28th May, 1975   *Parc des Princes, Paris*   *48,000*
Bayern Munich   **2**   **Leeds United**   **0**
Roth (71), Muller (81)
Bayern Munich: Maier, Beckenbauer, Schwarzenbeck, Durnberger,
Andersson (Weiss), Zobel, Roth, Kapellmann, Hoeness (Wunder), Muller,
Torstensson. Tr: Cramer
Leeds United: Stewart, Reaney, Gray F, Madeley, Hunter, Bremner, Giles,
Yorath (Gray E), Lorimer, Clarke, Jordan. Tr: Armfield

1976

12th May, 1976   *Hampden Park, Glasgow*   *63,000*
Bayern Munich   **1**   **Saint-Etienne**   **0**
Roth (57)

Bayern Munich: Maier, Hansen, Schwarzenbeck, Beckenbauer, Horsmann, Roth, Durnberger, Kapellmann, Rummenigge, Muller, Hoeness. Tr: Cramer
Saint-Etienne: Curkovic, Repellini, Piazza, Lopez, Joanvion, Bathenay, Santini, Larque, Revelli P, Revelli H, Sarramagna (Rocheteau). Tr: Herbin

1977

25th May, 1977   *Stadio Olimpico, Rome,*   52,000

Liverpool   **3**   **B. Monchengladbach**   **1**

McDermott (29), Smith (67), Neal (85)   Simonsen (50)

Liverpool: Clemence, Neal, Jones, Smith, Hughes, Case, Kennedy, Callaghan, McDermott, Keegan, Heighway. Tr: Paisley
Bor. Monchengladbach: Kneib, Vogts, Klinkhammer, Wittkamp, Schaffer, Wohlers (Hannes), Wimmer (Kulik), Stielike, Bonhof, Simonsen, Heynckes. Tr: Lattek

1978

10th May, 1978   *Wembley, London*   92,000

Liverpool   **1**   **Club Bruges**   **0**

Dalglish (64)

Liverpool: Clemence, Neal, Thompson, Hansen, Hughes, McDermott, Kennedy, Souness, Case (Heighway), Fairclough, Dalglish, Tr: Paisley
Club Bruges: Jensen, Bastijns, Krieger, Leekens, Maes (Volders), Cook, Decubber, Vandereycken, Ku (Sanders), Simoen, Sorensen. Tr: Happel

1979

30th May, 1979   *Olympiastadion, Munich*   57,000

Nottingham Forest   **1**   **Malmo**   **0**

Francis (45)

Nottingham Forest: Shilton, Anderson, Lloyd, Burns, Clark, Francis, McGovern, Bowyer, Robertson, Woodcock, Birtles. Tr: Clough
Malmo: Moller, Andersson R, Jonsson, Andersson M, Erlandsson, Tapper (Malmber), Ljungberg, Prytz, Kinnvall, Hansson (Andersson T), Cervin. Tr: Houghton

1980

28th May, 1980   *Bernabeu, Madrid*
50,000

Nottingham Forest   **1**   **SV Hamburg**   **0**

Robertson (21)

Nottingham Forest: Shilton, Anderson, Gray (Gunn), Lloyd, Burns, O'Neill, McGovern, Bowyer, Mills (O'Hare), Robertson, Birtles. Tr: Clough
SV Hamburg: Kargus, Kaltz, Nogly, Buljan, Jakobs, Hieronymus (Hrubesch), Magath, Memering, Keegan, Reimann, Milewski. Tr: Zebec.

1981

27th May, 1981   *Parc des Princes, Paris*   48,000

Liverpool   1   **Real Madrid**   0

Kennedy A (82)

Liverpool: Clemence, Neal, Thompson, Hansen, Kennedy A, Lee, McDermott, Souness, Kennedy R, Dalglish (Case), Johnson. Tr: Paisley
Real Madrid: Agustin, Cortes (Pineda), Navajas, Sabido, Del Bosque, Angel, Camacho, Stielike, Juanito, Santillana, Cunningham. Tr: Boskov

1982

26th May, 1982   *Feyenoord, Rotterdam*   46,000

Aston Villa   1   **Bayern Munich**   0

Withe (67)

Aston Villa: Rimmer (Spink), Swain, Evans, McNaught, Williams, Bremner, Cowans, Mortimer, Shaw, Withe, Morley. Tr: Barton
Bayern Munich: Muller, Dremmler, Weiner, Augenthaler, Horsmann, Mathy (Guttler), Breitner, Kraus (Niedermayer), Durnberger, Rummenigge, Hoeness. Tr: Csernai

1983

25th May, 1983   *Olympiako Stadio, Athens*   75,000

SV Hamburg   1   **Juventus**   0

Magath (7)

Hamburg: Stein, Kaltz, Hieronymous, Jakobs, Wehmeyer, Groh, Folff, Magath, Milewski, Bastrup (Von Heesen), Hrubesch. Tr: Happel
Juventus: Zoff, Gentile, Brio, Scirea, Cabrini, Bonini, Tardelli, Bettega, Platini, Rossi (Marocchino), Boniek. Tr: Trapattoni

1984

30th May, 1984   *Stadio Olimpico, Rome*   69,000

Liverpool   1   **Roma**   1

Neal (13)   Pruzzo (42)

Liverpool: Grobbelaar, Neal, Lawrenson, Hansen, Kennedy A, Johnston (Nicol), Lee, Souness, Whelan, Dalglish (Robinson), Rush. Tr: Fagan
Roma: Tancredi, Nappi, Bonetti, Righetti, Nela, Di Bartolonei, Falcao, Cerezo (Strukelj), Conti, Pruzzo (Chierico), Graziani. Tr: Liedholm
After extra time. Liverpool won 4-2 on penalties

1985

29th May, 1985   *Heysel, Brussels*   *58,000*
Juventus   **1**   **Liverpool**   **0**
Platini (56)
Juventus: Tacconi, Favero, Cabrini, Brio, Scirea, Bonini, Platini, Tardelli, Briaschi (Prandelli), Rossi (Vignola), Boniek. Tr: Trapattoni
Liverpool: Grobbelaar, Neal, Beglin, Lawrenson (Gillespie), Hansen, Nicol, Dalglish, Whelan, Wark, Rush, Walsh (Johnston). Tr: Fagan

1986

7th May, 1986   *Sanchez Pizjuan, Seville*   *70,000*
Steaua Bucharest   **0**   **Barcelona**   **0**
Steaua: Ducadam, Iovan, Belodedicik, Bumbescu, Barbulescu, Balint, Balan (Iordanescu), Boloni, Majaru, Lacatus, Piturca (Radu). Tr: Jenei
Barcelona: Urruti, Gerardo, Migueli, Alesanco, Julio Alberto, Victor, Marcos, Schuster (Moratalla), Pedraza, Archibald (Pichi Alonso), Carrasco. Tr: Venables
After extra time. Steaua won 2-0 on penalties

1987

27th May, 1987   *Prater, Vienna*   *56,000*
FC Porto   **2**   **Bayern Munich**   **1**
Madjer (77), Juary (79)   Kogi (24)
Porto: Mlynaraczyk, Joao Pinto, Eduardo Luis, Celso, Inacio (Frasco), Quim (Juary), Magalhaes, Madjer, Sousa, Andre, Futre. Tr: Jorge
Bayern Munich: Pfaff, Winklhofer, Nachtweih, Eder, Pfluger, Flick, Brehme, Matthaus, Rummenigge, Hoeness, Kogi. Tr: Lattek

1988

25th May, 1988   *Neckarstadion, Stuttgart*   *55,000*
PSV Eindhoven   **0**   **Benfica**   **0**
PSV Eindhoven: Van Breukelen, Gerets, Van Aerle, Koeman R, Nielsen, Heintze, Vanenburg, Linskens, Lerby, Kieft, Gillhaus (Janssen). Tr: Hiddink
Benfica: Silvino, Velose, Dito, Mozer, Alvaro, Elzo, Sheu, Chiquinho, Pacheco, Rui Aguas (Vando), Magnusson (Hajiri). Tr: Toni
After extra time. PSV Eindhoven won 6-5 on penalties

1989

24th May, 1989   *Nou Camp, Barcelona*   *97,000*
Milan   **4**   **Steaua Bucharest**   **0**
Gullit (17, 38), Van Basten (26, 46)
Milan: Galli G, Tassotti, Costacurta (Galli F), Baresi, Maldini, Colombo, Rijkaard, Ancelotti, Donadoni, Gullit, Van Basten. Tr: Sacchi

Steaua: Lung, Iovan, Petrescu, Bumbescu, Ungureanu, Hagi, Stoica, Minea, Rotariu (Balaci), Lacatus, Piturca. Tr: Iordanescu

1990

23rd May, 1990   *Prater, Vienna*   *57,000*
Milan   1   **Benfica**   **0**
Rijkaard (68)
Milan: Galli G, Tassotti, Costacurta, Baresi, Maldini, Colombo (Galli F), Rijkaard, Ancelotti (Massaro), Evani, Gullit, Van Basten. Tr: Sacchi
Benfica: Silvino, Jose Carlos, Aldair, Ricardo, Samuel, Vitor Paneira, Valdo, Thern, Hernani, Magnusson, Pacheco. Tr: Eriksson

1991

29th May, 1991   *San Nicola, Bari*   *50,000*
Red Star Belgrade   0   **Marseille**   **0**
Red Star Belgrade: Stajanovic, Belodedici, Najdoski, Sabanadzovic, Jugovic, Marovic, Mihajlovic, Binic, Savicevic (Stosic), Prosinecki, Pancev. Tr: Petrovic
Marseille: Olmeta, Amoros, Boli, Mozer, Di Meco (Stojkovic), Fournier (Vercruysse), Germain, Casonik, Pele, Papin, Waddle. Tr: Goethals
            After extra time. Red Star Belgrade won 5-3 on Penalties

1992

20th May, 1992   *Wembley, London*   *71,000*
Barcelona   1   **Sampdoria**   **0**
Koeman R (112)
Barcelona: Zubizarreta, Eusebio, Ferrer, Koeman R, Munoz, Juan Carlos, Baquero, Guardiola (Alexanco), Laudrup M, Salinas, Stoichkov, Tr: Cruyff
Sampdoria: Pagliuca, Mannini, Lanna, Vierchwood, Katanec, Lombardok, Cerezo, Pari, Bonetti (Invernizzi), Vialli (Buso), Mancini. Tr: Boskov

1993

26th May, 1993   *Munich*   *64,444*
Milan   0   **Marseille**   **1**
                                              Boli (43)
AC Milan: Rossi, Tassotti, Costacurta, Baresi, Maldini, Donadoni (Papin), Rijkaard, Albertini, Lentini, Van Basten (Eranio), Massaro. Tr: Capello
Marseille: Barthez, Angloma (Durand), Boli, Desailly, Di Meco, Pele, Sauzee, Deschamps, Eydelie, Boksic, Voller (Thomas). Tr: Goethals.

Cup-Winners' Cup 1992-93

Debutantes' Delight

It was quite remarkable that two teams making their respective debuts in the Cup-Winners' Cup should end up contesting the final itself, which will be remembered as much for the great humour of the Belgian supporters as for the football played. Antwerp's form in the competition had hardly been convincing. They had won just two of eight contests, slipping through once on penalties, once on the away goals rule and once after extra-time.

But, in former Spurs winger Nico Claesen and striker Alex Czerniatynski, they had players of palpable class. Parma, meanwhile, could rely on the world-class skills of Swedish international Tomas Brolin, recently recovered from a serious knee injury, and the guile of Alessandro Melli and Colombian goal ace Faustino Asprilla up-front.

As it was, a Wembley crowd of almost 40,000 were treated to an Italian performance par excellence. An early goal from defender Lorenzo Minotti after nine minutes gave the Serie A outfit exactly the start they were hoping for, with Minotti volleying home Luigi Apolloni's corner.

But only two minutes later, Antwerp were back on level terms. An attempted clearance from Daniele Zoratto struck Czerniatynski on the chest and the striker showed great composure to control the ball and stroke a magnificent pass to the advancing Francis Severeyns, who finished with a rising drive.

Parma regained their lead on the half-hour when Alessandro Melli headed home from a Rudy Taeymans centre. Melli found the target again just before the interval, but his effort was disallowed for offside.

Antwerp fought back in the second half as Parma continued to search for a third killer goal. Melli twice went close before Stefano Cuoghi accepted a pass from Georges Grun and beat Stevan Stojanovic from close range to seal a 3-1 victory.

English Chance

A 2-0 FA Cup victory had given Liverpool the opportunity to emulate the achievement of rivals Manchester United in 1991 by lifting the trophy that had previously been won by Merseyside neighbours Everton in 1985.

Graeme Souness's side kicked off their campaign against Cypriot Cup holders Apollon Limassol at Anfield. An early goal from Paul Stewart set the crowd's nerves at ease and another Stewart strike, plus a four-goal blast from Ian Rush, who surpassed Roger Hunt's European goal-scoring record in the process, clinched an impressive first-leg advantage of 6-1.

Limassol's task was not made any easier by the somewhat harsh dismissal of midfielder Marios Charalambous, and their resolve had all but disappeared by the time Liverpool travelled to Cyprus for the second leg and conjured a 2-1 victory, courtesy of goals from Rush, inevitably, and midfielder Don Hutchison.

Cardiff City had briefly entertained dreamy hopes of booking a place in the second round after a Chris Pike goal had helped the Bluebirds to a 1-1 draw at home to Admira Wacker from Poland. But the second leg slipped quietly away from Eddie May's side as they succumbed 2-0.

Scottish Cup-winners Airdrie fared little better, losing 1-0 at home to a late goal from Sparta Prague striker Sopko. The second leg went no better, with Sparta triumphing 2-1.

From Northern Ireland Glenavon distinguished themselves by holding eventual finalists Royal Antwerp 1-1 at home in front of 3,000 enthusiastic fans. Astonishingly the Irish side repeated the same feat in Belgium, with a 1-1 result after extra-time forcing a penalty shoot-out which the home side won 3-1.

From the south of Ireland, Bohemians from Dublin produced one of the shocks of the round by holding the mighty Steaua Bucharest to a goalless home draw. But the luck of the Irish did not hold out in the second leg as the Romanians triumphed 4-0.

Atletico Madrid posted their intent early on with a stunning 9-1 aggregate victory over Branik Maribor, and Monaco booked a second round berth, though hardly emphatically, with a 1-0 aggregate defeat of Miedz Legnica.

The second round tie that attracted most attention was the clash between reigning champions Werder Bremen and Sparta Prague, especially when Sparta clinched a 3-2 first-leg advantage. Then the Czech side offered little sign of nerves as they held on in the second leg for a 1-0 victory and a surprising place in the third round.

Liverpool, meanwhile, were in all sorts of trouble after a calamitous second round first leg trip to Spartak Moscow. Like Manchester United before them in the UEFA, whose downfall was precipitated by a miserable excursion to Moscow, Liverpool soon found themselves facing an uphill battle.

The main cause of their downfall was a disastrous defence which eventually conceded four goals, two of which were the direct result of catastrophic errors of judgement by goalkeeper Bruce Grobbelaar, who was eventually sent off for a professional foul. Goals from Mark Wright and Steve McManaman briefly offered the Merseysiders hope of a 2-2 draw, but with Grobbelaar's 82nd minute dismissal, Spartak added two more goals and the tie was effectively relinquished.

Graeme Souness's reaction after the game cost him a UEFA touchline ban for allegedly abusing the referee and, two weeks later, in front of 38,000

50

Liverpool fans at Anfield, the vulnerability of the Liverpool defence was cruelly exposed once more as the home side crashed to an embarrassing 2-0 defeat to leave the contest, the fourth English side to fail to get further than the second round of any of the competitions.

Another notable casualty in the second round was Monaco who, showing none of the form that had propelled them to the Cup-Winners' Cup final defeat against Werder Bremen last season, inexplicably crashed out 1-0 to Greek Cup-holders Olympiakos. But the thriller of the round was contested between Antwerp and Admira Wacker, with the Belgian side emerging 7-6 aggregate winners, thanks to three goals from Belgian international striker Alex Czerniatynski.

Parma, bidding to become the first Italian winners of the competition since Sampdoria in 1990, continued to make steady progress with a professional 2-0 removal of Boavista.

The quarter-final stages presented some intriguing possibilities, with Spartak Moscow facing a tough examination against Feyenoord. But the Dutch side were unable to recover from the ignominy of a 1-0 defeat in the home leg and eventually succumbed 4-1 on aggregate.

Antwerp sneaked through on the away goals rule against Steaua Bucharest following a 1-1 deadlock, Atletico Madrid were convincing 4-2 victors over Olympiakos and Parma progressed to the last four with a comfortable 2-0 disposal of Sparta Prague.

Atletico Madrid entertained Parma in the first leg of their semi-final and threw away a 1-0 advantage to go down 2-1, a defeat from which they never fully recovered. The second leg produced plenty of fireworks, with the Spanish side clinching a 1-0 victory in Italy, but going out on the away goals rule. At the final whistle, with defender Juanito already taking an early bath, midfielder Juan Vizcaino and Alfaro were dismissed amid chaotic scenes after the game.

In the other semi-final, Antwerp recovered from a 1-0 first-leg deficit to clinch a final berth with a 3-1 second-leg victory over Moscow Spartak. But this game was not without its fair share of incident, with Moscow midfielder Victor Onopko receiving his marching orders after 76 minutes.

Preliminary Round

Avenir Beggen Krings (1)	**B36 Thorshavn**	**1-0**	**1,500**
B36 Thorshavn Reynheim (9)	**Avenir Beggen** Krahen (28)	**1-1**	**665**

Avenir win 2-1 on aggregate

Maribor Branik Simundja (16, 30), Tarana (48), Bonkovski (76)	**Hamrun Spartans**	**4-0**	**5,000**
Hamrun Spartans Brincat (32, 59)	**Maribor Branik** Tarana (37)	**2-1**	**1,000**

Maribor win 5-2 on aggregate

Stromsgodset	**Hapoel Tel Aviv** Basson (81, 82)	**0-2**	**4,000**
Hapoel Tel Aviv Levin (17), Basson (69)	**Stromsgodset**	**2-0**	**2,000**

Hapoel win 4-0 on aggregate

Vaduz	**Chernomorets** Tsimbalar (44), Lebed (47), Sak (53), Gousev (81, 82)	**0-5**	**2,000**
Chernomorets Nikiforov (7, 44 pen, 79, 89), Yablonski (20),Tsimbaler (24), Lebed (78)	**Vaduz** Stuber (85)	**7-1**	**4,600**

Chernomoretz 12-1 on aggregate

1st Round

AIK Stockholm Simpson (51), Hallstrom (56) Yevtushenko (85)	**AGF Aarhus** Tofting (15), Christensen (36, 53)	**3-3**	**3,976**
AGF Aarhus Harder (67)	**AIK Stockholm** Simpson (20)	**1-1**	**9,000**

Aarhus win 4-4 on away goals rule

Airdrieonians	**Sparta Prague** Sopko (88)	**0-1**	**7,000**
Sparta Prague Vrabec (31), Vonasek (37)	**Airdrieonians** Black (55)	**2-1**	**8,989**

Sparta win 3-1 on aggregate

| Glenavon
Smith (44) | Royal Antwerp
Lehnhoff (46) | 1-1 | 3,000 |
| Royal Antwerp
Kiekens (65 pen) | Glenavon
Harris (80) | 1-1 | 7,000 |

Aggregate 2-2. Antwerp win 3-1 on penalties after extra time

| Werder Bremen
Rufer (19, 28), Bratseht (45) | Hannover
Wojcicki (26 pen) | 3-1 | 17,000 |
| Hannover
Daschner (29,33) | Werder Bremen
Rufer (19 pen) | 2-1 | 27,436 |

Werder Bremen win 4-3 on aggregate

| Bohemians (Dublin) | Steaua Bucharest | 0-0 | 4,500 |
| Steaua Bucharest
Andrasi (26, 34), Vladoiu (44), Viorel (85) | Bohemians (Dublin) | 4-0 | 15,000 |

Steaua win 4-0 on aggregate

| Maribor Branik | Atletico Madrid
Alfred (26), Garcia (43, 56) | 0-3 | 5,000 |
| Atletico Madrid
Alfaro (17), Juanito (44), Sabas (58 pen),
Pizo Gomez (69), Aguilera (80),
Tarana (58 og) | Maribor Branik
Bicarcik (22) | 6-1 | 3,000 |

Atletico win 9-1 on aggregate

| Cardiff City
Pike (59) | Admira Wacker
Abfalterer (44) | 1-1 | 9,624 |
| Admira Wacker
Marschall (47), Abfalterer (70) | Cardiff City | 2-0 | 4,700 |

Admira win 3-1 on aggregate

| Feyenoord
Kiprich (89) | Hapoel Tel Aviv | 1-0 | 15,000 |
| Hapoel Tel Aviv
Levin (2), Kakkon (50) | Feyenoord
Fraser (59) | 2-1 | 6,000 |

Aggregate 2-2. Feyenoord win on away goals rule

| Levski Sofia
Borimirov (52), Getov (70 pen) | Lucerne
Camenzind (9) | 2-1 | 8,000 |
| Lucerne
Camenzind (24) | Levski Sofia | 1-0 | 12,000 |

Aggregate 2-2. Lucerne win on away goals rule

Liverpool	Apollon	6-1	12,769
Stewart (4, 38), Rush (40, 50, 55, 74)	Spoljaric (83 pen)		
Apollon	Liverpool	1-2	12,000
Spoljaric (60)	Rush (62), Hutchison (68)		

Liverpool win 8-2 on aggregate

Miedz Legnica	Monaco	0-1	6,500
	Kjorkaeff (3)		
Monaco	Miedz Legnica	0-0	4,000

Monaco win 1-0 on aggregate

Spartak Moscow	Avenir Beggen	0-0	5,000
Avenir Beggen	Spartak Moscow	1-5	2,000
Novak (85)	Onopko (6), Piatnitski (9, 78), Radchenko (55), Popov (59)		

Spartak win 5-1 on aggregate

Parma	Ujpest Doza	1-0	11,600
Asprilla (48)			
Ujpest Doza	Parma	1-1	12,000
Hetesi (62)	Grun (53)		

Parma win 2-1 on aggregate

Trabzonspor	TPs Turun	2-0	22,500
Hami (51, 65)			
TPs Turun	Trabzonspor	2-2	2,000
Kajdu (1), Lehtonen (84)	Hami (14), Orhan (60)		

Trabzonspor win 4-2 on aggregate

Olympiakos	Chernomorets	0-1	30,000
	Sak (4)		
Chernomorets	Olympiakos	0-3	23,000
	Mitsidonas (15), Litovchenko (27), Protasov (80)		

Olympiakos win 3-1 on aggregate

Valur Reykjavik	Boavista	0-0	400
Boavista	Valur Reykjavik	3-0	15,000
Marlon (14, 81), Ricky (26)			

Boavista win 3-0 on aggregate

2nd Round

AGF Aarhus	**Steaua Bucharest**	**3-2**	**9,000**
S. Andersen (12), Christensen (19), M. Nielsen (89 pen)	Vladoiu (64), Dumitrescu (89)		
Steaua Bucharest	**AGF Aarhus**	**2-1**	**26,000**
Cristescu (81), Vladoiu (89)	Christensen (10)		

Aggregate 4-4. Steaua win on away goals rule

Admira Wacker	**Royal Antwerp**	**2-4**	**4,000**
Marschall (24), Bacher (41)	Czerniatynski (35, 73), Segers (53), Severeyns (62)		
Royal Antwerp	**Admira Wacker**	**3-4**	**7,000**
Czerniatynski (21), Severeyns (44), Van Rethy (96)	Bacher (46), Abfalterer (57) Ljung (63, 79)		

Antwerp win 7-6 on aggregate after extra time

Lucerne	**Feyenoord**	**1-0**	**16,100**
Rueda (74)			
Feyenoord	**Lucerne**	**4-1**	**21,000**
Taument (2), Blinker (16), Kiprich (46, 83 pen)	Nadig (12)		

Feyenoord win 4-2 on aggregate

Monaco	**Olympiakos**	**0-1**	**8,000**
	Vaitsis (86)		
Olympiakos	**Monaco**	**0-0**	**35,000**

Olympiakos win 1-0 on aggregate

Parma	**Boavista**	**0-0**	**15,000**
Boavista	**Parma**	**0-2**	**8,000**
	Di Chiara (11), Melli (78)		

Parma win 2-0 on aggregate

Spartak Moscow	**Liverpool**	**4-2**	**55,000**
Pisarev (10), Karpin (68, 82 pen), Ledyakhov (89)	Wright (67), McManaman (78)		
Liverpool	**Spartak Moscow**	**0-2**	**37,993**
	Radchenko (63), Piatnitski (89)		

Spartak win 6-2 on aggregate

Trabzonspor	**Atletico Madrid**	**0-2**	**20,000**
	Futre (38), Moya (60)		
Atletico Madrid	**Trabzonspor**	**0-0**	**9,000**

Atletico win 2-0 on aggregate

Werder Bremen	**Sparta Prague**	**2-3**	**10,747**
Neubarth (56), Rufer (81)	Sopko (25), Dvimik (36), Vonasek (90)		
Sparta Prague	**Werder Bremen**	**1-0**	**35,000**
Siegl (7)			

Sparta win 4-2 on aggregate

Quarter-Final

Royal Antwerp	**Steaua Bucharest**	**0-0**	**9,500**
Steaua Bucharest	**Royal Antwerp**	**1-1**	**15,000**
Dukitrescu (19)	Czerniatynski (82)		

Aggregate 1-1. Antwerp win on away-goals rule

Feyenoord	**Spartak Moscow**	**0-1**	**33,187**
	Piatnitski (36)		
Spartak Moscow	**Feyenoord**	**3-1**	**15,000**
Karpin (7, 78), Radchenko (87)	Kiprich (14)		

Spartak win 4-1 on aggregate

Olympiakos	**Atletico Madrid**	**1-1**	**55,000**
Vaitsis (64)	Moya (10)		
Atletico Madrid	**Olympiakos**	**3-1**	**40,000**
Manolo (10, 57), Alfaro (67)	Tsaluhidis (60)		

Atletico win 4-2 on aggregate

Sparta Prague	**Parma**	**0-0**	**24,900**
Parma	**Sparta Prague**	**2-0**	**20,000**
Melli (11), Asprilla (33)			

Parma win 2-0 on aggregate

Semi-Finals

Atletico Madrid	**Parma**	**1-2**	**50,000**
Luis Garcia (44)	Solozobal (og 57), Asprilla (61)		
Parma	**Atletico Madrid**	**0-1**	**21,915**
	Sabas (77)		

Aggregate 2-2. Parma win on away goals rule

| Spartak Moscow | Royal Antwerp | 1-0 | 60,000 |
| Piatnitski (36) | | | |

Royal Antwerp	Spartak Moscow	3-1	13,500
Czerniatynski (37), Jakovljevic (66),	Radchenko (10)		
Lehnhoff (78 pen)			

Antwerp win 3-2 on aggregate

Final
12th May 1993   *Wembley Stadium, London*

| Parma | Royal Antwerp | 3-1 | 37,393 |
| Minotti (9), Melli (30), Cuoghi (83) | Severeyns (12) | | |

Cup-Winners' Cup Final
Details 1955/56-1992/93

1961

1st Leg, 17th May, 1961   *Ibrox, Glasgow* *80,000*

Rangers **0** **Fiorentina** **2**

            Milani (12, 88)

Rangers: Ritchie, Shearer, Caldow, Davis, Paterson, Baxter, Wilson, McMillan, Scott, Brand, Hume

Fiorentina: Albertosi, Robotti, Castelletti, Gonfiantini, Orzan, Rimbaldo, Hamrin, Micheli, Da Costa, Milani, Petris

2nd Leg, 27th May, 1961   *Comunale, Florence* *50,000*

Fiorentina **2** **Rangers** **1**

Milani (12), Hamrin (86)   Scott (60)

Fiorentina: Albertosi, Robotti, Castelletti, Gonfiantini, Orzan, Rimbaldo, Hamrin, Micheli, Da Costa, Milani, Petris

Rangers: Ritchie, Shearer, Caldow, Davis, Paterson, Baxter, Scott, McMillan, Millar, Brand, Wilson

Fiorentina win 4-1 on aggregate

1962

10th May, 1962   *Hampden Park* *27,000*

Atletico Madrid **1** **Fiorentina** **1**

Peiro (11)   Hamrin (27)

Atletico Madrid: Madinabeytia, Rivilla, Calleja, Ramirez, Griffa, Glaria, Jones, Adelardo, Mendonca, Peiro, Collar

Fiorentina: Albertosi, Robotti, Castelletti, Malatrasi, Orzan, Marchesi, Hamrin, Ferretti, Milani, Dell-Angelo, Petris

Replay, 5th September, 1962   *Neckarstadion, Stuttgard* *38,000*

Atletico Madrid **3** **Fiorentina** **0**

Jones (8), Mendonca (27), Peiro (59)

Atletico: Madinabeytia, Rivilla, Calleja, Ramirez, Griffa, Glaria, Jones, Adelardo, Mendonca, Peiro, Collar

Fiorentina: Albertosi, Robotti, Castelletti, Malatrasi, Orzan, Marchesi, Hamrin, Ferretti, Milani, Dell-Angelo, Petris

1963

15th May, 1963   *Feyenoord Stadion*   *49,000*
Tottenham Hotspur   **5**   **Atletico Madrid**   **1**
Greaves (16, 80), White (35), Dyson (67, 85)   Collar (47)
Tottenham Hotspur: Brown, Baker, Norman, Henry, Blanchflower, Marchi,
Jones, White, Smith, Greaves, Dyson
Atletico Madrid: Madinabeytia, Rivilla, Griffa, Rodriguez, Ramiro, Glaria,
Jones, Adelardo, Chuzo, Mendonca, Collar

1964

13th May, 1964   *Heysel, Brussels*   *3,000*
Sporting Lisbon   **3**   **MTK Budapest**   **3**
Mascaranhas (40), Figueiredo (45, 80)   Sandor (19, 75), Kuti (73)
Sporting Lisbon: Carvalho, Gomez, Perdis, Battista, Carlos, Geo, Mendes,
Oswaldo, Mascaranghas, Figueiredo, Morais
MTK Budapest: Kovalik, Keszei, Dansky, Jenie, Nagy, Kovacs, Sandor,
Vasas, Kuti, Bodor, Halapi

Replay, 15th May, 1964   *Bosuil, Antwerp*   *19,000*
Sporting Lisbon   **1**   **MTK Budapest**   **0**
Morais (19)
Sporting Lisbon: Carvalho, Gomez, Perdis, Battista, Carlos, Geo, Mendes,
Oswaldo, Mascaranhas, Figueiredo, Morais
MTK Budapest: Kovalik, Keszei Dansky, Jenei, Nagy, Kovacs, Sandor,
Vasas, Kuti, Bodor, Halapi

1965

19th May, 1965   *Wembley, London*   *100,000*
West Ham United   **2**   **1860 Munich**   **0**
Sealey (70, 72)
West Ham United: Staden, Kirkup, Burkett, Moore, Peters, Brown, Sealey,
Boyce, Hurst, Dear, Sissons
1860 Munich: Radenkovic, Wagner, Kohlars, Reich, Bena, Luttrop, Heiss,
Kuppers, Brunnemeier, Grosser, Rebele

1966

5th May, 1966   *Hampden Park, Glasgow*   *41,000*
Borussia Dortmund   **2**   **Liverpool**   **1 aet**
Held (62), Libuda (109)   Hunt (68)
Borussia Dortmund: Tilkowski, Cyliax, Paul, Redder, Kurrat, Assauer,
Libuda, Schmidt, Held, Sturm, Emmerich
Liverpool: Lawrence, Lawler, Yeats, Byrne, Milne, Stevenson, Callaghan,
Hunt, Smith, St John, Thompson

1967

31st May, 1967   *Nuremberg*   *69,000*

Bayern Munich   **1**   **Rangers**   **0 aet**

Roth (108)

Bayern Munich: Maier, nowak, Kupferschmidt, Beckenbauer, Olk, Roth, Koulmann, Nafziger, Ohlhauser, Muller, Brenninger

Rangers: Martin, Johansen, Provan, McKinnon, Greig, Jardine, Smith D, Henderson, Hynd, Smith A, Johnston

1968

23rd May, 1968   *Feyenoord Stadion*   *53,000*

Milan   **2**   **Hamburg**   **0**

Hamrin (3, 19)

Milan: Cudicini, Anquilletti, Schnellinger, Rosato, Scala, Trapattoni, Lodetti, Hamrin, Sormani, Rivera, Prati

Hamburg: Ozcan, Sandmann, Schulx, Horst, Kurbjuhn, Dieckmann, Dramer, Dorfel B, Seeler, Honig, Dorfel G

1969

21st May, 1969   *St Jakob, Basle*   *19,000*

Slovan Bratislava   **3**   **Barcelona**   **2**

Cvetler (2), Hrivnak (30), Jan Capkovic (42)   Zaldua (16), Rexach (52)

Slovan Bratislava: Vencel, Filo, Horvath, Hrivnak, Zlocha, Hrdlicka, Josef Capkovic, Cvetler, Moder (Hatar), Jokl, Jan Capkovic

Barcelona: Sadurni, Franch (Pereda), Eladio, Rife, Olivella, Zabalza, Pellicer, Castro (Mendoza), Zaldua, Fuste, Rexach

1970

29th April, 1970   *Prater, Vienna*   *8,000*

Manchester City   **2**   **Gornik Zabrze**   **1**

Young (11), Lee (43)   Oslizlo (70)

Manchester City: Corrigan, Book, Booth, Heslop, Pardoe, Doyle (Bowyer), Towers, Oakes, Bell, Lee, Young

Gornik Zabrze: Kostka, Oslizlo, Florenski (Deja), Gorgon, Olek, Latocha, Szoltysik, Wilczek (Skowronek), Szarynski, Banas, Lubanski

1971

19th May, 1971   *Karaiskaki, Piraeus*   *42,000*

Chelsea   **1**   **Real Madrid**   **1**

Osgood (55)   Fleitas (74)

Chelsea: Bonetti, Boyle, Dempsey, Webb, Harris, Cooke, Hudson, Weller, Baldwin, Osgood (Smethurst), Houseman

Real Madrid: Borja, Jose Luis, Benito, Zoco, Zunzunegui, Pirri, Grosso, Velazquez (Gento), Fleitas, Amancio, Bueno (Grande)

Replay, 21st May, 1971   *Karaiskaki, Piraeus*   *35,000*
Chelsea   2   **Real Madrid**   1
Dempsey (32), Osgood (38)   Fleitas (74)
Chelsea: Bonetti, Boyle, Dempsey, Webb, Harris, Cooke, Hudson, Weller, Baldwin, Osgood (Smethurst), Houseman
Real Madrid: Borja, Jose Luis, Benito, Zoco, Zunzunegui, Pirri, Grosso, Velazquez (Gento), Fleitas, Amancio, Bueno (Grande)

1972

24th May, 1972   *Nou Camp, Barcelona*   *24,000*
Rangers   3   **Dinamo Moscow**   2
Stein (23), Johnston (40, 49)   Estrekov (60), Makovikov (87)
Rangers: McCloy, Jardine, Johnstone, Smith, Mathieson, Greig, Conn, MacDonald, McLean, Stein, Johnston
Dinamo Moscow: Pilgui, Basalev, Dolmatov, Zikov, Dobonosov (Gerschkovitch), Zhukov, Yakubik (Estrekov), Sabo, Baidatchini, Makovikov, Evriuschkin

1973

16th May, 1973   *Salonicia*   *45,000*
Milan   1   **Leeds United**   0
Chiarugi (5)
Milan: Vecchi, Sabadini, Zignoli, Anquilletti, Turone, Rosato (Dolci), Rivera, Benetti, Sogliano, Bigon, Chiarugi
Leeds Utd: Harvey, Reaney, Cherry, Bates, Madeley, Hunter, Gray E, Yorath (McQueen), Lorimer, Jordan, Jones

1974

8th May, 1974   *Feyenoord Stadion*   *4,000*
Magdeburg   2   **Milan**   0
(OG 43), Seguin (74)
Magdeburg: Schulze, Enge, Zapf, Tyll, Abraham, Seguin, Pommerenke, Gaube, Raugust, Sparwasser, Hoffmann
Milan: Pizzaballa, Sabadini, Anquilletti, Lanzi, Schnellinger, Benetti, Maldera, Rivera, Tresoldi, Bigon, Bergamaschi (Turin)

1975

14th May, 1975   *St Jakobs, Basle*   *10,000*

Dinamo Kiev   **3**   **Ferencvaros**   **0**

Onischenko (18, 39), Blokhin (67)

Dinamo Kiev: Rudakov, Troshkink, Matvienko, Reshko, Fomenko, Muntjan, Konkov, Burjak, Kolotov, Onischenko, Blokhin

Ferencvaros: Geczi, Martos, Megyesi, Pataki, Rab, Nyilasi (Onhaus), Juhasz, Mucha, Szabo, Mate, Magyar

1976

5th May, 1976   *Heysel, Brussels*   *58,000*

RSC Anderlecht   **4**   **West Ham United**   **2**

Rensenbrink (42, 73), Van der Elst (48, 87)   Holland (28), Robson (68)

RSC Anderlecht: Ruiter, Lomm, Van Binst, Thissen, Broos, Dockx, Coeck (Vercauteren), Haan, Van der Elst, Ressel, Rensenbrink

West Ham United: Day, Cloeman, Lampard (Taylor A), Taylor T McDowell, Bonds, Brooking, Paddon, Holland, Jennings, Robson

1977

11th May, 1977   *Amsterdam*   *66,000*

SV Hamburg   **2**   **RSC Anderlecht**   **0**

Volkert (78), Magath (88)

SV Hamburg: Kargus, Kaltz, Ripp, Nogly, Hidien, Memering, Magath, Keller, Steffenhagen, Reimann, Volkert

RSC Anderlecht: Ruiter, Van Binst, Van Den Daele, Thissen, Broos, Dockx (Van Poucke), Coeck, Haan, Vander Elst, Ressel, Rensenbrink

1978

3rd May, 1978   *Parc des Princes, Paris*   *48,000*

RSC Anderlecht   **4**   **Austria Vienna**   **0**

Rensenbrink (13, 41), Van Binst (45, 80)

RSC Anderlecht: De Bree, Van Binst, Thissen, Dusbaba, Broos, Vander Elst, Haan, Nielsen, Coeck, Vercauteren (Dockx), Rensenbrink

Austria Vienna: Baumgartner, Sara R, Sara J, Obermayer, Baumeister, Prohaska, Daxbacher (Martinez), Gasselich, Morels (Drazen), Pirkner, Parits

1979

16th May, 1979   *St Jakobs, Basle*   *58,000*

Barcelona   **4**   **Fortuna Dusseldorf 3** **aet**

Sanchez (5), Asensi (34), Rexach (104),   Allofs K (8), Seel (41, 114)
Krankl (111)

Barcelona: Artola, Zuviria, Migueli, Costas (Martinez), Albaladejo (Del la Cruz), Sanchez, Neeskens, Asensi, Rexach, Krankl, Carrasco

Fortuna Dusseldorf: Daniel, Baltes, Zewe, Zimmermann (Lund), Brei (Weik), Kohnen, Schmitz, Bommer, Allofs T, Allofs K, Seel

1980

15th May, 1980   *Heysel, Brussels*   36,000
Valencia   **0**   **Arsenal**   **0** **aet**

Valencia: Pereira, Carrette, Botubot, Arias, Tendollo, Solsona, Saura, Bonhof, Subirates (Castellanos), Kempes, Pablo
Arsenal: Jennings, Rice, Nelson, O'Leary, Young, Rix, Talbot, Price (Hollins), Brady, Sunderland, Stapleton

            After extra time. Valencia won 5-4 on penalties.

1981

13th May, 1981   *Rheinstadion, Dusseldorf*   9,000
Dinamo Tbilisi   **2**   **Carl Zeiss Jena**   **1**
Gutsayev (67), Daraselia (86)   Hoppe (63)

Dinamo Tbilisi: Gabelia, Kostave, Chivadze, Khisanishvili, Tavadze, Svanadze (Kakilashvili), Sulakvelidze, Daraselia, Gutsayev, Kipiani, Shengelia
Carl Zeiss Jena: Grapenthin, Brauer, Kurbjuweit, Schnuphase, Schilling, Hoppe (Overmann), Krause, Lindemann, Bielau (Topfer), Raab, Vogel

1982

12th May, 1982   *Nou Camp, Barcelona*   100,000
Barcelona   **2**   **Standard Liege**   **1**
Simonsen (44), Quini (63)   Vandermissen (7)

Barcelona: Urruti, Gerardo, Migueli, Alesanco, Manolo, Sanchez, Moratalla, Esteban, Simonsen, Quini, Carrasco
Standard Liege: Preud'homme, Gerets, Poel, Meeuws, Plessers, Vandermissen, Daerden, Haan, Botternon, Tahamata, Wendt

1983

11th May, 1983   *Nya Ullevi, Gothenburg*   17,000
Aberdeen   **2**   **Real Madrid**   **1 aet**
Black (4), Hewitt (112)   Juanito (15)

Aberdeen: Leighton, Rougvie, McLeish, Miller, McMaster, Cooper, Strachan, Simpson, McGhee, Black (Hewitt), Weir
Real Madrid: Agustin, Juan Jose, Metgod, Bonet, Camacho (San Jose), Angel, Gallego, Stielike, Isidro (Salguero), Juanito, Santillana

1984

16th May, 1984　　　　　　　　*St Jakobs, Basle*　　　60,000

Juventus　　　　　**2**　　　**FC Porto**　　　　　　**1**

Vignola (12), Boniek (41)　　　　　Sousa (29)

Juventus: Tacconik Gentile, Brio, Scirea, Cabrini, Tardelli, Bonini, Vignola (Aricola), Platini, Rossi, Boniek

FC Porto: Ze Beto, Joao Pinto, Lima Pereira, Enrico, Eduardo Luis (Costa), Magalhaes (Walsh), Frasco, Pacheco, Sousa, Gomes, Vermelinho

1985

15th May, 1985　　　　　　　*Feynoord Stadion*　　　50,000

Everton　　　　　**3**　　　**Rapid Vienna**　　　　**1**

Gray (57), Steven (72), Sheedy (85)　　　Krankl (83)

Everton: Southall, Stevens, Van den Hauwe, Ratcliffe, Mountfield, Reid, Steven, Bracewell, Sheedy, Gray, Sharp

Rapid Vienna: Konsel, Lainer, Weber, Garger, Brauneder, Hrstic, Kranjcar, Kienast, Weinhofer (Panenka), Pacult (Gross), Krankl

1986

2nd May, 1986　　　　　　　*Stade de Gerland, Lyon*　　39,000

Dinamo Kiev　　　　**3**　　　**Atletico Madrid**　　　**0**

Zavarov (5), Blokhin (85), Yevtushenko (88)

Dinamo Kiev: Chanov, Baltacha (Bal), Bessonov, Kuznetsov, Demianenko, Rats, Yakovenko, Yaremchuk, Zavarov (Yevtushenko), Belanov, Blokhin

Atletico Madrid: Fillol, Tomas, Arteche, Ruiz, Villaverde, Prieto, Ramos, Marina, Landaburu (Setien), Cabrera, Da Silva

1987

13th May, 1987　　　　　　*Olympiao Stadio, Athens*　　35,000

Ajax　　　　　　**1**　　　**Lokomotive Leipzig**　　**0**

Van Basten (21)

Ajax: Menzo, Silooy, Rijkaard, Verlaat, Boeve, Wouters, Winter, Muhren (Scholten), Van't Schip, Van Basten, Witschge (Bergkamp)

Lokomotive Leipzig: Muller, Kreer, Baum, Lindner, Zotzsche, Scholz, Liebers (Kuhn), Bredow, Marschal, Richter, Edmond (Leitzke)

1988

11th May, 1988　　　　　　　*Strasbourg*　　　　　40,000

KV Mechelen　　　**1**　　　**Ajax**　　　　　　　**0**

Den Boer (53)

KV Mechelen: Preud'homme, Clijsters, Sanders, Rutjes, Deferm, Hofkens (Theunis), Emmers, Koeman, De Wilde (Demesmeker), Den Boer, Ohana

Ajax: Menzo, Blind, Wouters, Larsson, Verlaat (Meijer), Van't Schip (Bergkamp), Winter, Muhren, Scholten, Bosman, Witschge

1989

10th May, 1989		*Wankdorf, Berne*	*45,000*
Barcelona	2	**Sampdoria**	0

Salinas (4), Recarte (79)

Barcelona: Zubizarreta, Alosio, Alesanco, Urbano, Milla (Soler), Armor, Eusebio Roberto, Lineker, Salinas, Berguiristain (Recarte)
Sampdoria: Pagliuca, Pellegrini L (Bonomi), Mannini (Pellegrinis), Lanna, Salsano, Pari, Victor, Cerezo, Dossena, Vialli, Mancini

1990

9th May, 1990		*Gothenburg*	*20,000*
Sampdoria	2	**RSC Anderlecht**	0 aet

Vialli (105, 107)

Sampdoria: Pagliuca, Pellegrini L, Mannini, Vierchwood, Carboni, Pari, Katanec (Salsano), Invernizzi (Lombardo), Dossena, Vialli, Mancini
RSC Anderlecht: De Wilde, Grun, Marchoul, Keshi, Kooiman, Veroort, Musonda, Gudjohnson, Jankovic (Oliveira), Degryse (Nilis), Van der Linden

1991

15th May, 1991		*Feyenoord Stadium*	*42,000*
Manchester United	2	**Barcelona**	1

Bruce (67), Hughes (74)   Koeman (79)

Manchester United: Sealey, Irwin, Bruce, Pallister, Blackmore, Phelan, Robson, Ince, Sharpe, Hughes, McClair
Barcelona: Busquets. Alesanco (Pinilla), Nando, Koeman R, Ferrer, Goikoetxea, Eusebio, Baquero, Beguiristain, Salinas, Laudrup

1992

6th May, 1992		*Estadio da Luz, Lisbon*	*15,000*
Werder Bremen	2	**Monaco**	0

Allofs (41), Rufer (54)

Werder Bremen: Rollmann, Wolter (Schaaf), Borowka, Bratseth, Bode, Bockenfeld, Eilts, Votova, Neubarth (Kohn), Rufer, Allofs
Monaco: Ettori, Valery (Djorkaeff), Petit, Mendy, Sonor, Dib, Gnako, Passi, Barros, Weah, Fofana (Clement)

1993

12th May, 1993   *Wembley, London*   *37,393*

Parma   **3**   **Royal Antwerp**   **1**

Minotti (9), Melli (30), Cuoghi (83)   Severeyns (12)

Parma: Ballotta, Benarrivo, Di Chiara, Minotti, Apolloni, Grun, Melli,
Zoratto (Pin), Osio (Pizzi), Cuoghi, Brolin
Royal Antwerp: Stojanovic, Kiekens, Broeckaert, Taeymans, Smidts,
Jakovljevic (Van Veirdeghem), Van Rethy, Segers (Moukrim), Severeyns,
Lehnhoff, Czerniatynski

UEFA Cup
1992-93

Re-Juvenated!

For Juve coach Giovanni Trapattoni, the UEFA Cup provided a fitting fillip to what was for him and his Juventus side, a most difficult and controversial season. Disappointing in Serie A having spent millions to acquire the likes of Baggio and Vialli, the pressure was on for a major success. Despite the undoubted talent in the Dortmund side, the final itself proved to be a very one-sided affair. Juve, going for their second UEFA Cup triumph in four seasons, established a powerful advantage in the first leg when they beat the Germans 3-1 in front of a stunned German audience. The Baggio duo – Roberto and Dino – inevitably grabbed all the headlines, with Roberto helping himself to two goals and Dino collecting the other. This after Michael Rummenigge had given the home side the perfect start after just two minutes.

Significantly, this first-leg lead was achieved without the assistance of England midfielder David Platt who, having spent most of a frustrating season playing out of position, was dropped for both the first and second legs of the final. Any conceivable worries that Juve fans might have nurtured about the possibility of their team throwing away their aggregate lead in the second leg were quickly dispelled when Dino Baggio punished the German defence with a powerful drive and sent the 60,000 fans in the Stadio Delle Alpi into ecstasy.

The same Baggio added a second goal five minutes before the interval when he converted a free-kick with a thumping header and Andreas Moller, formerly a Borussia player, added a third after 65 minutes when he somewhat fortuitously deflected an attempted clearance in to the German net.

As the home fans celebrated at the final whistle, a trophy had brought some relief and joy to a season that had been tarnished by controversy surrounding the club and their coach Giovanni Trapattoni. But the quality of the achievement was not to be underestimated. In winning the trophy, their first for three long years, Juventus became the only team to win the UEFA Cup three times since it replaced the Fairs Cup in 1972. Interestingly, all three triumphs came in periods under the guidance of Trapattoni.

The Real Thing

British clubs entered the UEFA Cup full of confidence. Manchester United, winners of the Rumbelows Cup, had emerged from a traumatic season when they had narrowly failed to clinch their first league title for 25 years, with a powerful young squad well-equipped for European competition.

But their high hopes for a repeat of the success they enjoyed in 1991 in the Cup-Winners competition were not to be. A goalless draw at home to Torpedo Moscow left United facing a tricky away leg in the Russian capital. Needing to score, the United attack failed to breach the Moscow rearguard, and despite extra-time, the only way of deciding the tie was the inevitable and odious penalty shoot-out, where Alex Ferguson's side capitulated 4-3.

Meanwhile Sheffield Wednesday, English football's other representatives in the competition, were continuing to develop as future title contenders under the watchful gaze of manager Trevor Francis. Wednesday it was who made the most impressive start, producing the highest score of the first round with an 8-1 demolition of Spora Luxembourg, with Paul Warhurst showing all the predatory instincts he demonstrated later in the season to collect a brace of goals. However, he narrowly escaped death when he swallowed his tongue. But the young striker/defender recovered in time to play in the second leg and notch another goal as Wednesday recorded a 10-2 aggregate victory.

They were joined in the second round by a much-relieved Celtic side who had miraculously negotiated a safe passage past Cologne. Trailing 2-0 from the first leg, Liam Brady's side conjured a memorable performance at Parkhead to win 3-0 thanks to goals from Paul McStay, Gerry Creaney and John Collins.

Hearts also kept the Scottish flag flying with a spirited fightback against Slavia Prague, clawing their way into the second round with a second leg 4-2 victory, following a 1-0 first-leg defeat.

Hibernian were not so fortunate. Having held Anderlecht 2-2 at home, the Scottish side were unable to produce the victory they needed, and a 1-1 draw in Holland meant they went out on the away goals rule.

Wednesday's next opponents in the competition produced a disastrous result. German Bundesliga side Kaiserslautern triumphed 3-1 at home and to make matters worse, England ace David Hirst was sent off in a bad-tempered encounter. A 2-2 draw at Hillsborough spelt the end for Wednesday and they were not to be the only British casualty. Celtic were dismissed by Borussia Dortmund 3-1 on aggregate and the exit of Hearts to a powerful Standard Liege side amounted to the end of British interest in the competition.

Napoli were a major casualty of the second round, ousted by an impressive Paris St Germain side 2-0 on aggregate, while UEFA Cup-holders Ajax, Juventus and Real Madrid continued to make ominously efficient progress towards the closing stages of the competition.

Final Draws

The quarter-final draw included most of the fancied teams in the competition, although Roma had quite a scare against Turkish side Galatasaray, who clinched a third round, second leg 3-2 victory, but lost 5-4 on aggregate.

Arguably the tie of the round was the clash between Italian giants Juventus and former Portuguese champions Benfica. Benfica won the first contest 2-1, but Juve responded with a 3-1 victory at home with two goals from Kohler and one from Dino Baggio.

Italian rivals Roma were dispatched by Borussia Dortmund 2-1 on aggregate and Spanish hopes ended with the disappearance over two legs of Real Madrid, with Paris St Germain recovering to win 4-1 in the second leg and clinch a 5-4 aggregate victory. Auxerre completed the quartet, setting up a semi-final clash with Borussia Dortmund following a good win over strongly fancied Ajax, who were tipped to retain the trophy they won last season when beating Torino in the final.

But, in what was to prove to be a sensational year for Italian clubs in European competitions, with the Serie A boasting a side in each of the finals, it was Juventus who overcame Paris St Germain to set up the mouthwatering prospect of a final against Borussia Dortmund, worthy victors over Auxerre.

1st Round

Austria Salzburg	**Ajax**	0-3	10,000
	Davids (53), Overmars (65), Kreek (79)		
Ajax	**Austria Salzburg**	3-1	12,500
Pettersson (26, 79), Bergkamp (49)	Reisinger (60)		

Ajax win 6-1 on aggregate

Benfica	**Belvedur Izola**	3-0	25,000
Vitor Paneira (43, 73), William (45 pen)			
Belvedur Izola	**Benfica**	0-5	4,000
	Pacheco (21, 46, 66), Joao Pinto (58), Cesar Brito (87)		

Benfica win 8-0 on aggregate

Caen	**Real Zaragoza**	3-2	7,000
Cravelaine (7, 14), Paille (37)	Sanjuan (37), Pardeza (79)		
Real Zaragoza	**Caen**	2-0	15,000
Montanier (24), Poyet (64)			

Zaragoza win 4-3 on aggregate

Dinamo Kiev	**Rapid Vienna**	1-0	17,000
Yakovenko (46)			
Rapid Vienna	**Dinamo Kiev**	3-2	16,000
Mandreko (8), Fjortoft (16, 38)	Leonenko (44 pen, 87)		

Aggregate 3-3, Kiev win on away goals

Dinamo Moscow Sklarov (34, 62), Timofeyev (46), Simotenkov (57), Tetradze (68)	**Rosenborg** Loken (75)	**5-1**	**7,250**
Rosenborg Ingebrigsten (7), Loken (48)	**Dinamo Moscow**	**2-0**	**10,218**

Moscow Dynamo win 5-3 on aggregate

Electroputere Craiova	**Panathinaikos** Franceskos (4), Warzycha (40, 53, 66), Maragos (70), Kalatzis (85)	**0-6**	**22,000**
Panathinaikos Saravakos (43), Warzycha (58), Kalatzis (67), Frantzekos (82)	**Electro're Craiova**	**4-0**	**8,000**

Panathinaikos win 10-0 on aggregate

FC Copenhagen Johansen (12, 54), Uldbjerg (28), Hoyer Nielson (69 pen), Larsen (86)	**MP Mikkeli**	**5-0**	**8,430**
MP Mikkeli Allen (63)	**FC Copenhagen** Nielsen (5), Johansen (17, 32, 44), Rasmussen (82)	**1-5**	**971**

Copenhagen win 10-1 on aggregate

Fenerbahce Aykut (14, 38), Tanju (55)	**Botev Plovdiv** Dermeciev (51)	**3-1**	**12,382**
Botev Plovdiv Iskrenov (5), Petrov (41)	**Fenerbahce** Ridvan (37, 78)	**2-2**	**8,000**

Fenerbahce win 5-3 on aggregate

Floriana	**Borussia Dortmund** M. Rummenigge (21)	**0-1**	**4,500**
Borussia Dortmund Zorc (10), Delia (18 o.g.), Franck (59), M Rummenigge (67), Mill (72, 79, 89)	**Floriana** Crawley (11, 17)	**7-2**	**11,790**

Dortmund win 8-2 on aggregate

Fram Reykjavik	**Kaiserslautern** Witeczek (29), Wegner (64), Kristinn Jonsson (66 o.g.)	**0-3**	**785**
Kaiserslautern Kuntz (29, 84), Witeczek (55, 57)	**Fram Reykjavik**	**4-0**	**23,197**

Kaiserslautern win 7-0 on aggregate

GKS Katowice	**Galatasaray**	**0-0**	**5,000**
Galatasaray Hakan (31), Falco (57)	**GKS Katowice** Macihevski (75)	**2-1**	**25,000**

Galatasatay win 2-1 on aggregate

Grasshoppers Zurich	Sporting Lisbon	1-2	10,750
A.Sutter (37 pen)	Balakov (45), Juskowiak (84)		
Sporting Lisbon	Grasshoppers Zurich	1-3	40,000
Cadete (84)	Elber (31, 110), Magnin (83)		

Grasshopper win 4-3 on aggregate, after extra time

Hibernian	RSC Anderlecht	2-2	14,213
Beaumont (4), McGinlay (75)	Degryse (39 pen), Van Vossen (67)		
RSC Anderlecht	Hibernian	1-1	25,000
Nilis (4)	Jackson (15)		

Aggregate 3-3, RSC Anderlecht win on away goals

IFK Norrkoping	Torino	1-0	8,601
Blom (80)			
Torino	IFK Norrkoping	3-0	22,500
Bruno (2), Casagrande (76), Aguilera (80)			

Torino win 3-1 on aggregate

Juventus	Anorthosis	6-1	5,000
R. Baggio (3), Moller (10), Vialli (43), Conte (44), Torricilli (75)	Kespaje (85)		
Anorthosis	Juventus	0-4	6,000
	Ravanelli (14), Kohler (39), Casiraghi (66, 87)		

Juventus win 10-1 on aggregate

Cologne	Celtic	2-0	15,000
Jensen (24), Ordenewitz (82)			
Celtic	Cologne	3-0	30,747
McStay (35), Creaney (39), Collins (79)			

Celtic win 3-2 on aggregate

KV Mechelen	Orebro	2-1	5,000
Eykelkamp (30), DeBoeck (63)	Milkvist (84)		
Orebro	KV Mechelen	0-0	5,085

Mechelen win 2-1 on aggregate

Lokomotiv Plovdiv	Auxerre	2-2	8,000
Sadukov (33 pen), Vidulov (57)	Baticout (3), Cocard (74)		
Auxerre	Lokomotiv Plovdiv	7-1	16,000
Baticle (2, 71), Cocard (11), Prunier (13, 48), Vahirua (28), Leaslandes (84)	Sadakov (21)		

Auxerre win 9-3 on aggregate

Manchester United	Torpedo Moscow	0-0	19,998
Torpedo Moscow	Manchester United	0-0	11,357

Aggregate 0-0, Torpedo win 4-3 on pens after extra time

Paris Saint-Germain   **PAOK Salonika**   **1-0** **25,000**
Weah (13, 24)
PAOK Salonika   **Paris Saint-Germain 0-2** **30,000**
                          Weah (15), Sassus (32)

Match abandoned after 46 min because of crowd problems
Paris Saint-Germain awarded tie and win 3-0 on aggregate

Polite. Timisoara   **Real Madrid**   **1-1** **26,000**
Cuc (62)   Alfonso (13)
Real Madrid   **Polite. Timisoara** **4-0** **40,000**
Alfonso (27), Luis Enrique (58),
Esnaider (65), Michel (87)

Real Madrid win 5-1 on aggregate

Sheffield Wednesday   **Spora Luxembourg** **8-1** **19,792**
Waddle (9), Anderson (23, 29),   Cruz (11)
Warhurst (31, 77), Bart Williams (60, 81),
Worthington (65)
Spora Luxembourg   **Sheffield Wednesday 1-2** **3,500**
Cruz (20)   Watson (18), Warhurst (36)

Sheffield Wednesday win 10-2 on aggregate

Sigma Olomouc   **Univ Craiova**   **1-0** **6,129**
Capka (87)
Univ Craiova   **Sigma Olomouc**   **1-2** **15,000**
Gane (21)   Kerber (23, 42)

Sigma win 3-1 on aggregate

Slavia Prague   **Heart of Midlothian** **1-0** **4,594**
Tatarchuk (85)
Heart of Midlothian   **Slavia Prague**   **4-2** **16,000**
Mackay (10), Baird (21), Levein (42),   Silhavy (14), Kuka (65)
Snodin (79)

Slavia win 4-3 on aggregate

Standard Liege   **Portadown**   **5-0** **12,000**
Asseiman (5, 44), Goossens (52, 65)
Leonard (56)
Portadown   **Standard Liege**   **0-0** **2,500**

Standard win 5-0 in aggregate

Vaci Izzo   **Groningen**   **1-0** **2,500**
Fuele (27)
Groningen   **Vaci Izzo**   **1-1** **5,000**
Huizingh (55)   Fuhle (43)

Vac win 2-1 on aggregate

Valencia	Napoli	1-5	34,000
Roberto (54)	Fonseca (20, 60, 63, 87, 89)		
Napoli	**Valencia**	**1-0**	**25,000**
Fonseca (7)			

Napoli win 6-1 on aggregate

Vitesse Arnhem	Derry City	3-0	10,000
Van der Brom (20, 56), Latuheru (89)			
Derry City	**Vitesse Arnhem**	**1-2**	**5,000**
Mooney (60)	Straal (44), Laamers (65)		

Vitesse win 5-1 on aggregate

Admira Wacker	Roma	1-4	8,500
Baur (36)	Giannini (17, 42), Caniggia (21), Muzzi (65)		
Roma	**Admira Wacker**	**1-0**	**23,000**
Hassler (50)			

Roma win 5-1 on aggregate

Widzew Lodz	Eintracht Frankfurt	2-2	7,600
Jozwiak (21), Koniarek (27)	Yeboah (67), Wolf (83)		
Eintracht Frankfurt	**Widzew Lodz**	**9-0**	**8,000**
Kruse (8, 14, 37), Yeboah (21, 22, 36, 69), Rahn (83), Bein (89)			

Frankfurt win 11-2 on aggregate

Vitoria Guimaraes	Real Sociedad	3-0	18,000
Kupressanin (15, 76), Barbosa (28)			
Real Sociedad	**Vitoria Guimaraes**	**2-0**	**19,200**
Lumbreras (6), Miguel Angel Fuentes (23)			

Vitoria win 3-2 on aggregate

Xamax Neuchatel	Frem Copenhagen	2-2	4,000
B Sutter (51), Manfreda (52)	Mikkelsen (17), Henchoz (21 o.g.)		
Frem Copenhagen	**Xamax Neuchatel**	**4-1**	**3,476**
Haren (17, 37), H. Jenssen (19), Thogersen (53)	Manfreda (24)		

Frem win 6-3 on aggregate

2nd Round

RSC Anderlecht	Dinamo Kiev	4-2	20,500
Nilis (23), Degryse (38), Versavel (51), Van Vossen (59)	Shkapenko (20), Leonenko (53)		
Dinamo Kiev	**RSC Anderlecht**	**0-3**	**40,000**
	Van Vossen (21), Nilis (61, 69)		

Anderlecht win 7-2 on aggregate

Auxerre **FC Copenhagen** **5-0 12,000**
Baticle (14, 40, 80), Martins (55),
Otokori (90)

FC Copenhagen **Auxerre** **0-2 5,061**
Cocard (67), Bonalair (88)

Auxerre win 7-0 on aggregate

Benfica **Vaci Izzo** **5-1 30,000**
Yuran (42), Isaias (55, 86), Szedlaczek (82)
Pencho (58 pen), William (79 pen)

Vaci Izzo **Benfica** **0-1 17,000**
Schwarz (13)

Benfica win 6-1 on aggregate

Borussia Dortmund **Celtic** **1-0 35,803**
Chapuisat (70)

Celtic **Borussia Dortmund** **1-2 31,578**
Creaney (13) Chapuisat (53), Zorc (58)

Dortmund win 3-1 on aggregate

Eintracht Frankfurt **Galatasaray** **0-0 40,000**

Galatasaray **Eintracht Frankfurt 1-0 32,500**
Ugur (5)

Galatasaray win 1-0 on aggregate

Fenerbahce **Sigma Olomouc** **1-0 32,195**
Ismail (37)

Sigma Olomouc **Fenerbahce** **7-1 10,152**
Hanus (9, 90), Kerbr (12), Barborik (34), Aykut (38)
Marosi (51), Fiala (76), Vadura (80)

Sigma win 7-2 on aggregate

Frem Copenhagen **Real Zaragoza** **0-1 2,852**
Poyet (12)

Real Zaragoza **Frem Copenhagen** **5-1 12,000**
Mateut (7, 38, 82), Seba (39, 70) Colding (73)

Zaragoza win 6-1 on aggregate

Heart of Midlothian **Standard Liege** **0-1 16,897**
Bettagno (6)

Standard Liege **Heart of Midlothian 1-0 17,000**
Wilmots (62)

Standard Liege win 2-0 on aggregate

Kaiserslautern **Sheffield Wednesday 3-1 20,802**
Funkel (5 pen), Marin (55), Hirst (5)
Witeczek (57)

Sheffield Wednesday   **Kaiserslautern**   **2-2 27,597**
D. Wilson (27), Sheridan (64)   Witeczek (62), Zeyer (76)
Kaiserslautern win 5-3 on aggregate

Napoli   **Paris Saint-Germain 0-2 19,000**
    Weah (15, 35)

Paris Saint-Germain   **Napoli**   **0-0 45,000**
Paris Saint-Germain win 2-0 on aggregate

Panathinaikos   **Juventus**   **0-1 75,000**
    Platt (68)

Juventus   **Panathinaikos**   **0-0 17,500**
Juventus win 1-0 on aggregate

Real Madrid   **Torpedo Moscow**   **5-2 43,000**
Hierro (8, 28, 32), Zamorano (52),   Shustikov (36), Grishin (39)
Michel (84 pen)

Torpedo Moscow   **Real Madrid**   **3-2 6,500**
Talalayev (11), Tishkov (62),   Zamorano (10), Hierro (56)
Mudraskov (77)
Madrid win 7-5 on aggregate

Roma   **Grasshoppers Zurich 3-0 35,000**
Carnevale (18), Rizzitelli (25), Giannini (41)

Grasshoppers Zurich   **Roma**   **4-3 9,000**
De Vicente (36 pen, 68),   Rizzitelli (7, 87), Caniggia (30)
A. Sutter (50), Gamperle (63)
AS Roma win 6-4 on aggregate

Torino   **Dinamo Moscow**   **1-2 30,000**
Timofeyev (55 o.g.)   Kasumov (44),
    Simutenkov (68)

Dinamo Moscow   **Torino**   **0-0 4,000**
Dinamo win 2-1 on aggregate

Vitoria Guimaraes   **Ajax**   **0-3 8,000**
    Davids (1), Pettersson (38),
    Bergkamp (48)

Ajax   **Vitoria Guimaraes**   **2-1 18,000**
Bergkamp (25), Alfen (61)   Mbote (57)
Ajax win 5-1 on aggregate

Vitesse Arnhem   **KV Mechelen**   **1-0 9,491**
Van Der Brom (33)

KV Mechelen   **Vitesse Arnhem**   **0-1 9,000**
    Cocu (73)
Vitesse win 2-0 on aggregate

3rd Round

Ajax	Kaiserslautern	2-0	42,000

Davids (1), Jonk (83)

Kaiserslautern	Ajax	0-1	27,000

Rob Alflen (43)

Ajax win 3-0 on aggregate

Borussia Dortmund	Real Zaragoza	3-1	36,800

Chapuisat (12), Zorc (23 pen), Povlsen (42)

Franco (51)

Real Zaragoza	Borussia Dortmund	2-1	35,000

Poyet (26), Brehme (90)

Chapuisat (51)

Borussia win 4-3 on aggregate

Moscow Dynamo	Benfica	2-2	6,000

Kalitvintsev (75), Dertkatch (88)

Isaias (35, 54)

Benfica	Moscow Dynamo	2-0	50,000

Isaias (51), Yuran (58)

Benfica win 4-2 on aggregate

Paris Saint-Germain	RSC Anderlecht	0-0	32,402

RSC Anderlecht	Paris Saint-Germain	1-1	19,000

Bosman (53)

Kombouare (75)

Paris win on away-goals rule. Aggregate 1-1

Roma	Galatasaray	3-1	23,980

Aldair (58, 90), Muzzi (80)

Hakan (85)

Galatasaray	Roma	3-2	30,000

Mustafa (27, 58), Arif (75)

Caniggia (8), Hassler (47)

Roma win 5-4 on aggregate

Sigma Olomouc	Juventus	1-2	15,000

Marosi (89)

Moller (23), D. Baggio (76)

Juventus	Sigma Olomouc	5-0	

Vialli (6, 50), Casiraghi (28), Moller (46), Ravanelli (69)

Juventus win 7-1 on aggregate

Standard Liege	Auxerre	2-2	18,000

Goossens (9, 48)

Verlaat (55), Baticle (71)

Auxerre	Standard Liege	2-1	19,000

Baticle (71), Dutuel (82)

Wilmots (88)

Auxerre win 4-3 on aggregate

| Vitesse Arnhem | Real Madrid | 0-1 | 13,000 |
| | Hierro (73) | | |

| Real Madrid | Vitesse Arnhem | 1-0 | 36,000 |
| Zamorano (31) | | | |

Real win 2-0 on aggregate

Quarter-Finals

Auxerre	Ajax	4-2	18,000
Verlaat (17), Martins (43), Vahirua (82),	Pettersson (3), Vink (44)		
Dutuel (89)			

| Ajax | Auxerre | 1-0 | 43,000 |
| de Boer (61) | | | |

Auxerre win 4-3 on aggregate

| Benfica | Juventus | 2-1 | 70,000 |
| Vitor Paneira (12, 76) | Vialli (59 pen) | | |

| Juventus | Benfica | 3-0 | 51,697 |
| Kohler (2), D. Baggio (45), Ravanelli (68) | | | |

Juventus win 4-2 on aggregate

Real Madrid	Paris Saint-Germain	3-1	50,000
B. Agueno (30), Zamorano (36),	Ginola (47)		
Michel (89)			

Paris Saint-Germain	Real Madrid	4-1	45,000
Weah (33), Ginola (80), Valdo (87),	Zamorano (89)		
Kombouare (90)			

Paris win 5-4 on aggregate

| Roma | Borussia Dortmund | 1-0 | 40,000 |
| Mihajlovic (66) | | | |

| Borussia Dortmund | Roma | 2-0 | 36,800 |
| Schulz (40), Sippel (46) | | | |

Dortmund win 2-1 on aggregate

Semi Finals

| Borussia Dortmund | Auxerre | 2-0 | 45,000 |
| Karl (58), Zorc (87) | | | |

| Auxerre | Borussia Dortmund | 2-0 | 18,400 |
| Martins (6), Verlaat (71) | | | |

Borussia Dortmund win 6-5 on penalties. 2-2 on aggregate

Juventus R. Baggio (3, 89)	**Paris Saint-Germain**	**2-1**	**42,793**
	Weah (23)		
Paris Saint-Germain	**Juventus** R. Baggio (77)	**0-1**	**48,000**

Juventus win 3-1 on aggregate

Final

Dortmund
Borussia Dortmund   **Juventus**   **1-3** **37,000**
M. Rummenigge (2)   D. Baggio (27), R. Baggio (31, 74)

19th May, 1993   Turin
Juventus   **Borussia Dortmund** **3-0** **60,000**
D. Baggio (5, 40), Moller (65)

Juventus win 6-1 on aggregate

UEFA Cup Final Details
1955/56-1992/93

1958

1st Leg, 5th March 1958   *Stamford Bridge, London*   *45,000*

London Select XI   **2**   **Barcelona**   **2**

Greaves (5), Langley (83)   Tejada (4), Martinez (43)

London: Kelsey, Sillett, Langley, Blanchflower, Norman, Koot, Groves, Greaves, Smith, Haynes, Robb

Barcelona: Estrems, Olivella, Segarra, Gracia, Gensana, Ribelles, Basora, Evaristo, Martinez, Villaverde, Tejada

2nd Leg, 1st May 1958   *Nou Camp, Barcelona*   *62,000*

Barcelona   **6**   **London Select XI**   **0**

Suarez (2 goals), Evaristo (2 goals), Martinez, Verges

Barcelona: Ramallets, Olivella, G Segarra, Verges, Brugue, Gensana, Tejada, Evaristo, Martinez, Suarez, Basora

London: Kelsey, Wright, Cantwell, Blanchflower, Brown, Bowen, Medwin, Groves, Smith, Bloomfield, Lewis

Barcelona win 8-2 on aggregate

1960

1st Leg, 29th March, 1960   *St. Andrews, Birmingham*   *40,000*

Birmingham City   **0**   **Barcelona**   **0**

Birmingham City: Schofield, Farmer, Allen, Watts, Smith, Neal, Astall, Gordon, Weston, Orritt, Hooper

Barcelona: Ramallets, Olivella, Gracia, Segarra, Rodri, Gensana, Coll, Kocsis, Martinez, Ribelles, Villaverde

2nd Leg, 4th March, 1960   *Nou Camp, Barcelona*   *70,000*

Barcelona   **4**   **Birmingham City**   **1**

Martinez (3), Czibor (6, 48), Coll (78)   Hooper (82)

Barcelona: Ramallets, Olivella, Gracia, Verges, Rodri, Segarra, Coll, Ribelles, Martinez, Kubala, Czibor

Birmingham City: Schofield, Farmer, Allen, Watts, Smith, Neal, Astall, Gordon, Weston, Murphy, Hooper

Barcelona win 4-1 on aggregate

1961

1st Leg, 27th September, 1961   St Andrews, Birmingham   21,000
Birmingham City 2   **Roma** 2
Hellawell (78), Orritt (85)   Manfredini (30, 56)
Birmingham City: Schofield, Farmer, Sissons, Hennessey, Foster, Beard,
Hellawell, Bloomfield, Harris, Orritt, Auld
Roma: Cudicini, Fontana, Corsini; Guiliano, Losi, Carpanesi, Orlando, Da
Costa, Manfredini, Angelillo, Menichelli

2nd Leg, 11th October, 1961   Stadio Olimpico, Rome   60,000
Roma 2   **Birmingham City** 0
Own Goal (56), Pestrin (90)
Roma: Cudicini, Fontana, Corsini, Carpanesi, Losi, Pestrin, Orlando,
Angelillo, Manfredini, Lojacono, Menichelli
Birmingham City: Schofield, Farmer, Sissons, Hennessey, Smith, Beard,
Hellawell, Bloomfield, Harris, Singer, Orrit.
Roma win 4-2 on aggregate

1962

1st Leg, 8th September, 1962   Luis Casanova, Valencia   56,000
Valencia 6   **Barcelona** 2
Yosu (14, 42), Guillot (35, 54, 67),   Kocsis (4, 20)
Nunez (74)
Valencia: Zamora, Piquer, Mestre, Sastre, Quincoces, Chicao, Nunez,
Ribelles, Waldo, Guillot, Yosu
Barcelona: Pesudo, Benitez, Rodri, Olivella, Verges, Gracia, Cubilla, Kocsis,
Re, Vilaverde, Camps

2nd Leg, 12th September, 1962   Nou Camp, Barcelona   60,000
Barcelona 1   **Valencia** 1
Kocsis (46)   Guillot (87)
Barcelona: Pesudo, Benitez, Garay, Fuste, Verges, Gracia, Cubilla, Kocsis,
Goyvaerts, Villaverde, Camps
Valencia: Zamora, Pique, Mestre, Sastre, Quincoces, Chicao, Nunez, Urtiaga,
Waldo, Guillot, Yosu
Valencia win 7-3 on aggregate

1963

1st Leg, 12th June, 1963   Dinamo Stadion, Zagreb   40,000
Dinamo Zagreb 1   **Valencia** 2
Zambata (13)   Waldo (64), Urtiaga (67)
Dinamo Zagreb: Skoric, Belin, Braun, Biscam, Markovic, Perusic, Kobesnac,
Zambata, Knez, Matus, Lamza

Valencia: Zamora, Piquer, Chicao, Paquito, Quincoces, Sastre, Manio, Sanchez-Lage, Waldo, Ribelles, Urtiaga

2nd Leg, 26th June, 1963   *Luis Casanova, Valencia*   *55,000*

Valencia   **2**   **Dinamo Zagreb**   **0**

Manio (68), Nunez (78)

Valencia: Zamora, Piquer, Chicao, Paquito, Quincoces, Sastre, Manio, Sanchez-Lage, Waldo, Ribelles, Nunez
Dinamo Zagreb: Skoric, Belin, Braun, Matus, Markovic, Perustic, Kobesnac, Lamza, Raus, Zambata, Knez
                    Valencia win 4-1 on aggregate

1964

25th June, 1964   *Nou Camp, Barcelona*   *50,000*

Real Zaragoza   **2**   **Valencia**   **1**

Villa (40), Marcelino (83)   Urtiaga (42)

Real Zaragoza: Yarza, Cortizo, Santamaria, Reija, Isasi, Pais, Canario, Duca, Marcelino, Villa, Lapetra
Valencia: Zamora, Arnal, Villegani, Paquito, Quincoces, Roterto, Suco, Guillot, Waldo, Urtiaga, Ficha
                    One match only – Real Zaragoza win 2-1

1965

23rd June, 1965   *Comunale, Turin*   *25,000*

Ferencvaros   **1**   **Juventus**   **0**

Fenyvesi (74)

Fenencvaros: Geczi, Novak, Horvath, Juhasz, Matrai, Orosz, Kraba, Vrga, Albert, Rakosi, Fenyvesi
Juventus: Anzolin, Gori, Sartri, Bercellino, Castano, Leoncini, Stachini, Del Sol, Combin, Mazzia, Menichelli
                    One match only – Ferencvaros win 1-0

1966

1st Leg, 14th September, 1966   *Nou Camp, Barcelona*   *70,000*

Barcelona   **0**   **Real Zaragoza**   **1**

                                        Canario (30)

Barcelona: Sadurni, Benitez, Eladio, Montesinos, Gallego, Torres, Zaballa, Muller, Zaldua, Fuste, Vidal
Real Zaragoza: Yarza, Irusquieta, Reija, Pais, Santamaria, Violeta, Canario, Santos, Marcelino, Villa, Lapertra

2nd Leg, 21st September, 1966   *La Romareda, Zaragoza*   *35,000*

Real Zaragoza   2   **Barcelona**   4

Marcelino (24, 87)   Pujol (3, 86, 120), Zaballa (89)

Real Zaragoza: Yarza, Irsquieta, Reija, Pais, Santamaria, Violeta, Canario,
Santos, Marcelino, Villa, Lapetra
Barcelona: Sadureni, Foncho, Eladio, Montesinos, Gallego, Torres, Zaballa,
Mas, Zaldua, Fuste, Pujol
                    Barcelona win 4-3 on aggregate

1967

1st Leg, 30th August, 1967   *Dinamo Stadion, Zagreb*   *40,000*

Dinamo Zagreb   2   **Leeds United**   0

Cercek (39, 59)

Dinamo Zagreb: Skoric, Gracanin, Brncic, Belin, Ramljak, Blaskovic,
Cercek, Piric, Zambata, Gucmirtl, Rora
Leeds Utd: Sprake, Reaney, Cooper, Bremner, Charlton, Hunter, Bates,
Lorimer, Belfitt, Gray, O'Grady

2nd Leg, 6th September, 1967   *Elland Road, Leeds*   *35,000*

Leeds United   0   **Dinamo Zagreb**   0

Leeds Utd: Sprake, Bell, Cooper, Bremner, Charlton, Hunter, Reaney, Belfitt,
Greenhoff, Giles, O'Grady
Dinamo Zagreb: Skoric, Gracanin, Brncic, Belin, Ramljak, Blaskovic,
Cercek, Piric, Zambata, Gucmirtl, Rora
                    Dinamo Zagreb win 2-0 on aggregate

1968

1st Leg, 7th September, 1968   *Elland Road, Leeds*   *76,000*

Leeds United   1   **Ferencvaros**   0

Jones (41)

Leeds Utd: Sprake, Reaney, Cooper, Bremner, Charlton, Hunter, Lorimer,
Madeley, Jones (Belfitt), Giles (Greenhoff), Gray
Ferencvaros: Geczi, Novak, Pancsics, Havasi, Juhasz, Szucs, Szoke, Varga,
Albert, Rakosi, Fenyvesi (Balint)

2nd Leg, 11th September, 1968   *Nepstadion, Budapest*   *76,000*

Ferencvaros   0   **Leeds United**   0

Ferencvaros: Geczi, Novak, Pancsics, Havasi, Juhasz, Szucs, Rakosi, Szoke
(Karaba), Varga, Albert, Katona
Leeds Utd: Sprake, Reaney, Cooper, Bremner, Charlton, Hunter, O'Grady,
Lorimer, Jones, Madeley, Hibbit (Bates)
                    Leeds United win 1-0 on aggregate

1969

1st Leg, 29th May, 1969   *St James' Park, Newcastle*   *60,000*

Newcastle United   **3**   **Ujpest Dozsa**   **0**

Moncur (63, 72), Scott (83)

Newcastle: McFaul, Craig, Clark, Gibb, Burton, Moncur, Scott, Robson, Davies, Arentoft, Sinclair (Foggon)

Ujpest Dozsa: Szentmilhalyi, Kaposzta, Solymosi, Bankuti, Nosko, Dunai E, Fazekas, Gorocs, Bene, Dunai A, Zambo

2nd Leg, 11th June, 1969   *Budapest*   *37,000*

Ujpest Dozsa   **2**   **Newcastle United**   **3**

Bene (31), Gorocs (44)   Moncur (46), Arentoft (50), Foggon (74)

Ujpesti Dozsa: Szentmilhalyi, Kaposzta, Solymosi, Bankuti, Nosko, Dunai E, Fazekas, Gorocs, Bene, Dunai A, Zambo

Newcastle: McFaul, Craig, Clark, Gibb, Burton, Moncur, Scott (Foggon), Arentoft, Robson, Davies, Sinclair

Newcastle United 6-2 on aggregate

1970

1st Leg, 22nd May, 1970   *Parc Astrid, Brussels*   *37,000*

RSC Anderlecht   **3**   **Arsenal**   **1**

Devrindt (25), Mulder (30, 74)   Kennedy (82)

RSC Anderlecht: Trappeniers, Heylens, Velkeneers, Kialunda, Cornelis (Peeters), Nordahl, Desanghere, Puis, Devrindt, Van Himst, Mulder

Arsenal: Wilson, Storey, McNab, Kelly, McLintock, Simpson, Armstrong, Sammels, Radford, George (Kennedy), Graham

2nd Leg, 28th April, 1970   *Highbury, London*   *51,000*

Arsenal   **3**   **RSC Anderlecht**   **0**

Kelly (25), Radford (75), Sammels (76)

Arsenal: Wilson, Storey, McNab, Kelly, McLintock, Simpson, Armstrong, Sammels, Radford, George, Graham

RSC Anderlecht: Trappeniers, Heylens, Velkeneers, Kialunda, Martens, Nordahl, Desanghere, Puis, Devrindt, Mulder, Van Himst

Arsenal win 4-3 on aggregate

1971

1st Leg, 28th May, 1971   *Comunale, Turin*   *65,000*

Juventus   **2**   **Leeds United**   **2**

Bettega (27), Capello (55)   Madeley (48), Bates (77)

Juventus: Piloni, Spinosl, Salvadore, Mardhetti, Furino, Morini, Haller, Capello, Causio, Anastasi (Novellini), Bettege

Leeds Utd: Sprake, Reaney, Cooper, Bremner, Charlton, Hunter, Lorimer, Clarke, Jones (Bates), Giles, Madeley

2nd Leg, 3rd June, 1971		*Elland Road, Leeds*	*42,000*

Leeds United   1   **Juventus**   1
Clarke (12)   Anastasi (20)

Leeds Utd: Sprake, Reaney, Cooper, Bremner, Charlton, Hunter, Lorimer, Clarke, Jones, Giles, Madeley (Bates)
Juventus: Tancredi, Spinosl, Salvadore, Mardhetti, Furino, Morini, Haller, Capello, Causio, Anastasi, Bettege
    Leeds United win on away goals rule. 3-3 on aggregate

1972

1st Leg, 3rd May, 1972   *Molineux, Wolverhampton*   *38,000*

Wolverhampton Wdrs   1   **Tottenham Hotspur**   2
McCalliog (72)   Chivers (57, 87)

Wolves: Parkes, Shaw, Taylor, Hegan, Munro, McAlle, McCalliog, Hibbitt, Richards, Dougan, Wagstaffe
Tottenham: Jennings, Kinnear, Knowles, Mullery, England, Beal, Gilzean, Perryman, Chivers, Peters, Coates (Pratt)

2nd Leg, 17th May, 1972   *White Hart Lane, London*   *54,000*

Tottenham Hotspur   1   **Wolverhampton Wdrs**   1
Mullery (30)   Wagstaffe (41)

Tottenham: Jennings, Kinnear, Knowles, Mullery, England, Beal, Gilzean, Perryman, Chivers, Peters, Coates
Wolves: Parkes, Shaw, Taylor, Hegan, Munro, McAlle, McCalliog, Hibbitt (Bailey), Richards, Dougan (Curran), Wagstaffe
    Tottenham win 3-2 on aggregate

1973

1st Leg, 10th June, 1973   *Anfield, Liverpool*   *41,000*

Liverpool   3   **Bor. Monchengladbach**   0
Keegan (21, 32), Lloyd (61)

Liverpool: Clemence, Lawler, Lindsay, Smith, Lloyd, Hughes, Keegan, Cormack, Toshack, Heighway (Hall), Callaghan
Borussia: Kleff, Michallik, Netzer, Bonhof, Vogts, Wimmer, Danner, Kulik, Jensen, Rupp (Simonsen), Heynckes

2nd Leg, 23rd June, 1973   *Bokelbergstadion, Monchen*   *35,000*

Bor. Monchengladbach   2   **Liverpool**   0
Heynckes (29, 40)

Borussia: Kleff, Surau, Netzer, Bonhof, Vogts, Wimmer, Danner, Kulik, Jensen, Rupp, Heynckes

Liverpool: Clemence, Lawler, Lindsay, Smith, Lloyd, Hughes, Keegan, Cormack, Heighway (Boersma), Toshack, Callaghan
Liverpool win 3-2 on aggregate

1974

1st Leg, 21st June, 1974　　　*White Hart Lane, London*　　　46,000

Tottenham Hotspur　　**2**　　**Feyenoord**　　**2**

England (39) Own Goal (64)　　　　Van Hanegem (43), de Jong (85)

Tottenham: Jennings, Evans, Naylor, Pratt, England, Beal, McGrath, Perryman, Peters, Chivers, Coates

Feyenoord: Treytel, Rijsbergen, Van Daele, Israel, Vos, de Jong, Jansen, Van Hanegem, Ressel, Schoemaker, Kristensen

2nd Leg, 29th May, 1974　　　*Feyenoord, Rotterdam*　　　59,000

Feyenoord　　**2**　　**Tottenham Hotspur**　　**0**

Rijsbergen (43), Ressel (84)

Feyenoord: Treytel, Rijsbergen, Van Daele, Israel, Vos, Ramljak, Jansen, de Jong, Ressel, Schoemaker, Kristensen (Boskamp) (Wery)

Tottenham: Jennings, Evans, Naylor, Pratt (Holder), England, Beal, McGrath, Perryman Peters, Chivers, Coates

Feyenoord win 4-2 on aggregate

1975

1st Leg, 7th May, 1975　　　*Rheinstadion, Dusseldorf*　　　42,000

Bor. Monchengladbach 0　　**FC Twente**　　**0**

Borussia: Kleff, Wittkamp, Stielike, Vogts, Surau, Bonhof, Wimmer, Danner (Del'Haye), Kulik (Schaffer), Simonsen, Jensen

FC Twente: Gross, Drost, Van Iessel, Overweg, Oranen, Thijssen, Pahlplatz, Van der Vall, Bos, Jeuring (Achterberg), Zuidema

2nd Leg, 21st May, 1975　　　*Diekman, Enschede*　　　21,000

FC Twente　　**1**　　**Bor. Monchengladbach 5**

Drost (76)　　　　Simonsen (2, 86), Heynckes (9, 50, 60)

FC Twente: Gross, Drost, Van Iessel, Overweg, Oranen, Bos (Muhren), Thijssen, Pahlplatz (Achterberg), Van der Vall, Jeuring, Zuidema

Borussia: Kleff, Wittkamp, Vogts, Surau (Schaffer), Kinkhammer, Bonhof, Wimmer (Koppel), Danner, Simonsen, Jensen, Heynckes

Bor. Monchengladbach win 5-1 on aggregate

1976

1st Leg, 28th April, 1976   *Anfield, Liverpool*   *49,000*

Liverpool   **3**   **Club Bruges**   **2**

Kennedy (59), Case (61), Keegan (65)   Lambert (5), Cools (15)

Liverpool: Clemence, Smith, Neal, Thompson, Hughes, Keegan, Kennedy, Callaghan, Fairclough, Heighway, Toshack (Case)
Bruges: Jensen, Bastijns, Krieger, Leekens, Volders, Cools, Vandereycken, Decubber, Van Gool, Lambert, Lefevre

2nd Leg, 19th May, 1976   *Olympiastadion, Bruges*   *32,000*

Club Bruges   **1**   **Liverpool**   **1**

Lambert (11)   Keegan (15)

Bruges: Jensen, Bastijns, Krieger, Leekens, Volders, Cools, Vandereycken, Decubber (Hinderyckx), Van Gool, Lambert (Sanders), Lefevre
Liverpool: Clemence, Smith, Neal, Thompson, Hughes, Keegan, Kennedy, Callaghan, Case, Heighway, Toshack (Fairclough)

Liverpool win 4-3 on aggregate

1977

1st Leg, 4th May, 1977   *Comunale, Turin*   *75,000*

Juventus   **1**   **Athletic Bilbao**   **0**

Tardelli (15)

Juventus: Zoff, Cuccureddu, Gentile, Scirea, Morini, Tardelli, Furino, Benetti, Causio, Boninsegna (Gori), Bettega
Athletic Bilbao: Iribar, Quaderra, Escalza, Guoicoechea, Guisasola, Villar, Irureta, Rojo M, Churruca, Dani, Rojo J

2nd Leg, 18th May, 1977   *San Mames, Bilbao*   *43,000*

Athletic Bilbao   **2**   **Juventus**   **1**

Churruca (11), Carlos (78)   Bettega (7)

Athletic Bilbao: Iribar, Lasa (Carlos), Guisasola, Alesanco, Escalza, Villar, Churruca, Irureta, Amarrortu, Dani, Rojo J
Juventus: Zoff, Cuccureddu, Morini, Scirea, Gentile, Causio, Tardelli, Furino, Benetti, Boninsegna (Spinosi), Bettega

Juventus win on away goals rule. 2-2 on aggregate

1978

1st Leg, 26th April, 1978   *Furiani, Bastia*   *15,000*

SEC Bastia   **0**   **PSV Eindhoven**   **0**

Bastia: Hiard, Burkhard, Guesdon, Orlanducci, Cazes, Papi, Lacuesta (Felix), Larios, Rep, Krimau, Mariot
PSV Eindhoven: Van Beveren, Van Draay, Drijgh, Stevens, Breandts, Poortvliet, Van der Duijlen, Van de Kerkhof W, Deijkers, Van de Kerkhof R, Lubse

2nd Leg, 9th May, 1978   *Philips Stadion, Eindhoven*   27,000
PSV Eindhoven   **3**   **SEC Bastia**   **0**
W. Van der Kerkhof (24), Deijkers (67)
Van der Kuijlen (69)
PSV Eindhoven: Van Beveren, Krijgh, Stevens, Van Draay (Deacy), Brandts,
Van de Kerkhof W, Poortvliet, Van der Kuijlen , Lubse, Keijkers, Van de
Kerkhof R
Bastia: Hiard (Weller), Marchioni, Orlanducci, Guesdon, Cazes, Lacuesta,
Larios, Papi, Rep, Krimau, Mariot (De Zerbi)
              PSV Eindhoven win 3-0 on aggregate

1979

1st Leg, 9th May, 1979   *Crevna Zvezda, Belgrade*   87,000
Red Star Belgrade   **1**   **Bor. Monchengladbach**   **1**
Sestic (21)   Own Goal (60)
Red Star: Stojanovic, Jovanovic, Miletovic, Jurisic, Jovin, Muslin
(Krmpotic), Petrovic, Blagojevic, Milosavljevic (Milovanovic), Savic, Sestic
Borussia: Kneib, Vogts, Hannes, Schaffer, Ringels, Schafer, Kulik, Nielsen
(Danner), Wohlers (Gores), Simonsen, Lienen

2nd Leg, 23rd May, 1979   *Rheinstadion, Dusseldorf*   45,000
Bor. Monchengladach   **1**   **Red Star Belgrade**   **0**
Simonsen (15)
Borussia: Kneib, Vogts, Hannes, Schaffer, Ringels, Schafer, Kulik (Koppel),
Gores, Wohlers, Simonsen, Lienen
Red Star: Stojanovic, Jovanovic, Miletovic, Jurisic, Jovin Muslin, Petrovic,
Blagojevic, Milovanovic (Sestic), Savic, Milosavljevic
              Bor. Monchengladbach win 2-1 on aggregate

1980

1st Leg, 7th May 1980
Bor. Monchengladbach   **3**   **Eintracht Frankfurt**   **2**
Kulik (44, 88), Matthaus (76)   Karger (37), Holzenbein (71)
Borussia: Kneib, Hannes, Schafer, Ringels, Matthaus, Kulik, Nielsen
(Thychosen), Del'Haye (Bodeker), Nickel, Lienen
Eintracht: Pahl, Pezzey, Neuberger, Korbel, Ehrmanntraut, Lorant,
Holzenbein (Nachtweih), Borchers, Nickel, Tscha, Kager (Trapp)

2nd Leg, 21st May 1980
Eintracht Frankfurt   **1**   **Bor. Monchengladbach**   **0**
Schaub (81)
Eintracht: Pahl, Pezzey, Neuberger, Korbel, Ehrmanntraut, Lorant,
Holzenbein, Borchers, Nickel, Tscha, Nachtweih (Schaub)

Borussia: Kneib, Bodeker, Hannes, Schafer, Ringels, Matthaus (Thychosen), Fleer, Kulik, Nielsen (Del'Haye), Nickel, Lienen

Eintracht Frankfurt win on away goals rule. 3-3 on aggregate

1981

1st Leg, 6th May, 1981　　　　　*Portman Road, Ipswich*　　　*27,000*

Ipswich Town　　　**3**　　　**AZ 67 Alkmaar**　　　**0**

Wark (28), Thijssen (46), Mariner (56)

Ipswich Town: Cooper, Mills, Osman, Butcher, McCall, Thijssen, Wark, Muhren, Mariner, Brazil, Gates

AZ 67 Alkmaar: Treytel, Van de Meer, Spelbos, Metgod, Hovenkamp, Peters, Jonker, Arntz, Nygaard (Welzl), Kist, Tol

2nd Leg, 20th May, 1981　　　　*Olympisch Stadion, Amsterdam*　　*28,000*

AZ 67 Alkmaar　　　**4**　　　**Ipswich Town**　　　**2**

Welzl (7), Metgod (25), Tol (40),　　　　　Thijssen (4), Wark (32)

AZ 67 Alkmaar: Treytel, Reijnders, Spelbos, Metgod, Hovenkamp, Peters, Arntz, Jonker, Nygaard, Welzl (Van den Dungen), Tol (Kist)

Ipswich Town: Cooper, Mills, Osman, Butcher, McCall, Thijssen, Wark, Muhren, Mariner, Brazil, Gates

Ipswich Town win 5-4 on aggregate

1982

1st Leg, 5th May, 1982　　　　　*Nya Ullevi, Gothenburg*　　　*42,000*

IFK Gothenburg　　　**1**　　　**SV Hamburg**　　　**0**

Tord Holmgren (87)

IFK Gothenburg: Wernersson, Svensson, Hysen, Karlsson C, Fredriksson, Tord Holmgren, Karlsson J, Stromberg, Corneliusson, Nilsson (Sandberg), Tommy Holmgren (Schiller)

Hamburg: Stein, Kaltz, Jakobs, Hieronymus, Groh, Hartwig, Wehmeyer, Magath, Von Heesen (Memering), Bastrup, Hrubesch

2nd Leg, 19th May, 1982　　　　*Volksparkstadin, Hamburg*　　*60,000*

SV Hamburg　　　**0**　　　**IFK Gothenburg**　　　**3**

　　　　　　　　　　　　　　Corneliusson (26), Nilsson (61), Fredriksson (63)

Hamburg: Stein, Kaltz (Hidien), Hieronymus, Groh, Wehmeyer, Hartwig, Memering, Magath, Von Heesen, Hrubesch, Bastrup

IFK Gothenburg: Wernersson, Svensson, Hysen (Schiller), Karlsson C, Fredriksson, Tord Holmgren, Stromberg, Karlsson J, Corneliusson (Sandberg), Nilsson, Tommy Holmgren

IFK win 4-0 on aggregate

1983

1st Leg, 4th May, 1983   *Heysel, Brussels*   55,000

RSC Anderlecht   **1**   **Benfica**   **0**

Brylle (29)

Anderlecht: Munaron, Hofkens, Peruzovic, Olsen, De Groote, Frimann, Coeck, Vercauteren, Lozano, Vandenbergh (Czerniatynski), Brylle
Benfica: Bento, Pietra, Alvaro, Humberto Coelho, Jose Luis, Sheu (Bastos Lopes), Frederico, Carlos Manuel, Chalana (Nene), Diamantino, Filipovic

2nd Leg, 18th May, 1983   *Estadio da Luz, Lisbon*   80,000

Benfica   **1**   **RSC Anderlecht**   **1**

Sheu (36)   Lozano (38)

Benfica: Bento, Pietra, Humberto Coelho, Bastos Lopes, Veloso (Alves), Carlos Manuel, Stromberg, Sheu (Filipovic), Chalana, Nene, Diamantino
Anderlecht: Munaron, Peruzovic, De Greef, Broos, Olsen, De Groot, Frimann, Lozano, Coeck, Vercauteren, Vandenbergh (Brylle)

Anderlecht win 2-1 on aggregate

1984

1st Leg, 9th April, 1984   *Parc Astrid, Brussels*   35,000

RSC Anderlecht   **1**   **Tottenham Hotspur**   **1**

Olsen (85)   Miller (57)

Anderlecht: Munaron, Grun, De Greef, Olsen, De Groot, Hofkens, Vandereycken, Scifo, Brylle, Vandenbergh (Arnesen), Czerniatynski (Vercauteren)
Tottenham: Parks, Thomas, Roberts, Hughton, Perryman, Miller, Stevens (Mabbutt), Hazard, Galvin, Archibald, Falco

2nd Leg, 23rd May, 1984   *White Hart Lane, London*   46,000

Tottenham Hotspur   **1**   **RSC Anderlecht**   **1**

Roberts (84)   Czerniatynski (60)

Tottenham: Parks, Thomas, Hughton, Roberts, Miller (Ardiles), Mabbutt (Dick), Hazard, Stevens, Galvin, Archibald, Falco
Anderlecht: Munaron, Hofkens, Grun, De Greef, Olsen, De Groot, Arnesen (Gudjohnsen), Vercauteren, Scifo, Czerniatynski (Brylle), Vandereycken

Tottenham won 4-3 on penalties – 2-2 on aggregate

1985

1st Leg, 8th May, 1985   *Sostoi, Szedesfehervar*   30,000

Videoton SC   **0**   **Real Madrid**   **3**

                            Michel (31), Santillana (77), Valdano (89)

Videoton: Disztl P, Borsanyi, Disztl L, Csuhay, Horvath, Palkovics, Vegh, Wittman, Vadasz, Novath (Gyenti), Burcsa

Real Madrid: Miguel Angel, Chendo, Sanchis, Stielike, Camacho, San Jose, Michel, Gallego, Butragueno (Juanito), Santillana (Salguero), Valdano

2nd Leg, 22nd May, 1985		*Bernabeu, Madrid*	*90,000*
Real Madrid	**0**	**Videoton SC**	**1**

Majer (86)

Real Madrid: Miguel Angel, Chendo, Sanchis, Stielike, Camacho, San Jose, Michel, Gallego, Butragueno, Santillana, Valdano (Juanito)
Videoton: Disztl P, Csuhay, Disztl L, Vegh, Horvath, Burcsa, Csongradi (Wittman), Vadasz, Szabo, Majer, Novath (Palkovics)
Real Madrid win 3-1 on aggregate

1986

1st Leg, 30th April, 1986		*Bernabeu, Madrid*	*85,000*
Real Madrid	**5**	**Cologne**	**1**

Sanchez (38), Gordillo (42), Allofs (29)
Valdano (51 84), Santillana (89)

Real Madrid: Agustin, Salguero, Solana, Camacho, Martin Vazquez (Santillana), Michel, Juanito, Gordillo, Butragueno, Sanchez, Valdano
Cologne: Schumacher, Geilis, Gielchen, Steiner, Prestin, Geilenkirchen, Honerbach, Bein (Hassler), Janssen, Littbarski (Dickel), Allofs

2nd Leg, 6th May, 1986		*Olympiastadion, Berlin*	*15,000*
Cologne	**2**	**Real Madrid**	**0**

Bein (22), Geilenkirchen (72)

Cologne: Schumacher, Prestin, Gielchen, Geilis (Schmitz), Geilenkirchen, Steiner, Bein, Honerbach, Janssen (Pisanti), Littbarski, Allofs
Real Madrid: Agustin, Chendo, Maceda, Solana, Camacho, Michel, Gallego, Valdano, Gordillo, Butragueno (Juanito), Sanchez (Santillana)
Real Madrid win 5-3 on aggregate

1987

1st Leg, 6th May, 1987		*Nya Ullevi, Gothenburg*	*50,000*
IFK Gothenburg	**1**	**Dundee United**	**0**

Pettersson (38)

IFK Gothenburg: Wernersson, Carlsson, Hysen, Larsson, Fredriksson, Johansson (Nilsson R), Tord Holmgren (Zetterlund), Andersson, Tommy Holmgren, Pettersson, Nilsson L
Dundee United: Thompson, Malpas, Narey, Hegarty (Clark), Holt, McInally, Kirkwood, Bowman, Bannon, Sturrock (Beaumont), Redford

2nd Leg, 20th May, 1987   *Tannadice Park, Dundee*   *21,000*
Dundee United   1   **IFK Gothenburg**   1
Clark (60)   Nilsson L (22)
Dundee United: Thompson, Malpas, Clark, Narey, Holt (Hegarty), McInally,
Ferguson, Kirkwood, Sturrock, Redford (Bannon), Gallacher
IFK Gothenburg: Wernersson, Carlsson, Hysen, Larsson, Fredriksson,
Nilsson R (Johansson), Tord Holmgren (Mordt), Andersson, Tommy
Holmgren, Pettersson, Nilsson L
IFK win 2-1 on aggregate

1988

1st Leg, 4th May, 1988   *Sarria, Barcelona*   *42,000*
Espanol   3   **Bayer Leverkusen**   0
Losada (45, 56), Soler (49)
Espanol: N'Kono, Job, Miguel Angel, Gallart, Soler, Orejuela (Golobart),
Urquiaga, Inaki, Valverde, Pichi Alonso (Lauridsen), Losada
Bayer: Volborn, Rolff, De Dayser, Reinhardt A, Hinterberger, Cha-Bum-Kun
(Gotz), Tita, Buncol, Falkenmayer (Reinhardt K), Waas, Tauber

2nd Leg, 18th May, 1988   *Leverkusen*   *22,000*
Bayer Leverkusen   3   **Espanol**   0
Tita (57), Gotz (63), Cha-Bum-Kun (81)
Bayer: Volborn, Rolff, Seckler, Reinhardt A, Reinhardt K, Schreier (Waas),
Buncol, Falkenmayer, Cha-Bum-Kun, Gotz, Tita (Tauber)
Espanol: N'Kono, Miguel Angel, Golobart (Ziniga), Urquiaga, Job, Orejuela
(Zubillaga), Inaki, Soler, Pichi Alonso, Losada
Bayer won 3-2 on penalties. 3-3 on aggregate

1989

1st Leg, 3rd May, 1989   *San Paola, Naples*   *83,000*
Napoli   2   **VfB Stuttgart**   1
Maradona (68), Careca (87)   Gaudino (17)
Napoli: Giuliani, Renica, Ferrera, Francini, Corradini (Crippa), Alemao, Fusi,
De Napoli, Careca, Maradona, Carnevale
Stuttgart: Immel, Allgower, Schmaler N, Hartmann, Buchwald, Schafer
Katanec, Sigurvinnson, Schroder, Walter (Zietsch), Gaudino

2nd Leg, 17th May, 1989   *Neckarstadion, Stuttgart*   *67,000*
VfB Stuttgart   3   **Napoli**   3
Klinsmann (27), Own Goal (70),   Alemao (18), Ferrera (39), Careca (62)
Schmaler (89)
Stuttgart: Immel, Allgower, Schmaler N, Hartmann, Schafer, Katanec,
Sigurvinnson, Schroder, Walter (Schmalero), Klinsmann, Gaudino

Napoli: Giuliani, Renica, Ferrera, Francini, Corradini, Alemao (Carranante), Fusi, De Napoli, Careca, Maradona, Carnevale
Napoli win 5-4 on aggregate

1990

1st Leg, 2nd May, 1990   *Comunale, Turin*   *45,000*

Juventus   **3**   **Fiorentina**   **1**

Galia (3), Casiraghi (59), De Agostini (73)   Buso (10)

Juventus: Tacconi, Napoli, De Agostini, Galia, Bruno (Alessio), Bonetti, Aleinikov, Barros, Marocchi, Casiraghi, Schillaci
Fiorentina: Landucci, Dell'Oglio, Volpecina, Pin, Battistini, Dunga, Nappi, Kubik (Malusci), Baggio R, Buso, Di Chiara

2nd Leg, 16th May, 1990   *Stadio Partenio, Avellino*   *32,000*

Fiorentina   **0**   **Juventus**   **0**

Fiorentina: Landucci, Dell'Oglio, Volpecina, Pin, Battistini, Dunga, Nappi (Zironelli), Kubik, Baggio R, Buso, Di Chiara
Juventus: Tacconi, Napoi, De Agostini, Galia, Bruno, Alessio, Aleinikov, Barros (Avallone), Marocchi, Casiraghi (Rosa), Schillaci
Juventus win 3-1 on aggregate

1991

1st Leg, 8th May, 1991   *Giuseppe Meazza, Milan*   *75,000*

Internazionale   **2**   **Roma**   **0**

Matthaus (55), Berti (67)

Internazionale: Zenga, Bergomi, Brehme, Battistini, Ferri, Paganin (Baresi), Bianchi, Berti, Matthaus, Klinsmann, Serena (Pizzi)
Roma: Cervone, Tempestilli, Nela, Berthold, Aldair (Carboni), Comi (Muzzi), Gerolin, Di Mauro, Giannini, Voller, Rizzitelli

2nd Leg, 22nd May, 1991   *Stadio Olimpico*   *71,000*

Roma   **1**   **Internazionale**   **0**

Rizzitelli (81)

Roma: Cervone, Tempestilli (Salsano), Gerolin, Berthold, Aldair, Nela, Desideri (Muzzi), Di Mauro, Giannini, Voller, Rizzitelli
Internazionale: Zenga, Bergomi, Brehme, Battistini, Ferri, Paganin, Bianchi, Berti, Matthaus, Klinsmann, Pizzi (Mandorlini)
Internazionale win 2-1 on aggregate

1992

1st Leg, 29th April, 1992   *Delle Alpi, Turin*   *65,000*

Torino   2   **Ajax**   2

Casagrande (65, 82)   Jonk (17), Pettersson (73)

Torino: Marchegiani, Bruno, Annoni, Cravero (Bresciani), Mussi (Sordo), Benedetti, Scifo, Vasquez M, Venturin, Lentini, Casagrande

Ajax: Menzo, Silooy, Blind, Jonk, De Boer, Winter, Kreek, Bergkamp, Van't Schip, Pettersson, Roy (Gronendijk)

2nd Leg, 13th May, 1992   *Olympisch Stadion, Amsterdam*   *42,000*

Ajax   0   **Torino**   0

Ajax: Menzo, Silooy, Blind, Jonk, De Boer, Winter, Kreek (Vink), Alflen, Van't Schip, Pettersson, Roy (Van Loen)

Torino: Marchegiani, Mussi, Cravero (Sordo), Benedetti, Fusi, Policano, Vasquez M, Scifo (Bresciani), Venturin, Casagrande, Lentini

            Ajax win on away goals rule. 2-2 on aggregate

1993

1st Leg, 5th May 1993   *Dortmund*   *37,000*

Borussia Dortmund   1   **Juventus**   3

M. Rummenigge (2)   D. Baggio (27), R. Baggio (31, 74)

Borussia: Kios, Grauer, Reuter, Schmidt, Lusch, Franck (Mill), Zorc (Karl), Rummenigge M, Poschner, Reinhardt, Chapuisat

Juventus: Peruzzi, Julio Cesar, Carrera, Kohler, De Marchi, Conte, Baggio D, Baggio R, (Di Canio), Marocchi, Vialli, Moller (Galia)

2nd Leg, 19th May, 1993   *Turin*   *60,000*

Juventus   3   **Borussia Dortmund**   0

D. Baggio (5, 40), Moller (65)

Juventus: Peruzzi, Carrera, Torricelli (Di Canio), De Marchi, Kohler, Julio Cesar, Moller, Baggio D, Vialli (Ravenelli), Baggio R, Marocchi

Borussia: Kios, Reinhardt, Schmidt, Schulz, Zelic, Poschner, Reuter (Lusch), Karl, Mill, Rummenigge M (Franck), Sippel

            Juventus win 6-1 on aggregate

Champions' Cup
Second Leg Outcomes 1955-93

First-leg: 0-0

2nd Leg Score	1-0	2-0	3-0	4-0	5-0	2-1	3-1	4-1
Occurrences	9	1	1	0	0	2	2	1
2nd Leg Score	5-1	3-2	4-2	5-2	4-3	5-3	5-4	0-0
Occurrences	0	1	0	0	0	0	0	4
2nd Leg Score	1-1	2-2	3-3	4-4	5-5	0-1	0-2	0-3
Occurrences	5	2	0	0	0	9	18	3
2nd Leg Score	0-4	0-5	1-2	1-3	1-4	1-5	2-3	2-4
Occurrences	4	3	5	1	2	2	1	0
2nd Leg Score	2-5	3-4	3-5	4-5	5>	<5		
Occurrences	0	0	0	0	0	3		

First-leg: 1-0

2nd Leg Score	1-0	2-0	3-0	4-0	5-0	2-1	3-1	4-1
Occurrences	6	3	2	1	0	2	2	1
2nd Leg Score	5-1	3-2	4-2	5-2	4-3	5-3	5-4	0-0
Occurrences	0	1	0	0	0	0	0	10
2nd Leg Score	1-1	2-2	3-3	4-4	5-5	0-1	0-2	0-3
Occurrences	9	1	1	0	0	3	25	13
2nd Leg Score	0-4	0-5	1-2	1-3	1-4	1-5	2-3	2-4
Occurrences	2	3	12	4	7	3	2	1
2nd Leg Score	2-5	3-4	3-5	4-5	5>	<5		
Occurrences	0	0	1	0	0	1		

First-leg: 2-0

2nd Leg Score	1-0	2-0	3-0	4-0	5-0	2-1	3-1	4-1
Occurrences	7	4	4	0	1	5	1	0
2nd Leg Score	5-1	3-2	4-2	5-2	4-3	5-3	5-4	0-0
Occurrences	0	3	2	0	0	0	0	5
2nd Leg Score	1-1	2-2	3-3	4-4	5-5	0-1	0-2	0-3
Occurrences	13	5	0	0	0	13	2	9
2nd Leg Score	0-4	0-5	1-2	1-3	1-4	1-5	2-3	2-4
Occurrences	4	0	7	5	3	1	5	0
2nd Leg Score	2-5	3-4	3-5	4-5	5>	<5		
Occurrences	0	0	0	0	0	0		

First-leg: 3-0

2nd Leg Score	1-0	2-0	3-0	4-0	5-0	2-1	3-1	4-1
Occurrences	9	5	3	0	0	4	2	1
2nd Leg Score	5-1	3-2	4-2	5-2	4-3	5-3	5-4	0-0
Occurrences	0	2	0	0	0	0	0	2
2nd Leg Score	1-1	2-2	3-3	4-4	5-5	0-1	0-2	0-3
Occurrences	5	2	0	0	0	9	9	2
2nd Leg Score	0-4	0-5	1-2	1-3	1-4	1-5	2-3	2-4
Occurrences	0	2	9	2	2	0	2	0
2nd Leg Score	2-5	3-4	3-5	4-5	5>	<5		
Occurrences	1	0	0	0	0	0		

First-leg: 1-1

2nd Leg Score	1-0	2-0	3-0	4-0	5-0	2-1	3-1	4-1
Occurrences	3	3	1	0	0	0	1	1
2nd Leg Score	5-1	3-2	4-2	5-2	4-3	5-3	5-4	0-0
Occurrences	0	2	1	0	0	0	0	6
2nd Leg Score	1-1	2-2	3-3	4-4	5-5	0-1	0-2	0-3
Occurrences	7	3	1	0	0	5	11	4
2nd Leg Score	0-4	0-5	1-2	1-3	1-4	1-5	2-3	2-4
Occurrences	3	2	10	1	3	4	0	0
2nd Leg Score	2-5	3-4	3-5	4-5	5>	<5		
Occurrences	1	0	0	0	1	5		

First-leg: 2-1

2nd Leg Score	1-0	2-0	3-0	4-0	5-0	2-1	3-1	4-1
Occurrences	5	6	0	0	0	7	1	2
2nd Leg Score	5-1	3-2	4-2	5-2	4-3	5-3	5-4	0-0
Occurrences	0	0	0	0	0	0	0	2
2nd Leg Score	1-1	2-2	3-3	4-4	5-5	0-1	0-2	0-3
Occurrences	7	2	2	0	0	8	10	3
2nd Leg Score	0-4	0-5	1-2	1-3	1-4	1-5	2-3	2-4
Occurrences	2	2	6	5	3	0	2	0
2nd Leg Score	2-5	3-4	3-5	4-5	5>	<5		
Occurrences	0	0	1	0	0	8		

First-leg: 3-1

2nd Leg Score	1-0	2-0	3-0	4-0	5-0	2-1	3-1	4-1
Occurrences	3	2	1	0	0	2	0	0
2nd Leg Score	5-1	3-2	4-2	5-2	4-3	5-3	5-4	0-0
Occurrences	0	1	1	0	0	0	0	4
2nd Leg Score	1-1	2-2	3-3	4-4	5-5	0-1	0-2	0-3
Occurrences	3	2	0	0	0	6	5	3
2nd Leg Score	0-4	0-5	1-2	1-3	1-4	1-5	2-3	2-4
Occurrences	1	0	6	3	1	0	1	1

2nd Leg Score	2-5	3-4	3-5	4-5	5>	<5
Occurrences	0	0	0	0	0	2

First-leg: 4-1

2nd Leg Score	1-0	2-0	3-0	4-0	5-0	2-1	3-1	4-1
Occurrences	1	1	0	0	0	1	1	0
2nd Leg Score	5-1	3-2	4-2	5-2	4-3	5-3	5-4	0-0
Occurrences	0	0	0	0	0	0	0	3
2nd Leg Score	1-1	2-2	3-3	4-4	5-5	0-1	0-2	0-3
Occurrences	3	1	0	0	0	4	2	2
2nd Leg Score	0-4	0-5	1-2	1-3	1-4	1-5	2-3	2-4
Occurrences	1	1	3	0	0	2	1	0
2nd Leg Score	2-5	3-4	3-5	4-5	5>	<5		
Occurrences	1	0	0	0	0	0		

First-leg: 5-1

2nd Leg Score	1-0	2-0	3-0	4-0	5-0	2-1	3-1	4-1
Occurrences	1	1	0	0	0	0	0	0
2nd Leg Score	5-1	3-2	4-2	5-2	4-3	5-3	5-4	0-0
Occurrences	0	0	0	0	0	0	0	0
2nd Leg Score	1-1	2-2	3-3	4-4	5-5	0-1	0-2	0-3
Occurrences	1	1	0	0	0	1	0	1
2nd Leg Score	0-4	0-5	1-2	1-3	1-4	1-5	2-3	2-4
Occurrences	0	0	4	0	0	0	0	0
2nd Leg Score	2-5	3-4	3-5	4-5	5>	<5		
Occurrences	0	0	0	0	1	0		

First-leg: 2-2

2nd Leg Score	1-0	2-0	3-0	4-0	5-0	2-1	3-1	4-1
Occurrences	2	1	0	0	0	1	0	0
2nd Leg Score	5-1	3-2	4-2	5-2	4-3	5-3	5-4	0-0
Occurrences	0	0	0	0	0	0	0	4
2nd Leg Score	1-1	2-2	3-3	4-4	5-5	0-1	0-2	0-3
Occurrences	2	0	0	0	0	3	3	1
2nd Leg Score	0-4	0-5	1-2	1-3	1-4	1-5	2-3	2-4
Occurrences	4	1	7	2	1	1	3	0
2nd Leg Score	2-5	3-4	3-5	4-5	5>	<5		
Occurrences	0	0	0	0	0	1		

First-leg: 3-2

2nd Leg Score	1-0	2-0	3-0	4-0	5-0	2-1	3-1	4-1
Occurrences	1	0	0	0	0	2	1	0
2nd Leg Score	5-1	3-2	4-2	5-2	4-3	5-3	5-4	0-0
Occurrences	1	0	0	0	0	0	0	3

2nd Leg Score	1-1	2-2	3-3	4-4	5-5	0-1	0-2	0-3
Occurrences	2	1	2	0	0	1	4	1
2nd Leg Score	0-4	0-5	1-2	1-3	1-4	1-5	2-3	2-4
Occurrences	2	1	3	0	0	0	0	1
2nd Leg Score	2-5	3-4	3-5	4-5	5>	<5		
Occurrences	0	0	0	0	0	1		

First-leg: 4-2

2nd Leg Score	1-0	2-0	3-0	4-0	5-0	2-1	3-1	4-1
Occurrences	0	0	1	0	0	0	0	0
2nd Leg Score	5-1	3-2	4-2	5-2	4-3	5-3	5-4	0-0
Occurrences	0	0	0	0	0	0	0	1
2nd Leg Score	1-1	2-2	3-3	4-4	5-5	0-1	0-2	0-3
Occurrences	0	0	1	1	0	0	2	0
2nd Leg Score	0-4	0-5	1-2	1-3	1-4	1-5	2-3	2-4
Occurrences	0	0	1	3	0	0	0	0
2nd Leg Score	2-5	3-4	3-5	4-5	5>	<5		
Occurrences	0	0	0	0	0	1		

First-leg: 5-2

2nd Leg Score	1-0	2-0	3-0	4-0	5-0	2-1	3-1	4-1
Occurrences	0	1	0	0	0	0	0	0
2nd Leg Score	5-1	3-2	4-2	5-2	4-3	5-3	5-4	0-0
Occurrences	0	0	0	0	0	0	0	0
2nd Leg Score	1-1	2-2	3-3	4-4	5-5	0-1	0-2	0-3
Occurrences	0	0	0	0	0	0	0	0
2nd Leg Score	0-4	0-5	1-2	1-3	1-4	1-5	2-3	2-4
Occurrences	0	0	0	1	0	0	0	0
2nd Leg Score	2-5	3-4	3-5	4-5	5>	<5		
Occurrences	0	0	0	0	0	0		

First-leg: 6-2

2nd Leg Score	1-0	2-0	3-0	4-0	5-0	2-1	3-1	4-1
Occurrences	0	0	1	0	0	0	0	0
2nd Leg Score	5-1	3-2	4-2	5-2	4-3	5-3	5-4	0-0
Occurrences	0	0	0	0	0	0	0	0
2nd Leg Score	1-1	2-2	3-3	4-4	5-5	0-1	0-2	0-3
Occurrences	0	0	0	0	0	0	0	0
2nd Leg Score	0-4	0-5	1-2	1-3	1-4	1-5	2-3	2-4
Occurrences	0	0	1	0	0	0	0	0
2nd Leg Score	2-5	3-4	3-5	4-5	5>	<5		
Occurrences	0	0	0	0	0	0		

First-leg: 3-3

2nd Leg Score	1-0	2-0	3-0	4-0	5-0	2-1	3-1	4-1
Occurrences	1	0	0	0	0	0	0	0
2nd Leg Score	5-1	3-2	4-2	5-2	4-3	5-3	5-4	0-0
Occurrences	0	0	0	0	0	0	0	0
2nd Leg Score	1-1	2-2	3-3	4-4	5-5	0-1	0-2	0-3
Occurrences	0	0	0	0	0	1	1	0
2nd Leg Score	0-4	0-5	1-2	1-3	1-4	1-5	2-3	2-4
Occurrences	0	1	1	0	0	0	0	0
2nd Leg Score	2-5	3-4	3-5	4-5	5>	<5		
Occurrences	1	0	0	0	0	1		

First-leg: 4-3

2nd Leg Score	1-0	2-0	3-0	4-0	5-0	2-1	3-1	4-1
Occurrences	0	0	0	0	0	0	0	0
2nd Leg Score	5-1	3-2	4-2	5-2	4-3	5-3	5-4	0-0
Occurrences	0	0	0	0	0	0	0	1
2nd Leg Score	1-1	2-2	3-3	4-4	5-5	0-1	0-2	0-3
Occurrences	1	0	1	0	0	0	1	0
2nd Leg Score	0-4	0-5	1-2	1-3	1-4	1-5	2-3	2-4
Occurrences	1	0	1	0	0	0	0	0
2nd Leg Score	2-5	3-4	3-5	4-5	5>	<5		
Occurrences	0	0	0	0	0			

First-leg: 5-3

2nd Leg Score	1-0	2-0	3-0	4-0	5-0	2-1	3-1	4-1
Occurrences	0	1	0	0	0	0	0	0
2nd Leg Score	5-1	3-2	4-2	5-2	4-3	5-3	5-4	0-0
Occurrences	0	0	0	0	0	0	0	0
2nd Leg Score	1-1	2-2	3-3	4-4	5-5	0-1	0-2	0-3
Occurrences	0	0	0	0	0	0	0	0
2nd Leg Score	0-4	0-5	1-2	1-3	1-4	1-5	2-3	2-4
Occurrences	0	0	0	0	0	1	0	0
2nd Leg Score	2-5	3-4	3-5	4-5	5>	<5		
Occurrences	0	1	0	0	0			

First-leg: 0-1

2nd Leg Score	1-0	2-0	3-0	4-0	5-0	2-1	3-1	4-1
Occurrences	1	0	0	0	0	0	1	0
2nd Leg Score	5-1	3-2	4-2	5-2	4-3	5-3	5-4	0-0
Occurrences	0	0	0	0	0	0	0	5
2nd Leg Score	1-1	2-2	3-3	4-4	5-5	0-1	0-2	0-3
Occurrences	5	2	0	0	0	2	4	4

2nd Leg Score	0-4	0-5	1-2	1-3	1-4	1-5	2-3	2-4
Occurrences	8	3	2	3	1	0	2	0
2nd Leg Score	2-5	3-4	3-5	4-5	5>	<5		
Occurrences	0	0	0	0	0	4		

First-leg: 0-2

2nd Leg Score	1-0	2-0	3-0	4-0	5-0	2-1	3-1	4-1
Occurrences	0	0	0	0	0	0	0	0
2nd Leg Score	5-1	3-2	4-2	5-2	4-3	5-3	5-4	0-0
Occurrences	0	0	0	0	0	0	0	2
2nd Leg Score	1-1	2-2	3-3	4-4	5-5	0-1	0-2	0-3
Occurrences	2	2	0	0	0	2	1	1
2nd Leg Score	0-4	0-5	1-2	1-3	1-4	1-5	2-3	2-4
Occurrences	2	3	2	4	0	2	0	3
2nd Leg Score	2-5	3-4	3-5	4-5	5>	<5		
Occurrences	1	0	0	0	0	3		

First-leg: 1-2

2nd Leg Score	1-0	2-0	3-0	4-0	5-0	2-1	3-1	4-1
Occurrences	4	0	0	0	0	0	0	0
2nd Leg Score	5-1	3-2	4-2	5-2	4-3	5-3	5-4	0-0
Occurrences	0	0	0	0	0	0	0	3
2nd Leg Score	1-1	2-2	3-3	4-4	5-5	0-1	0-2	0-3
Occurrences	5	0	1	0	0	5	1	3
2nd Leg Score	0-4	0-5	1-2	1-3	1-4	1-5	2-3	2-4
Occurrences	3	3	1	2	5	3	1	0
2nd Leg Score	2-5	3-4	3-5	4-5	5>	<5		
Occurrences	0	0	0	0	0	5		

First-leg: 1-3

2nd Leg Score	1-0	2-0	3-0	4-0	5-0	2-1	3-1	4-1
Occurrences	1	0	0	0	0	1	2	0
2nd Leg Score	5-1	3-2	4-2	5-2	4-3	5-3	5-4	0-0
Occurrences	0	0	0	0	0	0	0	1
2nd Leg Score	1-1	2-2	3-3	4-4	5-5	0-1	0-2	0-3
Occurrences	1	0	1	0	0	3	0	3
2nd Leg Score	0-4	0-5	1-2	1-3	1-4	1-5	2-3	2-4
Occurrences	2	1	4	1	1	0	1	0
2nd Leg Score	2-5	3-4	3-5	4-5	5>	<5		
Occurrences	0	0	1	0	0	1		

First-leg: 2-4

2nd Leg Score	1-0	2-0	3-0	4-0	5-0	2-1	3-1	4-1
Occurrences	0	0	0	0	0	0	0	0
2nd Leg Score	5-1	3-2	4-2	5-2	4-3	5-3	5-4	0-0
Occurrences	0	0	0	0	0	0	0	0
2nd Leg Score	1-1	2-2	3-3	4-4	5-5	0-1	0-2	0-3
Occurrences	0	0	0	0	0	0	1	1
2nd Leg Score	0-4	0-5	1-2	1-3	1-4	1-5	2-3	2-4
Occurrences	0	0	0	0	0	0	0	0
2nd Leg Score	2-5	3-4	3-5	4-5	5>	<5		
Occurrences	0	0	0	0	0	0		

First-leg: 3-4

2nd Leg Score	1-0	2-0	3-0	4-0	5-0	2-1	3-1	4-1
Occurrences	0	0	0	0	0	0	0	1
2nd Leg Score	5-1	3-2	4-2	5-2	4-3	5-3	5-4	0-0
Occurrences	0	0	0	0	0	0	0	0
2nd Leg Score	1-1	2-2	3-3	4-4	5-5	0-1	0-2	0-3
Occurrences	0	0	0	0	0	0	1	0
2nd Leg Score	0-4	0-5	1-2	1-3	1-4	1-5	2-3	2-4
Occurrences	0	0	1	0	0	0	0	0
2nd Leg Score	2-5	3-4	3-5	4-5	5>	<5		
Occurrences	0	0	0	0	0	1		

Qualification/Eliminations after First-leg Score

First-leg Score	No. Matches	Qualifications No.	Qualifications %	Eliminations No.	Eliminations %
0-0	79	25	31.65%	54	68.35%
1-0	116	54	46.55%	62	53.45%
2-0	99	81	81.82%	18	18.18%
3-0	73	68	93.15%	5	6.85%
1-1	79	22	27.85%	57	72.15%
2-1	90	40	44.44%	50	55.56%
3-1	48	37	77.08%	11	22.92%
4-1	28	23	82.14%	5	17.86%
5-1	13	13	100.00%	0	0.00%
2-2	37	5	13.51%	32	86.49%
3-2	26	13	50.00%	13	50.00%
4-2	11	8	72.73%	3	27.27%
5-2	2	2	100.00%	0	0.00%
6-2	2	2	100.00%	0	0.00%
3-3	7	1	14.29%	6	85.71%
4-3	6	4	66.67%	2	33.33%

5-3	4	2	50.00%	2	50.00%
0-1	46	1	2.17%	45	97.83%
0-2	30	0	0.00%	30	100.00%
1-2	45	0	0.00%	45	100.00%
1-3	26	1	3.85%	25	96.15%
2-4	2	0	0.00%	2	100.00%
3-4	4	1	25.00%	3	75.00%

Home Match Score Frequencies

Home Score	1-0	2-0	3-0	4-0	5-0	2-1	3-1	4-1
Number	208	217	151	81	52	189	89	62
Percentage	10	10	7	4	2	9	4	3
Home Score	5-1	3-2	4-2	5-2	4-3	5-3	5-4	0-0
Number	35	55	18	9	7	7	0	145
Percentage	2	2	1	0	0	0	0	7
Home Score	1-1	2-2	3-3	4-4	5-5	0-1	0-2	0-3
Number	166	70	19	2	0	114	69	40
Percentage	8	3	1	0	0	5	3	2
Home Score	0-4	0-5	1-2	1-3	1-4	1-5	2-3	2-4
Number	15	20	82	45	24	5	25	7
Percentage	1	1	4	2	1	0	1	0
Home Score	2-5	3-4	3-5	4-5	5>	<5		
Number	3	4	1	0	103	26		
Percentage	0	0	0	0	5	1		

Number of matches: 2165

Cup-Winners' Cup
Second Leg Outcomes 1960-93

First-leg: 0-0

2nd Leg Score	1-0	2-0	3-0	4-0	5-0	2-1	3-1	4-1
Occurrences	5	4	0	0	0	1	0	0
2nd Leg Score	5-1	3-2	4-2	5-2	4-3	5-3	5-4	0-0
Occurrences	1	0	0	1	0	0	0	2
2nd Leg Score	1-1	2-2	3-3	4-4	5-5	0-1	0-2	0-3
Occurrences	12	3	0	0	0	18	19	7
2nd Leg Score	0-4	0-5	1-2	1-3	1-4	1-5	2-3	2-4
Occurrences	4	3	5	4	1	0	1	0
2nd Leg Score	2-5	3-4	3-5	4-5	5>	<5		
Occurrences	1	0	0	0	0	2		

First-leg: 1-0

2nd Leg Score	1-0	2-0	3-0	4-0	5-0	2-1	3-1	4-1
Occurrences	9	5	0	1	0	6	0	0
2nd Leg Score	5-1	3-2	4-2	5-2	4-3	5-3	5-4	0-0
Occurrences	0	2	0	1	0	0	0	11
2nd Leg Score	1-1	2-2	3-3	4-4	5-5	0-1	0-2	0-3
Occurrences	10	4	0	0	0	7	22	5
2nd Leg Score	0-4	0-5	1-2	1-3	1-4	1-5	2-3	2-4
Occurrences	4	1	7	5	1	2	1	2
2nd Leg Score	2-5	3-4	3-5	4-5	5>	<5		
Occurrences	0	2	0	0	0	5		

First-leg: 2-0

2nd Leg Score	1-0	2-0	3-0	4-0	5-0	2-1	3-1	4-1
Occurrences	6	3	0	1	0	5	1	1
2nd Leg Score	5-1	3-2	4-2	5-2	4-3	5-3	5-4	0-0
Occurrences	0	1	0	0	0	1	0	7
2nd Leg Score	1-1	2-2	3-3	4-4	5-5	0-1	0-2	0-3
Occurrences	7	6	2	0	0	10	8	8
2nd Leg Score	0-4	0-5	1-2	1-3	1-4	1-5	2-3	2-4
Occurrences	4	3	9	6	5	1	2	0
2nd Leg Score	2-5	3-4	3-5	4-5	5>	<5		
Occurrences	0	1	0	0	0	2		

First-leg: 3-0

2nd Leg Score	1-0	2-0	3-0	4-0	5-0	2-1	3-1	4-1
Occurrences	2	4	4	0	0	0	2	0
2nd Leg Score	5-1	3-2	4-2	5-2	4-3	5-3	5-4	0-0
Occurrences	0	1	0	0	0	0	0	1
2nd Leg Score	1-1	2-2	3-3	4-4	5-5	0-1	0-2	0-3
Occurrences	7	4	0	0	0	0	7	8	1
2nd Leg Score	0-4	0-5	1-2	1-3	1-4	1-5	2-3	2-4
Occurrences	3	1	7	0	0	0	1	2
2nd Leg Score	2-5	3-4	3-5	4-5	5>	<5		
Occurrences	0	0	0	0	0	0		

First-leg: 1-1

2nd Leg Score	1-0	2-0	3-0	4-0	5-0	2-1	3-1	4-1
Occurrences	4	1	1	0	0	3	2	0
2nd Leg Score	5-1	3-2	4-2	5-2	4-3	5-3	5-4	0-0
Occurrences	0	1	0	0	0	0	0	8
2nd Leg Score	1-1	2-2	3-3	4-4	5-5	0-1	0-2	0-3
Occurrences	10	3	0	0	0	17	15	2
2nd Leg Score	0-4	0-5	1-2	1-3	1-4	1-5	2-3	2-4
Occurrences	6	1	9	8	3	1	2	0
2nd Leg Score	2-5	3-4	3-5	4-5	5>	<5		
Occurrences	0	0	1	0	0	7		

First-leg: 2-1

2nd Leg Score	1-0	2-0	3-0	4-0	5-0	2-1	3-1	4-1
Occurrences	2	1	1	0	0	2	1	1
2nd Leg Score	5-1	3-2	4-2	5-2	4-3	5-3	5-4	0-0
Occurrences	0	1	0	0	0	0	0	4
2nd Leg Score	1-1	2-2	3-3	4-4	5-5	0-1	0-2	0-3
Occurrences	4	3	0	0	0	12	9	6
2nd Leg Score	0-4	0-5	1-2	1-3	1-4	1-5	2-3	2-4
Occurrences	2	0	4	3	2	0	1	1
2nd Leg Score	2-5	3-4	3-5	4-5	5>	<5		
Occurrences	0	0	0	1	0	2		

First-leg: 3-1

2nd Leg Score	1-0	2-0	3-0	4-0	5-0	2-1	3-1	4-1
Occurrences	3	1	1	0	0	1	2	0
2nd Leg Score	5-1	3-2	4-2	5-2	4-3	5-3	5-4	0-0
Occurrences	0	0	0	0	0	0	0	3
2nd Leg Score	1-1	2-2	3-3	4-4	5-5	0-1	0-2	0-3
Occurrences	2	1	0	0	0	5	3	1
2nd Leg Score	0-4	0-5	1-2	1-3	1-4	1-5	2-3	2-4
Occurrences	1	0	3	1	1	1	0	1

2nd Leg Score	2-5	3-4	3-5	4-5	5>	<5
Occurrences	0	0	0	0	1	0

First-leg: 4-1

2nd Leg Score	1-0	2-0	3-0	4-0	5-0	2-1	3-1	4-1
Occurrences	0	1	0	1	0	1	0	1
2nd Leg Score	5-1	3-2	4-2	5-2	4-3	5-3	5-4	0-0
Occurrences	0	0	0	0	0	0	0	0
2nd Leg Score	1-1	2-2	3-3	4-4	5-5	0-1	0-2	0-3
Occurrences	1	0	0	0	0	3	2	0
2nd Leg Score	0-4	0-5	1-2	1-3	1-4	1-5	2-3	2-4
Occurrences	0	1	1	0	0	0	0	0
2nd Leg Score	2-5	3-4	3-5	4-5	5>	<5		
Occurrences	0	0	0	0	0	0		

First-leg: 5-1

2nd Leg Score	1-0	2-0	3-0	4-0	5-0	2-1	3-1	4-1
Occurrences	1	0	0	0	0	1	0	0
2nd Leg Score	5-1	3-2	4-2	5-2	4-3	5-3	5-4	0-0
Occurrences	1	0	0	0	0	0	0	1
2nd Leg Score	1-1	2-2	3-3	4-4	5-5	0-1	0-2	0-3
Occurrences	2	0	0	0	0	2	0	0
2nd Leg Score	0-4	0-5	1-2	1-3	1-4	1-5	2-3	2-4
Occurrences	0	0	1	0	0	0	1	0
2nd Leg Score	2-5	3-4	3-5	4-5	5>	<5		
Occurrences	0	0	0	0	1	0		

First-leg: 2-2

2nd Leg Score	1-0	2-0	3-0	4-0	5-0	2-1	3-1	4-1
Occurrences	1	0	0	0	0	0	0	0
2nd Leg Score	5-1	3-2	4-2	5-2	4-3	5-3	5-4	0-0
Occurrences	0	0	0	0	0	0	0	1
2nd Leg Score	1-1	2-2	3-3	4-4	5-5	0-1	0-2	0-3
Occurrences	1	0	0	0	0	2	2	3
2nd Leg Score	0-4	0-5	1-2	1-3	1-4	1-5	2-3	2-4
Occurrences	3	1	2	3	3	1	1	0
2nd Leg Score	2-5	3-4	3-5	4-5	5>	<5		
Occurrences	0	0	0	0	0	1		

First-leg: 3-2

2nd Leg Score	1-0	2-0	3-0	4-0	5-0	2-1	3-1	4-1
Occurrences	1	0	0	0	0	3	1	0
2nd Leg Score	5-1	3-2	4-2	5-2	4-3	5-3	5-4	0-0
Occurrences	0	0	0	0	0	0	0	0

2nd Leg Score	1-1	2-2	3-3	4-4	5-5	0-1	0-2	0-3
Occurrences	1	1	1	0	0	1	3	1
2nd Leg Score	0-4	0-5	1-2	1-3	1-4	1-5	2-3	2-4
Occurrences	1	0	6	1	0	1	0	0
2nd Leg Score	2-5	3-4	3-5	4-5	5>	<5		
Occurrences	1	1	0	0	0	0		

First-leg: 4-2

2nd Leg Score	1-0	2-0	3-0	4-0	5-0	2-1	3-1	4-1
Occurrences	0	1	0	0	0	1	1	1
2nd Leg Score	5-1	3-2	4-2	5-2	4-3	5-3	5-4	0-0
Occurrences	0	0	0	0	0	0	0	1
2nd Leg Score	1-1	2-2	3-3	4-4	5-5	0-1	0-2	0-3
Occurrences	0	0	0	0	0	0	1	1
2nd Leg Score	0-4	0-5	1-2	1-3	1-4	1-5	2-3	2-4
Occurrences	0	0	1	1	0	0	0	0
2nd Leg Score	2-5	3-4	3-5	4-5	5>	<5		
Occurrences	0	0	0	0	0	0		

First-leg: 5-2

2nd Leg Score	1-0	2-0	3-0	4-0	5-0	2-1	3-1	4-1
Occurrences	0	0	0	0	0	0	0	0
2nd Leg Score	5-1	3-2	4-2	5-2	4-3	5-3	5-4	0-0
Occurrences	0	1	0	0	0	0	0	0
2nd Leg Score	1-1	2-2	3-3	4-4	5-5	0-1	0-2	0-3
Occurrences	0	0	0	0	0	0	0	0
2nd Leg Score	0-4	0-5	1-2	1-3	1-4	1-5	2-3	2-4
Occurrences	0	0	0	0	0	0	0	0
2nd Leg Score	2-5	3-4	3-5	4-5	5>	<5		
Occurrences	0	0	0	0	0	0		

First-leg: 6-2

2nd Leg Score	1-0	2-0	3-0	4-0	5-0	2-1	3-1	4-1
Occurrences	0	0	0	0	0	0	0	0
2nd Leg Score	5-1	3-2	4-2	5-2	4-3	5-3	5-4	0-0
Occurrences	0	0	0	0	0	0	0	0
2nd Leg Score	1-1	2-2	3-3	4-4	5-5	0-1	0-2	0-3
Occurrences	1	0	0	0	0	0	0	0
2nd Leg Score	0-4	0-5	1-2	1-3	1-4	1-5	2-3	2-4
Occurrences	0	1	0	0	0	0	0	0
2nd Leg Score	2-5	3-4	3-5	4-5	5>	<5		
Occurrences	0	0	0	0	0	0		

First-leg: 3-3

2nd Leg Score	1-0	2-0	3-0	4-0	5-0	2-1	3-1	4-1
Occurrences	0	0	0	0	0	0	0	0
2nd Leg Score	5-1	3-2	4-2	5-2	4-3	5-3	5-4	0-0
Occurrences	0	0	0	0	0	0	0	0
2nd Leg Score	1-1	2-2	3-3	4-4	5-5	0-1	0-2	0-3
Occurrences	1	0	0	0	0	0	0	1
2nd Leg Score	0-4	0-5	1-2	1-3	1-4	1-5	2-3	2-4
Occurrences	1	0	0	0	0	0	0	0
2nd Leg Score	2-5	3-4	3-5	4-5	5>	<5		
Occurrences	0	0	0	0	0	0		

First-leg: 4-3

2nd Leg Score	1-0	2-0	3-0	4-0	5-0	2-1	3-1	4-1
Occurrences	1	0	0	0	0	0	0	0
2nd Leg Score	5-1	3-2	4-2	5-2	4-3	5-3	5-4	0-0
Occurrences	0	0	0	0	0	0	0	0
2nd Leg Score	1-1	2-2	3-3	4-4	5-5	0-1	0-2	0-3
Occurrences	0	0	1	0	0	0	0	0
2nd Leg Score	0-4	0-5	1-2	1-3	1-4	1-5	2-3	2-4
Occurrences	0	0	0	1	0	0	0	0
2nd Leg Score	2-5	3-4	3-5	4-5	5>	<5		
Occurrences	0	0	0	0	0	0		

First-leg: 5-3

2nd Leg Score	1-0	2-0	3-0	4-0	5-0	2-1	3-1	4-1
Occurrences	0	1	0	0	0	0	0	0
2nd Leg Score	5-1	3-2	4-2	5-2	4-3	5-3	5-4	0-0
Occurrences	0	0	0	0	0	0	0	0
2nd Leg Score	1-1	2-2	3-3	4-4	5-5	0-1	0-2	0-3
Occurrences	0	0	0	0	0	0	0	0
2nd Leg Score	0-4	0-5	1-2	1-3	1-4	1-5	2-3	2-4
Occurrences	0	0	0	0	0	0	0	0
2nd Leg Score	2-5	3-4	3-5	4-5	5>	<5		
Occurrences	0	0	0	0	0	0		

First-leg: 0-1

2nd Leg Score	1-0	2-0	3-0	4-0	5-0	2-1	3-1	4-1
Occurrences	1	1	2	0	0	1	0	0
2nd Leg Score	5-1	3-2	4-2	5-2	4-3	5-3	5-4	0-0
Occurrences	0	0	0	0	0	0	0	3
2nd Leg Score	1-1	2-2	3-3	4-4	5-5	0-1	0-2	0-3
Occurrences	6	1	1	0	0	11	8	9
2nd Leg Score	0-4	0-5	1-2	1-3	1-4	1-5	2-3	2-4

106

2nd Leg Score							
Occurrences	3	3	5	2	0	0	1	0
2nd Leg Score	2-5	3-4	3-5	4-5	5>	<5		
Occurrences	0	1	0	0	0	6		

First-leg: 0-2

2nd Leg Score	1-0	2-0	3-0	4-0	5-0	2-1	3-1	4-1
Occurrences	0	0	0	0	0	1	0	0
2nd Leg Score	5-1	3-2	4-2	5-2	4-3	5-3	5-4	0-0
Occurrences	0	1	0	0	0	0	0	2
2nd Leg Score	1-1	2-2	3-3	4-4	5-5	0-1	0-2	0-3
Occurrences	2	1	0	0	0	5	2	2
2nd Leg Score	0-4	0-5	1-2	1-3	1-4	1-5	2-3	2-4
Occurrences	3	4	4	1	1	0	0	0
2nd Leg Score	2-5	3-4	3-5	4-5	5>	<5		
Occurrences	0	1	0	0	0	6		

First-leg: 1-2

2nd Leg Score	1-0	2-0	3-0	4-0	5-0	2-1	3-1	4-1
Occurrences	1	0	0	0	0	0	0	0
2nd Leg Score	5-1	3-2	4-2	5-2	4-3	5-3	5-4	0-0
Occurrences	0	0	0	0	0	0	0	1
2nd Leg Score	1-1	2-2	3-3	4-4	5-5	0-1	0-2	0-3
Occurrences	6	1	0	0	0	9	3	2
2nd Leg Score	0-4	0-5	1-2	1-3	1-4	1-5	2-3	2-4
Occurrences	2	0	2	2	0	0	0	1
2nd Leg Score	2-5	3-4	3-5	4-5	5>	<5		
Occurrences	0	1	0	0	0	1		

First-leg: 1-3

2nd Leg Score	1-0	2-0	3-0	4-0	5-0	2-1	3-1	4-1
Occurrences	0	0	0	0	0	0	0	0
2nd Leg Score	5-1	3-2	4-2	5-2	4-3	5-3	5-4	0-0
Occurrences	0	0	0	0	0	0	0	0
2nd Leg Score	1-1	2-2	3-3	4-4	5-5	0-1	0-2	0-3
Occurrences	2	0	0	0	0	2	2	3
2nd Leg Score	0-4	0-5	1-2	1-3	1-4	1-5	2-3	2-4
Occurrences	2	1	0	2	0	0	0	1
2nd Leg Score	2-5	3-4	3-5	4-5	5>	<5		
Occurrences	0	0	0	0	0	1		

First-leg: 2-4

2nd Leg Score	1-0	2-0	3-0	4-0	5-0	2-1	3-1	4-1
Occurrences	1	0	0	0	0	0	0	1
2nd Leg Score	5-1	3-2	4-2	5-2	4-3	5-3	5-4	0-0
Occurrences	0	0	0	0	1	0	0	0

2nd Leg Score	1-1	2-2	3-3	4-4	5-5	0-1	0-2	0-3
Occurrences	0	0	0	0	0	0	0	0
2nd Leg Score	0-4	0-5	1-2	1-3	1-4	1-5	2-3	2-4
Occurrences	0	0	1	1	0	0	0	0
2nd Leg Score	2-5	3-4	3-5	4-5	5>	<5		
Occurrences	0	0	0	0	0	0		

First-leg: 3-4

2nd Leg Score	1-0	2-0	3-0	4-0	5-0	2-1	3-1	4-1
Occurrences	0	0	0	0	0	1	0	0
2nd Leg Score	5-1	3-2	4-2	5-2	4-3	5-3	5-4	0-0
Occurrences	0	0	0	0	0	0	0	0
2nd Leg Score	1-1	2-2	3-3	4-4	5-5	0-1	0-2	0-3
Occurrences	2	0	0	0	0	0	0	0
2nd Leg Score	0-4	0-5	1-2	1-3	1-4	1-5	2-3	2-4
Occurrences	0	0	0	0	0	0	0	0
2nd Leg Score	2-5	3-4	3-5	4-5	5>	<5		
Occurrences	0	0	0	0	0	0		

Qualification/Eliminations after First-leg Score

First-leg Score	No. Matches	Qualifications		Eliminations	
		No.	%	No.	%
0-0	94	26	27.66%	68	72.34%
1-0	113	60	53.09%	53	46.90%
2-0	100	70	70.00%	30	30.00%
3-0	55	50	90.90%	5	9.09%
1-1	106	19	17.92%	87	82.07%
2-1	63	26	41.26%	37	58.73%
3-1	32	24	75.00%	8	25.00%
4-1	12	11	91.67%	1	8.33%
5-1	11	11	100.00%	0	0.00%
2-2	25	1	4.00%	24	96.00%
3-2	24	9	37.50%	15	62.50%
4-2	9	6	66.66%	3	33.33%
5-2	1	1	100.00%	0	0.00%
6-2	2	1	50.00%	1	50.00%
3-3	3	0	0.00%	3	100.00%
4-3	3	2	66.67%	1	33.33%
5-3	1	1	100.00%	0	0.00%
0-1	65	4	6.15%	61	93.84%
0-2	35	0	0.00%	35	100.00%
1-2	31	0	0.00%	31	100.00%

1-3	16	0	0.00%	16	100.00%
2-4	5	1	20.00%	4	80.00%
3-4	3	0	0.00%	3	100.00%

Home Match Score Frequencies

Home Score	1-0	2-0	3-0	4-0	5-0	2-1	3-1	4-1
Number	235	217	114	74	39	138	77	32
Percentage	12	11	6	4	2	7	4	2
Home Score	5-1	3-2	4-2	5-2	4-3	5-3	5-4	0-0
Number	22	36	19	5	10	2	1	147
Percentage	1	2	1	0	1	0	0	8
Home Score	1-1	2-2	3-3	4-4	5-5	0-1	0-2	0-3
Number	192	57	8	1	0	114	63	33
Percentage	10	3	0	0	0	6	3	2
Home Score	0-4	0-5	1-2	1-3	1-4	1-5	2-3	2-4
Number	11	5	67	28	23	10	25	6
Percentage	1	0	3	1	1	1	1	0
Home Score	2-5	3-4	3-5	4-5	5>	<5		
Number	5	4	2	0	84	18		
Percentage	0	0	0	0	4	1		

Number of matches: 1924

UEFA Cup
Second Leg Outcomes 1956-93

First-leg: 0-0

2nd Leg Score	1-0	2-0	3-0	4-0	5-0	2-1	3-1	4-1
Occurrences	8	4	0	0	0	5	2	0
2nd Leg Score	5-1	3-2	4-2	5-2	4-3	5-3	5-4	0-0
Occurrences	1	1	0	0	0	0	0	7
2nd Leg Score	1-1	2-2	3-3	4-4	5-5	0-1	0-2	0-3
Occurrences	15	2	0	0	0	21	21	7
2nd Leg Score	0-4	0-5	1-2	1-3	1-4	1-5	2-3	2-4
Occurrences	4		14	7	2	2	5	1
2nd Leg Score	2-5	3-4	3-5	4-5	5>	<5		
Occurrences	0	1	0	0	0	5		

First-leg: 1-0

2nd Leg Score	1-0	2-0	3-0	4-0	5-0	2-1	3-1	4-1
Occurrences	15	1	5	2	0	10	9	1
2nd Leg Score	5-1	3-2	4-2	5-2	4-3	5-3	5-4	0-0
Occurrences	0	4	2	2	0	0	0	21
2nd Leg Score	1-1	2-2	3-3	4-4	5-5	0-1	0-2	0-3
Occurrences	25	8	2	0	0	22	36	12
2nd Leg Score	0-4	0-5	1-2	1-3	1-4	1-5	2-3	2-4
Occurrences	10	6	28	7	6	4	9	3
2nd Leg Score	2-5	3-4	3-5	4-5	5>	<5		
Occurrences	1	0	0	0	1	4		

First-leg: 2-0

2nd Leg Score	1-0	2-0	3-0	4-0	5-0	2-1	3-1	4-1
Occurrences	8	9	0	0	1	8	4	1
2nd Leg Score	5-1	3-2	4-2	5-2	4-3	5-3	5-4	0-0
Occurrences	1	3	0	0	0	0	0	15
2nd Leg Score	1-1	2-2	3-3	4-4	5-5	0-1	0-2	0-3
Occurrences	21	11	2	0	0	28	16	20
2nd Leg Score	0-4	0-5	1-2	1-3	1-4	1-5	2-3	2-4
Occurrences	5	4	21	1	2	3	2	0
2nd Leg Score	2-5	3-4	3-5	4-5	5>	<5		
Occurrences	1	0	0	0	1	6		

First-leg: 3-0

2nd Leg Score	1-0	2-0	3-0	4-0	5-0	2-1	3-1	4-1
Occurrences	7	2	2	1	1	5	5	3
2nd Leg Score	5-1	3-2	4-2	5-2	4-3	5-3	5-4	0-0
Occurrences	1	4	0	0	0	0	0	3
2nd Leg Score	1-1	2-2	3-3	4-4	5-5	0-1	0-2	0-3
Occurrences	10	4	1	1	0	14	14	6
2nd Leg Score	0-4	0-5	1-2	1-3	1-4	1-5	2-3	2-4
Occurrences	2	1	8	11	2	2	2	1
2nd Leg Score	2-5	3-4	3-5	4-5	5>	<5		
Occurrences	0	1	0	0	2	1		

First-leg: 1-1

2nd Leg Score	1-0	2-0	3-0	4-0	5-0	2-1	3-1	4-1
Occurrences	6	5	2	0	0	7	2	2
2nd Leg Score	5-1	3-2	4-2	5-2	4-3	5-3	5-4	0-0
Occurrences	0	2	1	0	0	0	0	16
2nd Leg Score	1-1	2-2	3-3	4-4	5-5	0-1	0-2	0-3
Occurrences	7	1	0	0	0	22	15	5
2nd Leg Score	0-4	0-5	1-2	1-3	1-4	1-5	2-3	2-4
Occurrences	10	2	19	11	3	2	5	1
2nd Leg Score	2-5	3-4	3-5	4-5	5>	<5		
Occurrences	2	1	0	0	0	3		

First-leg: 2-1

2nd Leg Score	1-0	2-0	3-0	4-0	5-0	2-1	3-1	4-1
Occurrences	13	0	1	0	1	4	4	0
2nd Leg Score	5-1	3-2	4-2	5-2	4-3	5-3	5-4	0-0
Occurrences	0	2	0	0	1	0	0	5
2nd Leg Score	1-1	2-2	3-3	4-4	5-5	0-1	0-2	0-3
Occurrences	16	4	2	1	0	21	14	19
2nd Leg Score	0-4	0-5	1-2	1-3	1-4	1-5	2-3	2-4
Occurrences	3	3	6	6	4	1	3	3
2nd Leg Score	2-5	3-4	3-5	4-5	5>	<5		
Occurrences	1	1	0	0	3			

First-leg: 3-1

2nd Leg Score	1-0	2-0	3-0	4-0	5-0	2-1	3-1	4-1
Occurrences	9	3	1	0	0	3	1	3
2nd Leg Score	5-1	3-2	4-2	5-2	4-3	5-3	5-4	0-0
Occurrences	0	0	0	1	0	1	0	6
2nd Leg Score	1-1	2-2	3-3	4-4	5-5	0-1	0-2	0-3
Occurrences	5	5	0	0	0	9	7	6

2nd Leg Score	0-4	0-5	1-2	1-3	1-4	1-5	2-3	2-4
Occurrences	4	3	11	3	4	4	2	1

2nd Leg Score	2-5	3-4	3-5	4-5	5>	<5		
Occurrences	0	0	0	0	1	1		

First-leg: 4-1

2nd Leg Score	1-0	2-0	3-0	4-0	5-0	2-1	3-1	4-1
Occurrences	6	1	0	0	0	3	2	0
2nd Leg Score	5-1	3-2	4-2	5-2	4-3	5-3	5-4	0-0
Occurrences	0	0	0	0	0	0	0	3
2nd Leg Score	1-1	2-2	3-3	4-4	5-5	0-1	0-2	0-3
Occurrences	3	3	1	0	0	2	8	1
2nd Leg Score	0-4	0-5	1-2	1-3	1-4	1-5	2-3	2-4
Occurrences	2	1	2	5	0	1	1	1

2nd Leg Score	2-5	3-4	3-5	4-5	5>	<5		
Occurrences	0	0	0	1	0	1		

First-leg: 5-1

2nd Leg Score	1-0	2-0	3-0	4-0	5-0	2-1	3-1	4-1
Occurrences	2	0	0	0	0	3	3	1
2nd Leg Score	5-1	3-2	4-2	5-2	4-3	5-3	5-4	0-0
Occurrences	0	1	0	0	0	0	0	1
2nd Leg Score	1-1	2-2	3-3	4-4	5-5	0-1	0-2	0-3
Occurrences	2	3	0	0	0	3	4	0
2nd Leg Score	0-4	0-5	1-2	1-3	1-4	1-5	2-3	2-4
Occurrences	1	0	0	2	2	0	2	0

2nd Leg Score	2-5	3-4	3-5	4-5	5>	<5		
Occurrences	0	0	0	0	0	1		

First-leg: 2-2

2nd Leg Score	1-0	2-0	3-0	4-0	5-0	2-1	3-1	4-1
Occurrences	4	3	0	0	0	1	0	0
2nd Leg Score	5-1	3-2	4-2	5-2	4-3	5-3	5-4	0-0
Occurrences	0	2	0	0	0	0	0	6
2nd Leg Score	1-1	2-2	3-3	4-4	5-5	0-1	0-2	0-3
Occurrences	4	1	0	1	0	10	5	4
2nd Leg Score	0-4	0-5	1-2	1-3	1-4	1-5	2-3	2-4
Occurrences	1	2	9	1	5	1	3	2

2nd Leg Score	2-5	3-4	3-5	4-5	5>	<5		
Occurrences	0	0	0	0	1	3		

First-leg: 3-2

2nd Leg Score	1-0	2-0	3-0	4-0	5-0	2-1	3-1	4-1
Occurrences	2	1	1	0	0	4	0	0
2nd Leg Score	5-1	3-2	4-2	5-2	4-3	5-3	5-4	0-0
Occurrences	0	1	0	1	0	0	0	6

2nd Leg Score	1-1	2-2	3-3	4-4	5-5	0-1	0-2	0-3
Occurrences	3	1	0	0	0	11	6	2
2nd Leg Score	0-4	0-5	1-2	1-3	1-4	1-5	2-3	2-4
Occurrences	4	0	5	3	0	0	0	0
2nd Leg Score	2-5	3-4	3-5	4-5	5>	<5		
Occurrences	0	0	0	0	2	3		

First-leg: 4-2

2nd Leg Score	1-0	2-0	3-0	4-0	5-0	2-1	3-1	4-1
Occurrences	1	2	0	0	0	1	1	0
2nd Leg Score	5-1	3-2	4-2	5-2	4-3	5-3	5-4	0-0
Occurrences	0	0	1	1	0	0	0	2
2nd Leg Score	1-1	2-2	3-3	4-4	5-5	0-1	0-2	0-3
Occurrences	1	1	1	0	0	4	4	1
2nd Leg Score	0-4	0-5	1-2	1-3	1-4	1-5	2-3	2-4
Occurrences	0	0	2	0	1	0	0	0
2nd Leg Score	2-5	3-4	3-5	4-5	5>	<5		
Occurrences	2	0	0	0	0			

First-leg: 5-2

2nd Leg Score	1-0	2-0	3-0	4-0	5-0	2-1	3-1	4-1
Occurrences	2	0	0	0	0	1	0	0
2nd Leg Score	5-1	3-2	4-2	5-2	4-3	5-3	5-4	0-0
Occurrences	0	0	0	0	0	0	0	0
2nd Leg Score	1-1	2-2	3-3	4-4	5-5	0-1	0-2	0-3
Occurrences	0	0	0	0	0	1	0	1
2nd Leg Score	0-4	0-5	1-2	1-3	1-4	1-5	2-3	2-4
Occurrences	0	0	0	1	2	1	1	0
2nd Leg Score	2-5	3-4	3-5	4-5	5>	<5		
Occurrences	0	0	0	0	0			

First-leg: 6-2

2nd Leg Score	1-0	2-0	3-0	4-0	5-0	2-1	3-1	4-1
Occurrences	0	0	0	0	0	0	0	0
2nd Leg Score	5-1	3-2	4-2	5-2	4-3	5-3	5-4	0-0
Occurrences	0	0	0	0	0	0	0	0
2nd Leg Score	1-1	2-2	3-3	4-4	5-5	0-1	0-2	0-3
Occurrences	2	0	0	0	0	0	0	0
2nd Leg Score	0-4	0-5	1-2	1-3	1-4	1-5	2-3	2-4
Occurrences	1	0	0	0	0	0	0	0
2nd Leg Score	2-5	3-4	3-5	4-5	5>	<5		
Occurrences	0	0	0	0	0			

First-leg: 3-3

2nd Leg Score	1-0	2-0	3-0	4-0	5-0	2-1	3-1	4-1
Occurrences	0	0	0	0	0	1	0	0
2nd Leg Score	5-1	3-2	4-2	5-2	4-3	5-3	5-4	0-0
Occurrences	0	0	0	0	0	0	0	0
2nd Leg Score	1-1	2-2	3-3	4-4	5-5	0-1	0-2	0-3
Occurrences	1	2	0	0	0	1	0	1
2nd Leg Score	0-4	0-5	1-2	1-3	1-4	1-5	2-3	2-4
Occurrences	0	0	0	0	0	1	0	0
2nd Leg Score	2-5	3-4	3-5	4-5	5>	<5		
Occurrences	1	0	0	0	0	0		

First-leg: 4-3

2nd Leg Score	1-0	2-0	3-0	4-0	5-0	2-1	3-1	4-1
Occurrences	0	0	0	0	0	0	0	0
2nd Leg Score	5-1	3-2	4-2	5-2	4-3	5-3	5-4	0-0
Occurrences	0	0	0	0	0	0	0	0
2nd Leg Score	1-1	2-2	3-3	4-4	5-5	0-1	0-2	0-3
Occurrences	0	0	0	0	0	1	1	1
2nd Leg Score	0-4	0-5	1-2	1-3	1-4	1-5	2-3	2-4
Occurrences	0	0	1	1	1	0	0	0
2nd Leg Score	2-5	3-4	3-5	4-5	5>	<5		
Occurrences	0	0	0	0	0	0		

First-leg: 5-3

2nd Leg Score	1-0	2-0	3-0	4-0	5-0	2-1	3-1	4-1
Occurrences	0	0	0	0	0	0	0	0
2nd Leg Score	5-1	3-2	4-2	5-2	4-3	5-3	5-4	0-0
Occurrences	0	0	0	0	0	0	0	1
2nd Leg Score	1-1	2-2	3-3	4-4	5-5	0-1	0-2	0-3
Occurrences	0	0	0	0	0	0	0	0
2nd Leg Score	0-4	0-5	1-2	1-3	1-4	1-5	2-3	2-4
Occurrences	0	0	0	0	0	0	0	0
2nd Leg Score	2-5	3-4	3-5	4-5	5>	<5		
Occurrences	0	0	0	0	0	0		

First-leg: 0-1

2nd Leg Score	1-0	2-0	3-0	4-0	5-0	2-1	3-1	4-1
Occurrences	1	4	0	1	0	0	0	0
2nd Leg Score	5-1	3-2	4-2	5-2	4-3	5-3	5-4	0-0
Occurrences	0	0	1	0	0	0	0	9
2nd Leg Score	1-1	2-2	3-3	4-4	5-5	0-1	0-2	0-3
Occurrences	11	2	0	0	0	17	13	11
2nd Leg Score	0-4	0-5	1-2	1-3	1-4	1-5	2-3	2-4
Occurrences	8	4	6	5	3	2	2	1

2nd Leg Score	2-5	3-4	3-5	4-5	5>	<5
Occurrences	0	0	0	0	1	5

First-leg: 0-2

2nd Leg Score	1-0	2-0	3-0	4-0	5-0	2-1	3-1	4-1
Occurrences	3	0	0	1	0	2	1	0
2nd Leg Score	5-1	3-2	4-2	5-2	4-3	5-3	5-4	0-0
Occurrences	0	0	0	0	0	0	0	3
2nd Leg Score	1-1	2-2	3-3	4-4	5-5	0-1	0-2	0-3
Occurrences	3	1	0	0	0	6	5	3
2nd Leg Score	0-4	0-5	1-2	1-3	1-4	1-5	2-3	2-4
Occurrences	4	1	8	2	2	1	0	0
2nd Leg Score	2-5	3-4	3-5	4-5	5>	<5		
Occurrences	0	0	0	0	0	8		

First-leg: 1-2

2nd Leg Score	1-0	2-0	3-0	4-0	5-0	2-1	3-1	4-1
Occurrences	1	0	0	0	0	1	2	0
2nd Leg Score	5-1	3-2	4-2	5-2	4-3	5-3	5-4	0-0
Occurrences	0	0	0	0	0	0	0	10
2nd Leg Score	1-1	2-2	3-3	4-4	5-5	0-1	0-2	0-3
Occurrences	10	2	0	0	0	5	8	6
2nd Leg Score	0-4	0-5	1-2	1-3	1-4	1-5	2-3	2-4
Occurrences	1	2	7	7	3	2	1	0
2nd Leg Score	2-5	3-4	3-5	4-5	5>	<5		
Occurrences	0	1	0	0	0	2		

First-leg: 1-3

2nd Leg Score	1-0	2-0	3-0	4-0	5-0	2-1	3-1	4-1
Occurrences	1	1	0	0	0	0	0	0
2nd Leg Score	5-1	3-2	4-2	5-2	4-3	5-3	5-4	0-0
Occurrences	0	0	0	0	0	0	0	2
2nd Leg Score	1-1	2-2	3-3	4-4	5-5	0-1	0-2	0-3
Occurrences	2	1	1	0	0	5	4	1
2nd Leg Score	0-4	0-5	1-2	1-3	1-4	1-5	2-3	2-4
Occurrences	3	1	5	3	1	2	0	2
2nd Leg Score	2-5	3-4	3-5	4-5	5>	<5		
Occurrences	0	0	0	0	0	5		

First-leg: 2-4

2nd Leg Score	1-0	2-0	3-0	4-0	5-0	2-1	3-1	4-1
Occurrences	1	0	0	0	0	0	0	0
2nd Leg Score	5-1	3-2	4-2	5-2	4-3	5-3	5-4	0-0
Occurrences	0	0	0	0	0	0	0	1

2nd Leg Score	1-1	2-2	3-3	4-4	5-5	0-1	0-2	0-3
Occurrences	0	0	0	0	0	1	0	1
2nd Leg Score	0-4	0-5	1-2	1-3	1-4	1-5	2-3	2-4
Occurrences	1	0	2	0	1	0	0	0
2nd Leg Score	2-5	3-4	3-5	4-5	5>	<5		
Occurrences	0	0	0	0	0			

First-leg: 3-4

2nd Leg Score	1-0	2-0	3-0	4-0	5-0	2-1	3-1	4-1
Occurrences	0	0	0	0	0	0	0	0
2nd Leg Score	5-1	3-2	4-2	5-2	4-3	5-3	5-4	0-0
Occurrences	0	0	0	0	0	0	0	0
2nd Leg Score	1-1	2-2	3-3	4-4	5-5	0-1	0-2	0-3
Occurrences	0	0	0	0	0	0	0	0
2nd Leg Score	0-4	0-5	1-2	1-3	1-4	1-5	2-3	2-4
Occurrences	0	0	0	0	1	0	1	0
2nd Leg Score	2-5	3-4	3-5	4-5	5>	<5		
Occurrences	0	0	0	1	0			

Qualification/Eliminations after First-leg Score

First-leg Score	No. Matches	Qualifications No.	%	Eliminations No.	%
0-0	137	41	29.93%	96	70.07%
1-0	259	153	59.07%	106	40.93%
2-0	197	148	75.13%	49	24.87%
3-0	117	106	90.60%	11	9.40%
1-1	152	31	20.39%	121	79.61%
2-1	141	62	43.97%	79	56.03%
3-1	94	63	67.02%	31	32.98%
4-1	48	42	87.50%	6	12.50%
5-1	31	29	93.55%	2	6.45%
2-2	69	13	18.84%	56	81.16%
3-2	55	22	40.00%	33	60.00%
4-2	27	19	70.37%	8	29.63%
5-2	10	6	60.00%	4	40.00%
6-2	4	3	75.00%	1	25.00%
3-3	8	2	25.00%	6	75.00%
4-3	6	0	0.00%	6	100.00%
5-3	1	1	100.00%	0	0.00%
0-1	107	9	8.41%	98	91.59%
0-2	56	2	3.57%	54	96.43%
1-2	72	4	5.56%	68	94.44%
1-3	40	0	0.00%	40	100.00%

| 2-4 | 8 | 0 | 0.00% | 8 | 100.00% |
| 3-4 | 3 | 0 | 0.00% | 3 | 100.00% |

Home Match Score Frequencies

Home Score	1-0	2-0	3-0	4-0	5-0	2-1	3-1	4-1
Number	485	397	235	130	74	309	179	99
Percentage	13	11	6	3	2	8	5	3

Home Score	5-1	3-2	4-2	5-2	4-3	5-3	5-4	0-0
Number	62	101	47	18	14	1	3	258
Percentage	2	3	1	0	0	0	0	7

Home Score	1-1	2-2	3-3	4-4	5-5	0-1	0-2	0-3
Number	310	129	21	6	0	201	98	44
Percentage	8	3	1	0	0	5	3	1

Home Score	0-4	0-5	1-2	1-3	1-4	1-5	2-3	2-4
Number	20	17	147	77	30	7	42	18
Percentage	1	0	4	2	1	0	1	1

Home Score	2-5	3-4	3-5	4-5	5>	<5
Number	10	5	4	0	132	30
Percentage	0	0	0	0	4	1

Number of matches: 3760

Champions' Cup Win Statistics

Appearances, Winners, Runners-up by Country

	Final Appearances		The Winners		The Runners-up	
1.	Italy	16	Italy	8	Italy	9
2.	Spain	13	England	8	Spain	6
3.	England	10	Italy	7	Germany	5
4.	Germany	9	Spain	7	Portugal	5
5.	Portugal	8	Holland	5	France	4
6.	Holland	6	Germany	4	England	2
7.	France	5	Portugal	3	Yugoslavia	1
8.	Scotland	2	France	1	Holland	1
9.	Romania	2	Scotland	1	Scotland	1
10.	Yugoslavia	2	Romania	1	Greece	1
11.	Greece	1	Yugoslavia	1	Belgium	1
12.	Belgium	1			Sweden	1
13.	Sweden	1			Romania	1
	Total	76	Total	38	Total	38

The Winners by Country

Country	Apps	Winning Teams (Years)
Albania	–	–
Austria	–	–
Belgium	–	–
Bulgaria	–	–
Cyprus	–	–
Czechoslovakia	–	–
Denmark	–	–
East Germany	–	–
England	8	Manchester United (1968), Liverpool (1977, 1978, 1981, 1984), Nottingham Forest (1979, 1980), Aston Villa (1982)
Finland	–	–
France	1	Marseille (1993)
Greece	–	–
Germany	4	West: Bayern Munich (1974, 1975, 1976), SV Hamburg (1983)

Holland	5	Feyenoord (1970), Ajax (1971, 1972, 1973), PSV Eindhoven (1988)
Hungary	–	–
Iceland	–	–
Italy	7	Milan (1963, 1969, 1989, 1990), Internazionale (1964, 1965), Juventus (1985)
Luxembourg	–	–
Malta	–	–
Northern Ireland	–	–
Norway	–	–
Poland	–	–
Portugal	3	Benfica (1961, 1962), FC Porto (1987)
Republic of Ireland	–	–
Romania	1	Steaua Bucharest (1986)
Scotland	1	Celtic (1967)
Spain	7	Real Madrid (1956, 1957, 1958, 1959, 1960, 1966), Barcelona (1992)
Sweden	–	–
Switzerland	–	–
Turkey	–	–
USSR	–	–
Yugoslavia	1	Red Star Belgrade (1991)

The Winners – Classification by Results

Pos	Club	Cnty	Wins	Years
1	Real Madrid	Esp	6	1956, 1957, 1958, 1959, 1960, 1966
2	Milan	Ita	4	1963, 1969, 1989, 1990
	Liverpool	Eng	4	1977, 1978, 1981, 1984
4	Ajax	Hol	3	1971, 1972, 1973
5	Bayern Munich	FRG	3	1974, 1975, 1976
6	Benfica	Por	2	1961, 1962
	Internazionale	Ita	2	1964, 1965
	Nottingham Forest	Eng	2	1979, 1980
9	Celtic	Sco	1	1967
	Manchester United	Eng	1	1968
	Feyenoord	Hol	1	1970
	Aston Villa	Eng	1	1982
	SV Hamburg	FRG	1	1983
	Juventus	Ita	1	1985
	Steaua Bucharest	Rom	1	1986
	FC Porto	Por	1	1987
	PSV Eindhoven	Hol	1	1988

Red Star Belgrade	Yug	1	1991
Barcelona	Esp	1	1992
Marseille	Fra	1	1993

The European Champions Cup Finalists

Pos'n	Club	Cnty	Apps	Wins
1	Real Madrid	Esp	9	6
2	Benfica	Por	7	2
3	Milan	Ita	6	4
4	Liverpool	Eng	5	4
5	Ajax	Hol	4	3
6	Bayern Munich	Frg	5	3
7	Internazionale	Ita	4	3
8	Juventus	Ita	3	1
	Barcelona	Esp	3	1
10	Nottingham Forest	Eng	2	2
11	Celtic	Sco	2	1
	SV Hamburg	Frg	2	1
	Steaua Bucharest	Rom	2	1
	Marseille	Fra	2	1
15	Stade de Reims	Fra	2	0
16	Manchester United	Eng	1	1
	Feyenoord	Hol	1	1
	Aston Villa	Eng	1	1
	FC Porto	Por	1	1
	PSV Eindhoven	Ned	1	1
	Red Star Belgrade	Yug	1	1
22	Fiorentina	Ita	1	0
	Eintracht Frankfurt	Frg	1	0
	Partizan Belgrade	Yug	1	0
	Panithaniakos	Gre	1	0
	Atletico Madrid	Esp	1	0
	Leeds United	Eng	1	0
	Saint-Etienne	Fra	1	0
	Borussia Monchengladbach	FRG	1	0
	Club Bruges	Bel	1	0
	Malmo	Swe	1	0
	Roma	Ita	1	0

Cup-Winners' Cup
Win Statistics

Appearances, Winners, Runners-up by Country

	Final Appearances		*The Winners*		*The Runners-up*	
1.	Spain	11	England	6	Spain	6
2.	England	10	Italy	6	England	4
3.	Italy	10	Spain	5	Italy	3
4.	Germany	10	Germany	5	Germany	5
5.	Belgium	5	USSR	3	Belgium	4
6.	Scotland	4	Belgium	3	Scotland	2
7.	USSR	4	Scotland	2	Hungry	2
8.	Portugal	2	Portugal	1	Austria	2
9.	Hungary	2	Czechoslovakia	1	Poland	1
10.	Austria	2	Holland	1	USSR	1
11.	Holland	2			Portugal	1
12.	Czechoslovakia	1			Holland	1
13.	Poland	1			France	1
14	Belgium	1				
	Total	66	Total	33	Total	33

The Winners by Country

Country	Apps	Winning Teams (Years)
Albania	–	–
Austria	–	–
Belgium	3	RSC Anderlecht (1976, 1978), KV Mechelen (1988)
Bulgaria	–	–
Cyprus	–	–
Czechoslovakia	1	Slovan Bratislava (1969)
Denmark	–	–
England	6	Tottenham Hotspur (1963), West Ham United (1965), Manchester City (1970), Chelsea (1971), Everton (1985), Manchester United (1991)
Finland		

France	–	–
Germany	5	Werder Bremen (1992)
		East: Magdeburg (1974)
		West: Borussia Dortmund (1966), Bayern Munich (1967), SV Hamburg (1977)
Greece	–	–
Holland	1	Ajax (1987)
Hungary	–	–
Iceland	–	–
Italy	6	Fiorentina (1961), Milan (1968, 1973), Juventus (1984), Sampdoria (1990), Parma (1993)
Luxembourg	–	–
Malta	–	–
Northern Ireland	–	–
Norway	–	–
Poland	–	–
Portugal	1	Sporting Lisbon (1964)
Republic of Ireland	–	–
Romania	–	–
Scotland	2	Rangers (1972), Aberdeen (1983)
Spain	5	Atletico Madrid (1962), Barcelona (1979, 1982, 1989), Valencia (1980)
Sweden	–	–
Switzerland	–	–
Turkey	–	–
USSR	3	Dinamo Kiev (1975, 1986), Dinamo Tbilisi (1981)
Wales	–	–
Yugoslavia	–	–

The Winners – Classification by Results

Pos'n	Club	Cnty	Wins	Years
1	Barcelona	Esp	3	1979, 1982, 1989
2	Milan	Ita	2	1968, 1973
3	Dinamo Kiev	Urs	2	1975, 1986
4	RSC Anderlecht	Bel	2	1976, 1978
5	Fiorentina	Ita	1	1961
6	Atletico Madrid	Esp	1	1962

7	Tottenham Hotspur	Eng	1	1963
8	Sporting Lisbon	Por	1	1964
9	West Ham United	Eng	1	1965
10	Borussia Dortmund	Frg	1	1966
11	Bayern Munich	Frg	1	1967
12	Slovan Bratislava	Tch	1	1969
13	Manchester City	Eng	1	1970
14	Chelsea	Eng	1	1971
15	Rangers	Sco	1	1972
16	Magdeburg	GDR	1	1974
17	SV Hamburg	FRG	1	1977
18	Valencia	Esp	1	1980
19	Dinamo Tbilisi	URS	1	1981
20	Aberdeen	Sco	1	1983
21	Juventus	Ita	1	1984
22	Everton	Eng	1	1985
23	Ajax	Hol	1	1987
24	KV Mechelen	Bel	1	1988
25	Sampdoria	Ita	1	1990
26	Manchester United	Eng	1	1991
27	Werder Bremen	Ger	1	1992
28	Parma	Ita	1	1993

The Cup-Winners' Cup Finalists

Pos'n	Club	Cnty	Apps	Wins
1	Barcelona	Esp	5	3
2	RSC Anderlecht	Bel	4	2
3	Milan	Ita	3	2
4	Atletico Madrid	Esp	3	1
	Rangers	Sco	3	1
6	Dinamo Kiev	URS	2	2
7	Fiorentina	Ita	2	1
	West Ham United	Eng	2	1
	SV Hamburg	Ger	2	1
	Ajax	Hol	2	1
	Sampdoria	Ita	2	1
12	Real Madrid	Esp	2	0
13	Tottenham Hotspur	Eng	1	1

Sporting Lisbon	Por	1	1
Borussia Dortmund	FRG	1	1
Bayern Munich	FRG	1	1
Slovan Bratislava	Tch	1	1
Manchester City	Eng	1	1
Chelsea	Eng	1	1
Magdeburg	GDR	1	1
Valencia	Esp	1	1
Dinamo Tbilisi	URS	1	1
Aberdeen	Sco	1	1
Juventus	Ita	1	1
Everton	Eng	1	1
KV Mechelen	Bel	1	1
Manchester United	Eng	1	1
Werder Bremen	Ger	1	1
Parma	Ita	1	1
30 MTK-VM	Hun	1	0
1860 Munich	FRG	1	0
Liverpool	Eng	1	0
Gornik Zabrze	Pol	1	0
Dinamo Moscow	URS	1	0
Leeds United	Eng	1	0
Ferencvaros	Hun	1	0
Austria Vienna	Aut	1	0
Fortuna Düsseldorf	FRG	1	0
Arsenal	Eng	1	0
Carl Zeiss Jena	GDR	1	0
Standard Liege	Bel	1	0
FC Porto	Por	1	0
Rapid Vienna	Aut	1	0
Lokomotive Leipzig	GDR	1	0
Monaco	Fra	1	0
Royal Antwerp	Bel	1	0

UEFA Cup Win Statistics

Appearances, Winners, Runners-up by Country

	Final Appearances		The Winners		The Runners-up	
1.	England	15	England	9	England	6
2.	Spain	13	Spain	8	Germany	6
3.	Italy	11	Italy	6	Spain	5
4.	Germany	10	Germany	4	Italy	5
5.	Hungary	4	Holland	3	Hungary	3
6.	Belgium	4	Sweden	2	Belgium	3
7.	Holland	5	Hungary	1	Yugoslavia	2
8.	Yugoslavia	3	Portugal	1	Holland	2
9.	Sweden	2	Belgium	1	France	1
10.	France	1			Portugal	1
11.	Portugal	1			Scotland	1
12.	Scotland	1				
	Total	70	Total	35	Total	35

The Winners by Country

Country	Apps	Winning Teams (Years)
Albania	–	–
Austria	–	–
Belgium	1	RSC Anderlecht (1983)
Bulgaria	–	–
Cyprus	–	–
Czechoslovakia	–	–
Denmark	–	–
England	9	Leeds Utd (1968, 1971), Newcastle Utd (1969), Arsenal (1970), Tott Hotspur (1972, 1984), Liverpool (1973, 1976), Ipswich Town (1981)
Finland	–	–
France	–	–
Germany	4	West: Bor. Monchengladbach (1975, 1979), Eintracht Frankfurt (1980), Bayer Leverkusen (1988)
Greece	–	–

Holland	3	Feyenoord (1974), PSV Eindhoven (1978), Ajax (1992)
Hungary	1	Ferencvaros (1965)
Iceland	–	–
Italy	5	Roma (1961), Juventus (1977, 1990), Napoli (1989), Internazionale (1991), Juventus (1993)
Luxembourg	–	–
Malta	–	–
Northern Ireland	–	–
Norway	–	–
Poland	–	–
Portugal	–	–
Republic of Ireland	–	–
Romania	–	–
Scotland	–	–
Spain	8	Barcelona (1958, 1960, 1966), Valencia (1962, 1963), Real Zaragoza (1964), Real Madrid (1985, 1986)
Sweden	1	IFK Gothenburg (1982, 1987)
Switzerland	–	–
Turkey	–	–
USSR	–	–
Wales	–	–
Yugoslavia	1	Dinamo Zagreb (1967)

The Winners – Classification by Results

Pos'n	Club	Cnty	Wins	Years
1	Barcelona	Esp	3	1958, 1960, 1966
	Juventus	Ita	3	1977, 1990, 1993
3	Valencia	Esp	2	1962, 1963
	Leeds United	Eng	2	1968, 1971
	Tottenham Hotspur	Eng	2	1972, 1984
	Liverpool	Eng	2	1973, 1976
	B. Monchengladbach	Frg	2	1975, 1979
	IFK Gothenburg	Swe	2	1982, 1987
	Real Madrid	Esp	2	1985, 1986
10	Roma	Ita	1	1961
	Real Zaragoza	Esp	1	1964
	Ferencvaros	Hun	1	1965

Dinamo Zagreb	Yug	1	1967	
Newcastle United	Eng	1	1969	
Arsenal	Eng	1	1970	
Feyenoord	Hol	1	1974	
PSV Eindhoven	Hol	1	1978	
Eintracht Frankfurt	FRG	1	1980	
Ipswich Town	Eng	1	1981	
RSC Anderlecht	Bel	1	1983	
Bayer Leverkusen	FRG	1	1988	
Napoli	Ita	1	1989	
Internazionale	Ita	1	1991	
Ajax	Hol	1	1992	

The UEFA Cup Finalists

Pos'n	Club	Cnty	Apps	Wins
1	Juventus	Ita	5	3
2	Barcelona	Esp	4	3
3	Borussia Monchengladbach	FRG	4	2
4	Valencia	Esp	3	2
	Leeds United	Eng	3	2
	Tottenham Hotspur	Eng	3	2
7	RSC Anderlecht	Bel	3	1
8	Liverpool	Eng	2	2
	IFK Gothenburg	Swe	2	2
	Real Madrid	Esp	2	2
11	Roma	Ita	2	1
	Real Zaragoza	Esp	2	1
	Ferencvaros	Hun	2	1
	Dinamo Zagreb	Yug	2	1
15	Birmingham City	Eng	2	0
16	Newcastle United	Eng	1	1
	Arsenal	Eng	1	1
	Feyenoord	Hol	1	1
	PSV Eindhoven	Hol	1	1
	Eintracht Frankfurt	FRG	1	1
	Ipswich Town	Eng	1	1
	Bayer Leverkusen	FRG	1	1
	Napoli	Ita	1	1
	Internazionale	Ita	1	1

25	Ajax	Hol	1	0
	Chelsea	Eng	1	0
	Ujpest Dozsa	Hun	1	0
	Wolverhampton Wanderers	Eng	1	0
	FC Twente	Hol	1	0
	Club Bruges	Bel	1	0
	Athletic Bilbao	Esp	1	0
	SEC Bastia	Fra	1	0
	Red Star Belgrade	Yug	1	0
	AZ'67 Alkmaar	Hol	1	0
	SV Hamburg	FRG	1	0
	Benfica	Por	1	0
	Videoton	Hun	1	0
	Cologne	FRG	1	0
	Dundee United	Sco	1	0
	Español	Esp	1	0
	VFB Stuttgart	FRG	1	0
	Fiorentina	Ita	1	0
	Torino	Ita	1	0
	Borussia Dortmund	Ger	1	0

A-Z of CLUBS
COMPETING IN EUROPE

The following section contains details of all clubs competing in the three European cup competitions. The clubs are arranged alphabetically by name irrespective of the competition they are hoping to win. Each entry is arranged to provide you with the maximum amount of relevant information and can be broken down into four sections. Firstly, the club name followed by country or origin and then the competition in which they are playing. The code used here is:

C1	Champions' Cup
C2	Cup-Winners' Cup
C3	UEFA Cup

This is followed by a brief history of the club.

Secondly, details relating to club name, date of formation, address and stadium are provided wherever possible. This is followed by the club's Euro record and provides the PWDLFA details of the club in each of the competitions. Again the C1, C2, C3 key is used to identify the various competitions. Finally, the seasons in which the club concerned entered each of these competitions is provided.

Wherever possible I have used the common form of club name. This has posed a few headaches, not least because of the amount of TV coverage now given to European football. For example, the live coverage of Italian football by BSkyB and Channel 4 in recent years has meant that it is now common-place to use the name Fiorentina whereas Florence was more popular five years ago, likewise Milan rather than AC Milan and Internazionale rather than Inter Milan.

There have also been a large number of club name-changes in recent years, not least due to the restructuring of Eastern Europe and the former Soviet states. As an example, Dynamo Tbilisi is a very famous name – however the club is now called Iberya Tbilisi. Austrian clubs can also pose a problem as they now tend to include sponsors' names in their club names. Name-change details are normally given in club histories in an effort to assist! Please bear all this in mind when searching for a particular club entry.

Compiling details for some of the minor former Soviet states has been very difficult and there are a number of gaps and discrepancies. For example, various reference works show that the Ukraine club Karpaty Lvov was formed in 1963 and competed in Europe in 1970-71. However, other works show that the club SKA Karpaty Lvov was relegated from the USSR 1st League at the end of 1989 but no longer existed in 1990. However, a club called Karpaty Lvov already played in the 2nd League in 1989! Any firm details from readers would be greatly appreciated for future editions.

AaB Aalborg (Denmark) C3

No League honours but Cup winners in 1966 and 1977. Their European debut came in the 1966-67 Cup-Winners' Cup.

Full Name: Aalborg Boldspilkub A/S   **Founded:** 1885
Address: Hornevej 2, Oster Uttrup, 9220 Aalborg Ost, Denmark
Phone: 98-153333
Stadium: Aalborg Stadion   **Capacity:** 20,000

Euro Record		P	W	D	L	F	A
	C1	0	0	0	0	0	0
	C2	6	1	1	4	3	12
	C3	0	0	0	0	0	0
	Total	6	1	1	4	3	12

C1: (0) None
C2: (3) 66-67, 70-71, 87-88
C3: (0) None

Aberdeen (Scotland) C2

Founded by members of Victoria United and Orion. Joined the League in 1906 and have never been relegated. Four times League champions and seven times Cup winners. Their European debut came in the 1967-68 Cup-Winners' Cup.

Full Name: Aberdeen FC   **Founded:** 1903
Address: Pittodrie Park, Aberdeen, AB2 1QH
Phone: (0224) 632328
Stadium: Pittodrie Park   **Capacity:** 21,779
Colours: Red, Red., Red

Euro Record		P	W	D	L	F	A
	C1	12	5	4	3	14	12
	C2	35	20	5	10	69	32
	C3	34	12	9	13	42	45
	Total	81	37	18	26	125	89

C1: (3) 80-81, 84-85, 85-86
C2: (7) 67-68, 70-71, 78-79, 82-83, 83-84, 86-87, 90-91
C3: (11) 68-69, 71-72, 72-73, 73-74, 77-78, 79-80, 81-82, 87-88, 88-89, 89-90, 91-92

Admira Wacker (Austria) C3

Founded as Admira Wien and merged with Waker Wien (founded 1908) in 1971. Nine times League champions, five times Cup winners. Their European debut came in the 1964-65 Cup Winners' Cup.

Full Name: FC Baumit Admira Wacker   **Founded:** 1905
Address: Johann-Steinbock-Strasse 1, 2344 Maria Enzersdorf, Austria
Phone: 2236-23479
Stadium: Bundesstadion   **Capacity:** 18,600
Colours: White, White, White

Euro Record		P	W	D	L	F	A
	C1	2	0	1	1	0	1
	C2	12	5	2	5	18	16
	C3	14	7	1	6	15	19
	Total	28	12	4	12	33	36

C1: (1) 66-67
C2: (3) 64-65, 89-90, 92-93
C3: (4) 73-74, 82-83, 87-88, 90-91

AEK Athens (Greece) C1

Founded by Greek refugees from Constantinople. Nine times League champions and eight times Cup winners. Reached the UEFA Cup semi-finals in the 1976-77 season. In the last four seasons in the League they have finished 2nd, 3rd, 1st and 1st again.

Full Name: AEK FC Athens   **Founded:** 1924
Address: Tritis Septemvriou 144, GR-11251 Athens, Greece
Phone: 1-8215645
Stadium: Neas Filadelfias   **Capacity:** 33,494

Euro Record		P	W	D	L	F	A
	C1	24	7	6	11	37	48
	C2	6	2	0	4	7	11
	C3	38	14	5	19	41	58
	Total	68	23	11	34	85	117

C1: (7) 63-64, 68-69, 71-72, 78-79, 79-80, 89-90, 92-93
C2: (3) 64-65, 66-67, 83-84
C3: (10) 70-71, 72-73, 75-76, 76-77, 77-78, 82-83, 85-86, 86-87, 88-89, 91-92

AIK Stockholm (Sweden)   C1

League founder members in 1924. Nine times League champions, most recently in the season finishing in late 1992. Four times Cup winners. European debut in the Fairs Cup 1965-66. In the last four seasons in the League they have finished 8th, 8th, 6th and 1st. Their first entry into the Champions' Cup this season.

Full Name: Allmanna Idrotts Klubben   **Founded:** 1891
Address: Box 1408, S-171 27 Solna, Sweden
Phone: 8-735 80 80
Stadium: Rasunda Stadion   **Capacity:** 27,500

Euro Record	P	W	D	L	F	A
C1	0	0	0	0	0	0
C2	8	2	4	2	21	10
C3	16	5	5	6	20	26
Total	24	7	9	8	41	36

C1: (0) None
C2: (3) 76-77, 85-86, 92-93
C3: (6) 65-66, 68-69, 73-74, 75-76, 84-85, 87-88

Ajax (Holland)   C2

Twenty-three times League champions and 11 times Cup winners. First Dutch club to play in the Cup-Winners' Cup, 1961-62. World Club Championship winners in 1972. In the last four seasons in the League they have finished 1st, 2nd, 2nd and 3rd.

Full Name: Ajax   **Founded:** 1900
Address: Middenweg 401, Postbus 41885, 1098 AV Amsterdam
Phone: 2-6654440/6946515
Stadium: De Meer   **Capacity:** 19,500
Colours: White/Red, White, White/Red

Euro Record	P	W	D	L	F	A
C1	75	42	15	18	141	74
C2	22	15	1	6	41	18
C3	58	34	7	17	117	53
Total	155	91	23	41	299	145

C1: (15) 57-58, 60-61, 66-67, 68-69, 70-71, 71-72, 72-73, 73-74, 77-78, 79-80, 80-81, 82-83, 83-84, 85-86
C2: (4) 61-62, 81-82, 86-87, 87-88
C3: (9) 69-70, 74-75, 75-76, 76-77, 78-79, 84-85, 88-89, 89-90, 91-92, 92-93

Albpetrol (Albania) C2

First time into Europe. Cup runners-up to the League champions, in 1993.

Full Name: Alpetrol
Address:
Stadium:

Euro Record	P	W	D	L	F	A
C1	0	0	0	0	0	0
C2	0	0	0	0	0	0
C3	0	0	0	0	0	0
Total	0	0	0	0	0	0

C1: (0) None
C2: (0) None
C3: (0) None

Apoel Nicosia (Cyprus) C2

Founded as the Greek Football and Athletic Club. League founder members in 1935 and champions 15 times, 12 times Cup winners. In the Cup-Winners' Cup, a competition in which they were the first entrant from Cyprus (1963-64), they have reached the 2nd round twice. In the last four seasons in the League they have finished 1st, 3rd, 1st and 4th.

Full Name: Apoel FC **Founded:** 1926
Address: Kennedy Avenue, PO Box 1133, Nicosia, Cyprus
Phone: 2-495222
Stadium: Makarion **Capacity:** 20,000
Colours: Yellow/Blue, Blue, Yellow

Euro Record	P	W	D	L	F	A
C1	12	2	2	8	10	30
C2	18	2	2	14	13	61
C3	8	0	3	5	8	21
Total	38	4	7	27	31	112

C1: (6) 65-66, 73-74, 80-81, 86-87, 90-91, 92-93
C2: (7) 63-64, 68-69, 69-70, 76-77, 78-79, 79-80, 84-85
C3: (4) 77-78, 81-82, 85-86, 88-89

Apollon (Cyprus)   C3

League champions once, in 1991, Cup winners four times. In the Champions'
Cup they reached the 2nd round in 1992, their European debut having been in
the 1966-67 Cup-Winners' Cup. In the last four seasons in the League they
have finished 5th, 1st, 3rd and 2nd.

Full Name: Apollon FC   **Founded:** 1954
Address: 1 Mesolongiou Str., Limassol, Cyprus
Phone: 5-363702
Stadium: Tsirion   **Capacity:** 20,000

Euro Record	P	W	D	L	F	A
C1	6	1	0	5	4	19
C2	10	1	1	8	6	39
C3	4	0	2	2	4	12
Total	20	2	3	15	14	70

C1: (1)   91-92
C2: (5)   66-67, 67-68, 82-83, 86-87, 92-93
C3: (2)   84-85, 89-90

Arsenal (England)   C2

Founded by workers at Royal Arsenal and soon known as Woolwich Arsenal.
Took present title in 1913. Joined League in 1892 and members of top
division without a break since 1913. Ten League championships and six times
Cup winners. European debut in 1963-64 Fairs Cup. Fairs Cup winners in
1970, beaten Cup-Winners' Cup finalists in 1980.

Full Name: Arsenal FC   **Founded:** 1886
Address: Highbury, London, N5 1BU
Phone: 071-226-0304
Stadium: Arsenal Stadium   **Capacity:** 29,000
Colours: Red & White, White, Red & White

Euro Record	P	W	D	L	F	A
C1	10	5	1	4	21	10
C2	9	4	5	0	13	5
C3	36	19	6	11	66	33
Total	55	28	12	15	100	48

C1: (2)   71-72, 91-92
C2: (1)   79-80
C3: (6)   63-64, 69-70, 70-71, 78-79, 81-82, 82-83

Aston Villa (England) C3

Founded by cricketers in 1874 Villa were founder members of the League in 1888. Champions seven times, the sixth in 1909-10, the seventh in 1980-81. Seven times Cup winners, the last in 1957. European debut in the 1975-76 UEFA Cup. Champions' Cup winners in 1982.

Full Name: Aston Villa FC   **Founded:** 1874
Address: Villa Park, Trinity Road, Birmingham, B6 6HE
Phone: 021-3272299
Stadium: Villa Park   **Capacity:** 40,000
Colours: Claret/Blue, White, Blue

Euro Record	P	W	D	L	F	A
C1	15	9	3	3	24	10
C2	0	0	0	0	0	0
C3	18	8	4	6	31	21
Total	33	17	7	9	55	31

C1: (2)   81-82, 82-83
C2: (0)   None
C3: (4)   74-75, 77-78, 83-84, 90-91

Atletico Madrid (Spain) C3

Founded as a branch of Athletico Bilbao. League founder members 1928-29. Recovered after the Civil War by amalgamating with an airmen's team to become Atletico Aviation de Madrid. Early in 1947 changed back to original name. Has eight League championships and eight Cup wins. First Spanish club to play in the Cup-Winners' Cup, 1961-62, a competition they won. World Club champions 1974.

Full Name: Club Atletico de Madrid   **Founded:** 1903
Address: Estadio Vicente Calderon, Paseo Virgen del Puerto 67, Puerta 8, 28005 Madrid, Spain
Phone: 91-2664707
Stadium: Vicente Calderon   **Capacity:** 62,000
Colours: Red/White, Blue, Red/White

Euro Record	P	W	D	L	F	A
C1	39	21	7	11	65	39
C2	62	38	12	12	118	57
C3	43	19	4	20	60	59
Total	144	78	23	43	243	155

C1: (5)   58-59, 66-67, 70-71, 73-74, 77-78
C2: (9)   61-62, 62-63, 65-66, 72-73, 75-76, 76-77, 85-86, 91-92, 92-93
C3: (14)   63-64, 64-65, 67-68, 68-69, 71-72, 74-75, 79-80, 81-82, 83-84, 84-85, 86-87, 88-89, 89-90, 90-91

Austria Vienna (Austria) C1

Originally known as Amateure (League champions 1924 and 1926) until 1926. Twice Mitropa Cup winners in the 1930s. Joined with Wiener Athletik Club in 1972. Twenty-one times League champions and 21 times Cup Winners. Represented Austria in the first Cup-Winners' Cup, 1960-61.

Full Name: FK Austria-Memphis   **Founded:** 1911
Address: Wiener Prater Stadion, Meiereistrasse, Sektor D, 1020 Vienna
Phone: (01) 2186491
Stadium: Prater   **Capacity:** 12,000

Euro Record

	P	W	D	L	F	A
C1	55	21	11	23	83	83
C2	35	9	12	14	36	52
C3	20	8	5	7	38	34
Total	110	38	28	44	157	169

C1: (14) 61-62, 62-63, 63-64, 69-70, 70-71, 76-77, 78-79, 79-80, 80-81, 81-82, 84-85, 85-86, 86-87, 92-93
C2: (7) 60-61, 67-68, 71-72, 74-75, 77-78, 82-83, 90-91
C3: (5) 72-73, 83-84, 87-88, 88-89, 89-90

Avenir Beggen (Luxembourg) C1

The capital city club have won the championship five times, the Cup four times. Their European debut came in the 1969-70 Champions' Cup. In the last four seasons in the League they have finished 2nd, 4th, 2nd and 1st.

Full Name: FC Avenir Beggen   **Founded:** 1915
Address: BP 382, 2013 Luxembourg
Phone: 78253
Stadium: Beggen   **Capacity:** 4,800
Colours: Yellow/Black, Black, Yellow

Euro Record

	P	W	D	L	F	A
C1	8	0	0	8	0	44
C2	12	1	2	9	7	42
C3	6	1	0	5	2	22
Total	26	2	2	22	9	108

C1: (4) 69-70, 82-83, 84-85, 86-87
C2: (5) 74-75, 83-84, 87-88, 88-89, 92-93
C3: (3) 75-76, 85-86, 90-91

Bangor (Northern Ireland) C2

Their Cup win in 1993 was their first, the previous best having been as runners-up in 1938-39.

Full Name: Bangor FC **Founded:** 1918
Address: 2 Belmont Drive, Co. Down, BT19 1NH
Phone: (0247) 469826
Stadium: Clandeboye Park **Capacity:** 5,000

Euro Record		P	W	D	L	F	A
	C1	0	0	0	0	0	0
	C2	0	0	0	0	0	0
	C3	2	0	0	2	0	6
	Total	2	0	0	2	0	6

C1: (0) None
C2: (0) None
C3: (1) 91-92

Barcelona (Spain) C1

Founded by a Swiss emigrant. Original members and first champions of the Spanish League in 1929, having been the first Cup winners in 1902. Now has 13 League titles and 22 Cup wins. Were Spain's first representative in the Fairs Cup, taking part in the first competition, 1956-58.

Full Name: Futbol Club Barcelona **Founded:** 1899
Address: Aristides Maillol s/n, 08028 Barcelona
Phone: 3-330-9411
Stadium: Nou Camp **Capacity:** 115,000
Colours: Blue/Dark and Red stripes, Blue/Dark and Red, Blue/Dark Red

Euro Record		P	W	D	L	F	A
	C1	50	28	11	11	92	45
	C2	76	45	14	17	164	82
	C3	122	59	27	36	228	144
	Total	248	132	52	64	484	271

C1: (6) 59-60, 60-61, 74-75, 85-86, 91-92, 92-93
C2: (12) 63-64, 68-69, 71-72, 78-79, 79-80, 81-82, 82-83, 83-84, 84-85, 88-89, 89-90, 90-91
C3: (19) 56-58, 58-60, 60-61, 61-62, 62-63, 64-65, 65-66, 66-67, 67-68, 69-70, 70-71, 72-73, 73-74, 75-76, 76-77, 77-78, 80-81, 86-87, 87-88

Bayer Leverkusen (Germany) C2

No domestic honours before winning the Cup in 1993. Won the UEFA Cup in 1988 on their European debut, beating Espanol on penalties. In the last four seasons they have finished 5th and 8th in the West German League, 6th and 5th in the united German League.

Full Name: TSV Bayer O4 Leverkusen   **Founded:** 1904
Address: Postfach 120 140, 5090 Leverkusen
Phone: 214-46030
Stadium: Ulrich-Haberland-stadion   **Capacity:** 25,350
Colours: White, White, White

Euro Record		P	W	D	L	F	A
	C1	0	0	0	0	0	0
	C2	0	0	0	0	0	0
	C3	24	11	9	4	31	16
	Total	24	11	9	4	31	16

C1: (0) None
C2: (0) None
C3: (4) 86-87, 87-88, 88-89, 90-91

Bayern Munich (Germany) C3

One German championship, 1932, and one West German Cup win before joining the Bundesliga in 1965. Subsequently won 11 League championships and won the Cup seven times. World Club Championship winners 1976. In the last four seasons they have finished 1st and 2nd in the West German League, 10th and 2nd.

Full Name: FC Bayern Munich   **Founded:** 1900
Address: Sabener Strasse 51, 8000 Munich, 90, Germany
Phone: 89-69931-2
Stadium: Olympiastadion   **Capacity:** 73,132
Colours: Red, Red, Red

Euro Record		P	W	D	L	F	A
	C1	94	58	18	18	210	87
	C2	39	19	14	6	67	36
	C3	49	26	8	15	101	59
	Total	182	103	40	39	378	182

C1: (13) 69-70, 72-73, 73-74, 74-75, 75-76, 76-77, 80-81, 81-82, 85-86, 86-87, 87-88, 89-90, 90-91
C2: (5) 66-67, 67-68, 71-72, 82-83, 84-85
C3: (7) 62-63, 70-71, 77-78, 79-80, 83-84, 88-89, 91-92

Beitar Jerusalem (Israel) C1

Twice League champions and five times Cup winners. In 1976 took part in the summer Inter-Toto in Switzerland. No other European experience.

Full Name: Beitar   **Founded:** 1924
Address:
Stadium:

Euro Record		P	W	D	L	F	A
	C1	0	0	0	0	0	0
	C2	0	0	0	0	0	0
	C3	0	0	0	0	0	0
	Total	0	0	0	0	0	0

C1: (0) None
C2: (0) None
C3: (0) None

Belzers (Liechtenstein) C2

This club has no European experience.

Full Name: **Founded:**
Address:
Stadium:

Euro Record		P	W	D	L	F	A
	C1	0	0	0	0	0	0
	C2	0	0	0	0	0	0
	C3	0	0	0	0	0	0
	Total	0	0	0	0	0	0

C1: (0) None
C2: (0) None
C3: (0) None

Benfica (Portugal) C2

Founded by a soccer fan who had learnt the game from Englishmen in the capital. In 1907 came together with two other Lisbon clubs to become Sport Lisboa e Benfica. League founder members 1935 and third in the first season. 29 times League champions and not out of the top two since 1985. 25 times Cup winners. Portugal's first winner of a European competition.

Full Name: Sport Lisboa e Benfica   **Founded:** 1904
Address: Avenida General Norton de Matos, 1500 Lisbon, Portugal
Phone: 1-7622129
Stadium: Sport Lisboa e Benfica   **Capacity:** 120,000
Colours: Red, White, Red

Euro Record	P	W	D	L	F	A
C1	133	67	29	37	266	139
C2	28	13	8	7	42	19
C3	36	18	10	8	58	33
Total	197	98	47	52	366	191

C1: (22) 57-58, 60-61, 61-62, 62-63, 63-64, 64-65, 65-66, 67-68, 68-69, 69-70, 71-72, 72-73, 73-74, 75-76, 76-77, 77-78, 81-82, 83-84, 84-85, 87-88, 89-90, 91-92
C2: (5) 70-71, 74-75, 80-81, 85-86, 86-87
C3: (7) 66-67, 78-79, 79-80, 82-83, 88-89, 90-91, 92-93

Besiktas (Turkey) C2

Eight times League champions and three times Cup winners. Their European debut came in the 1958-59 Champions' Cup.

Full Name: Besiktas SK   **Founded:** 1903
Address: Spor Cad. 92, Akaretler, Istanbul
Phone: 1-1615804
Stadium: Inonu   **Capacity:** 38,000
Colours: White/Black, White, White/Black

Euro Record	P	W	D	L	F	A
C1	20	4	4	12	15	36
C2	8	1	1	6	5	19
C3	8	2	1	5	5	13
Total	36	7	6	23	25	68

C1: (9) 58-59, 60-61, 66-67, 67-68, 82-83, 86-87, 90-91, 91-92, 92-93
C2: (4) 75-76, 77-78, 84-85, 89-90
C3: (4) 74-75, 85-86, 87-88, 88-89

Boavista FC (Portugal) C3

The Oporto-based club were League runners-up in 1975-76, their highest ever finishing position, and they have also recorded a third place, 1991-92. Four times Cup winners (all since 1975), one bringing them their European debut in the 1975-76 Cup-Winners' Cup

Full Name: Boavista Futebol Clube **Founded:** 1903
Address: No Estadio do Bessa, Rua O Primeiro de Janeiro, 4100 Porto
Phone: 2-698159/668506
Stadium: Bessa **Capacity:** 23,421

Euro Record		P	W	D	L	F	A
	C1	0	0	0	0	0	0
	C2	16	6	6	4	25	13
	C3	22	7	4	11	22	31
	Total	38	13	10	15	47	44

C1: (0) None
C2: (4) 75-76, 76-77, 79-80, 92-93
C3: (7) 77-78, 80-81, 81-82, 85-86, 86-87, 89-90, 91-92

Boby Brno (Czech) C2

Known as Zbrojovaka Brno until 1992. League champions once, 1978. Took part in the first Cup-Winners' Cup, 1960-61, and were Czechoslovakia's first Fairs Cup entrant the following season. In the last four seasons in the League they have finished 12th, 16th (and relegated), Czech Second Division Champions, and 7th.

Full Name: FC Boby Brno **Founded:** 1913
Address: Drobneho 45, 65 631 Brno
Phone: 5-750786
Stadium: Za Luzankami **Capacity:** 35,000

Euro Record		P	W	D	L	F	A
	C1	4	1	3	0	7	5
	C2	4	1	1	2	3	4
	C3	33	16	4	13	55	43
	Total	41	18	8	15	65	52

C1: (0) 78-79
C2: (1) 60-61
C3: (8) 61-62, 62-63, 63-64, 64-65, 65-66, 66-67, 79-80, 80-81

Bohemians (Rep. Ireland) C3

Founder members of the Northern Ireland League and runners-up 1921-22.
Seven times champions, the last in 1977-78. All-Ireland Cup winners in 1907-
08 and five times winners of the Northern Ireland Cup. Their European debut
came in the 1970-71 Cup-Winners' Cup. Reached the 2nd round of the Cup-
Winners' Cup in 1976-77 and the Champions' Cup in 1978-79.

Full Name: Bohemian FC   **Founded:** 1890
Address: Dalymount Park, Philsboro, Dublin 7
Phone: 01-868 0923
Stadium: Dalymount Park   **Capacity:** 40,000

Euro Record		P	W	D	L	F	A
	C1	6	1	2	3	4	13
	C2	8	2	2	4	6	13
	C3	14	1	4	9	8	27
	Total	28	4	8	16	18	53

C1: (2)   75-76, 78-79
C2: (3)   70-71, 76-77, 92-93
C3: (7)   72-73, 74-75, 77-78, 79-80, 84-85, 85-86, 87-88

Bordeaux (France) C3

Four times League champions and three times Cup winners. They reached the
semi-final of the Champions' Cup in 1985 and the same stage of the Cup-
Winners' Cup in 1987. In the last four seasons in the League they have
finished 2nd, 10th (but were relegated for financial irregularities), 1st in
Division 2(B) and 4th.

Full Name: Girondins de Bordeaux   **Founded:** 1881
Address: Rue Joliot-Curie, 33186 Le Haillan
Phone: 56-086363
Stadium: Parc Lescure   **Capacity:** 50,000
Colours: Navy Blue, Navy Blue, Navy Blue

Euro Record		P	W	D	L	F	A
	C1	16	6	8	2	17	12
	C2	10	6	1	3	14	10
	C3	38	17	4	17	52	59
	Total	64	29	13	22	83	81

C1: (3)   84-85, 85-86, 87-88
C2: (2)   68-69, 86-87
C3: (10)   64-65, 65-66, 66-67, 67-68, 69-70, 81-82, 82-83, 83-84, 88-89,
90-91

Borussia Dortmund (Germany)　　C3

Three pre-Bundesliga West German championships and subsequently twice
runners-up. Twice West German Cup winners. In the last four seasons they
have finished 4th and 10th in the West German League, 2nd and 4th. UEFA
Cup losing finalists in 1992-93.

Full Name: BV Borussia Dortmund　　　　　　**Founded:** 1909
Address:　　Westfalenstadion, Strobelallee, Postfach 10059,
　　　　　　　　4600 Dortmund 1
Phone:　　　231-22083/4
Stadium:　　Westfalenstadion　　　　　　　　**Capacity:** 53,870
Colours:　　Yellow, Black, Yellow

Euro Record		P	W	D	L	F	A
	C1	18	8	3	7	44	30
	C2	15	9	3	3	32	15
	C3	30	16	1	13	44	40
	Total	63	33	7	23	120	85

C1: (3)　56-57, 57-58, 63-64
C2: (3)　65-66, 66-67, 89-90
C3: (5)　64-65, 82-83, 87-88, 90-91, 92-93

Botev Plovdiv (Bulgaria)　　C3

Founded 1912 as Botev. Known as Trakia from 1967, when amalgamated
with Spartak and Akademik Plovdiv, until 1990. Spartak split away again in
1982. Three times League champions. Their European debut came in the
1962-63 Cup-Winners' Cup, qualification coming as holders of the Soviet
Army Cup. In the last four seasons they have finished 7th, 5th, 4th and 3rd.

Full Name: FC Botev　　　　　　　　　　**Founded:** 1912
Address:　　Bul D. Blagoev 10, 4000 Plovdiv
Phone:　　　32-226375/226987
Stadium:　　Christa Botev　　　　　　　　**Capacity:** 40,000

Euro Record		P	W	D	L	F	A
	C1	8	2	1	5	8	11
	C2	12	6	2	4	23	18
	C3	16	3	5	8	24	28
	Total	36	11	8	17	55	57

C1: (3)　63-64, 67-68, 85-86
C2: (3)　62-63, 81-82, 84-85
C3: (8)　66-67, 68-69, 70-71, 78-79, 86-87, 87-88, 88-89, 92-93

Brondby IF (Denmark) C3

Five League titles and a Cup win, all achieved since 1985. Their European debut came in the 1986-87 Champions' Cup. They reached the UEFA Cup semi-finals in 1990-91, the furthest any Danish club has ever been in European competition.

Full Name: Brondbyernes Idraets Forening **Founded:** 1964
Address: Gildhoj 6, 2605 Brondby, Denmark
Phone: 42-630810/459394
Stadium: Brondby stadion **Capacity:** 14,000
Colours: Yellow, Blue, Blue

Euro Record		P	W	D	L	F	A
	C1	14	4	5	5	18	18
	C2	0	0	0	0	0	0
	C3	14	7	3	4	20	11
	Total	28	11	8	9	38	29

C1: (4) 86-87, 88-89, 89-90, 91-92
C2: (0) None
C3: (2) 87-88, 90-91

Cagliari (Italy) C3

Founded as Calgliari FC. In 1924 became CS Calgliari and in 1934 adopted current name. Promoted to the First Division for the first time in 1964. League runners-up 1968-69 and champions the following season. Their European debut came in the 1969-70 UEFA Cup.

Full Name: Cagliari Calcio **Founded:** 1920
Address: Via Tela 30, 09128 Cagliari
Phone: 70-489375
Stadium: Sant' Elia **Capacity:** 43,117

Euro Record		P	W	D	L	F	A
	C1	4	2	0	2	5	5
	C2	0	0	0	0	0	0
	C3	6	1	1	4	5	7
	Total	10	3	1	6	10	12

C1: (1) 70-71
C2: (0) None
C3: (2) 69-70, 72-73

Cardiff City (Wales) C2

Founded as Riverside from the cricket club of that name. Took their present name in 1908. Joined the English League in 1920 and were runners-up in 1924. Welsh Cup winners 22 times, once English Cup winners (1927). Cup-Winners Cup semi-finalists 1967-68. In the last four seasons in Division Four of the English League they have finished 21st, 13th, 9th and, in the new Division Three, 1st.

Full Name: Cardiff City   **Founded:** 1899
Address: Ninian Park, Sloper Road, Leckwith, Cardiff, CF1 8SX
Phone: 0222-398636
Stadium: Ninian Park

Euro Record		P	W	D	L	F	A
	C1	0	0	0	0	0	0
	C2	47	16	14	17	64	53
	C3	0	0	0	0	0	0
	Total	47	16	14	17	64	53

C1: (0)   None
C2: (13)   64-65, 65-66, 67-68, 68-69, 69-70, 70-71, 71-72, 73-74, 74-75, 76-77, 77-78, 88-89, 92-93
C3: (0)   None

Celtic (Scotland) C3

Founded by Irish Catholics in east Glasgow to raise funds for poor children. Founder members of the League in 1890-91 and third in the first season. Thirty five times League champions and never relegated. A record 29 times Cup winners. Their European debut came in the 1962-63 Fairs Cup. First club from Scotland to win a European trophy.

Full Name: Celtic FC   **Founded:** 1888
Address: 95 Kerrydale Street, Glasgow G40 3RE
Phone: (041) 5542611   **Stadium:** Celtic Park   **Capacity:** 51,907
Colours: Green and White hoops, White, Green and White

Euro Record		P	W	D	L	F	A
	C1	78	42	15	21	143	73
	C2	34	19	4	11	68	31
	C3	24	8	6	10	33	33
	Total	136	69	25	42	244	137

C1: (15)   66-67, 67-68, 68-69, 69-70, 70-71, 71-72, 72-73, 73-74, 74-75, 77-78, 79-80, 81-82, 82-83, 86-87, 88-89
C2: (7)   63-64, 65-66, 75-76, 80-81, 84-85, 85-86, 89-90
C3: (7)   62-63, 64-65, 76-77, 83-84, 87-88, 91-92, 92-93

Cork City (Rep. Ireland) C1

League runners-up in 1990-91 and champions in 1992-93. Twice Cup runners-up. Their European debut came in the 1989-90 Cup-Winners' Cup.

Full Name: Cork City FC   **Founded:** 1984
Address: Turner's Cross, Cork, Republic of Ireland
Phone: (021) 885694
Stadium: Turner's Cross   **Capacity:** 20,000

Euro Record	P	W	D	L	F	A
C1	0	0	0	0	0	0
C2	2	0	0	2	0	6
C3	2	0	1	1	1	3
Total	4	0	1	3	1	9

C1: (0) None
C2: (1) 89-90
C3: (1) 91-92

Croatia Zagreb (Croatia) C1

Founded as Dinamo Zagreb in 1945 as successors to Gradjanska, first League champions in 1923, which had closed down during the War. Dinamo won four Yugoslavian League championships and won the Yugoslavian Cup eight times. Changed their name in 1991 to HASK Gradanski Zagreb, and more recently to Croatia Zagreb. Their European debut came in the first Fairs Cup, 1956-58. They were Yugoslavia's representative in the first Cup Winners' Cup, 1960-61, when they reached the semi-final.

Full Name: Croatia Zagreb   **Founded:** 1945
Address: Maksimirska 128, YU-41000, Zagreb
Phone: 41-223-234
Colours: Blue, Blue, Blue

Euro Record	P	W	D	L	F	A
C1	4	1	1	2	4	7
C2	29	10	6	13	28	34
C3	67	24	18	25	101	85
Total	100	35	25	40	133	126

C1: (2) 58-59, 82-83
C2: (8) 60-61, 63-64, 64-65, 65-66, 69-70, 73-74, 80-81, 83-84
C3: (14) 56-58, 58-60, 61-62, 62-63, 66-67, 67-68, 68-69, 70-71, 71-72, 76-77, 77-78, 79-80, 88-89, 90-91

Crusaders (Northern Ireland)　　C3

Twice League champions and twice Cup winners, all between 1967 and 1976.
Their European debut came in the 1967-68 Cup-Winners' Cup.

Full Name: Crusaders FC　　　　　　**Founded:** 1898
Address:　St. Vincent Street, Shore Road, Belfast BT15
Phone:　　(0232) 37077
Stadium:　Seaview　　　　　　**Capacity:** 9,000

Euro Record		P	W	D	L	F	A
	C1	4	0	0	4	0	19
	C2	6	0	2	4	5	18
	C3	0	0	0	0	0	0
	Total	10	0	2	8	5	37

C1: (2)　73-74, 76-77
C2: (3)　67-68, 68-69, 80-81
C3: (0)　None

CSKA Sofia (Bulgaria)　　C2

The Army club played under various names, including CDNA Sofia between
1949 and 1966, as other clubs were absorbed. Following disbanding in 1985,
reformed as Stredets in 1985, became CFKA Stredets in 1987, and CSKA
Sofia in 1989. 27 times League champions, six times Cup winners. Bulgaria's
first entrant in the Champions' Cup, 1956-57. Champions' Cup semi-finalists
twice and Cup-Winners' Cup semi-finalists once. In the last four seasons in
the League they have finished 1st, 2nd, 1st and 2nd.

Full Name: FC CSKA　　　　　　**Founded:** 1948
Address:　Bul.Dragan Zankov 3, Sofia, Bulgaria
Phone:　　2-662036
Stadium:　Stadion Narodna Anna　　**Capacity:** 35,000
Colours:　Red, Red, Red

Euro Record		P	W	D	L	F	A
	C1	88	36	15	37	128	130
	C2	20	10	0	10	39	29
	C3	12	3	3	6	13	22
	Total	120	49	18	53	180	181

C1: (22)　56-57, 57-58, 58-59, 59-60, 60-61, 61-62, 62-63, 66-67, 69-70,
　　　　　71-72, 72-73, 73-74, 75-76, 76-77, 80-81, 81-82, 82-83, 83-84,
　　　　　87-88, 89-90, 90-91, 92-93
C2: (4)　65-66, 70-71, 74-75, 88-89
C3: (6)　77-78, 78-79, 79-80, 84-85, 86-87, 91-92

Cwmbran Town (Wales) C1

Founder members and first champions of the League of Wales in 1993. In the previous three seasons had finished 4th, 9th and 7th in the Welsh National League. No European experience.

Full Name: Cwmbran Town FC   **Founded:** 1955
Address: Stebonheath Park, Gwent, Wales
Stadium: Stebonheath Park   **Capacity:** 13,200

Euro Record	P	W	D	L	F	A
C1	0	0	0	0	0	0
C2	0	0	0	0	0	0
C3	0	0	0	0	0	0
Total	0	0	0	0	0	0

C1: (0)   None
C2: (0)   None
C3: (0)   None

DAC Dunjaska Streda (Slovakia) C3

Czechoslovakian Cup winners once, 1967, which brought them their European debut in the Cup-Winners' Cup. In the last four seasons they have finished, in the Czechoslovakian League, 14th, 4th, 9th and 4th.

Full Name: Diac Pol'Nogospodar Dunjaska Streda   **Founded:** 1905
Address: Sportova 491/16, 929 01 Dunjaska Streda
Phone: 709-24650
Stadium: Dac   **Capacity:** 11,400

Euro Record	P	W	D	L	F	A
C1	0	0	0	0	0	0
C2	4	3	0	1	9	4
C3	4	1	0	3	7	7
Total	8	4	0	4	16	11

C1: (0)   None
C2: (1)   87-88
C3: (1)   88-89

Degerfors IF (Sweden) C2

A club from the regionalised First Division East, promoted from the Second division in 1990. They played in the top section earlier, however, and have twice been League runners-up, the last time in 1963. Their Cup final victory in 1993 gave them their first domestic honour. No European experience.

Full Name: Deferfors Idrottsforening **Founded:** 1907
Address:
Stadium: Storavalla
Colours: Red/White
Euro Record

	P	W	D	L	F	A
C1	0	0	0	0	0	0
C2	0	0	0	0	0	0
C3	0	0	0	0	0	0
Total	0	0	0	0	0	0

C1: (0) None
C2: (0) None
C3: (0) None

Deportivo La Coruna (Spain) C3

Highest League position, runners-up, achieved in 1949-50. Promoted as Division Two runners-up in 1990-91, they survived the relegation play-offs in 1991-92 to qualify this season for European football for the first time having topped the Spanish League for some time.

Full Name: Real Club Deportivo La Coruna **Founded:** 1904
Address: Plaza de Pontevedra 19-1, 15003 Coruna
Phone: 981-259500
Stadium: Riazor **Capacity:** 28,956
Euro Record

	P	W	D	L	F	A
C1	0	0	0	0	0	0
C2	0	0	0	0	0	0
C3	0	0	0	0	0	0
Total	0	0	0	0	0	0

C1: (0) None
C2: (0) None
C3: (0) None

Dinamo Bucharest (Romania)　　C3

Founded on the merger of Ciocanul and Unirea Tricolour, the 1941 League champions and themselves a 1926 amalgamation of Unirea and Tricolour. Fourteen subsequent League championships and seven Cup wins. They were Romania's first representative in Europe, taking part in the 1956-57 Champions' Cup. They reached the Cup Winners' Cup semi-finals in 1989-90.

Full Name: FC Dinamo Bucharest　　**Founded:** 1948
Address: Stefan cel Mare 9, Bucharest
Phone: 990-105700
Stadium: Dinamo　　　　　　　**Capacity:** 18,000
Colours: Red, Red, Red

Euro Record		P	W	D	L	F	A
	C1	56	22	9	25	85	87
	C2	20	8	4	8	25	18
	C3	26	10	5	11	44	31
	Total	102	40	18	44	154	136

C1: (14)　56-57, 62-63, 63-64, 64-65, 65-66, 71-72, 73-74, 75-76, 77-78, 82-83, 83-84, 84-85, 90-91, 92-93
C2: (5)　68-69, 86-87, 87-88, 88-89, 89-90
C3: (8)　66-67, 70-71, 74-75, 76-77, 79-80, 81-82, 85-86, 91-92

Dinamo Minsk (Bielorussia)　　C1

Known as Dinamo, Spartak and, until 1962, as Belarus. Soviet Champions once, in 1982, which gave them their European debut in the following season's Champions' Cup. Reached the quarter-final of the UEFA Cup 1984-85. In the last three seasons of the Soviet League finished 9th, 12th and 8th, and were 1992 Bielorussia champions.

Full Name: Dinamo Minsk　　　　**Founded:** 1928
Address: Ul Kirova 8, Minsk
Phone: 221133
Stadium: Dinamo　　　　　　　**Capacity:** 50,862

Euro Record		P	W	D	L	F	A
	C1	6	3	2	1	13	8
	C2	6	2	3	1	6	4
	C3	14	7	2	5	22	13
	Total	26	12	7	7	41	25

C1: (1)　83-84
C2: (1)　87-88
C3: (4)　84-85, 86-87, 88-89, 92-93

Dinamo Moscow (Russia) C3

Founded 1923, but their origins were in the 1880's when formed by British cotton mill owners. The Orekhovo Klub Sport became Morozovsti, a prominent Moscow League club, later being adopted by the Soviet Electrical Trade Union. Eleven times Soviet champions and six times Cup winners. Their European debut came in the 1971-72 Cup Winners' Cup, a competition in which they were losing finalists.

Full Name: Dinamo Moscow   **Founded:** 1923
Address: Lenningradski Pr. 36, 125190 Moscow, Russia
Phone: 2145463
Stadium: Dinamo   **Capacity:** 50,475

Euro Record

	P	W	D	L	F	A
C1	0	0	0	0	0	0
C2	29	15	8	6	46	25
C3	26	9	7	10	30	28
Total	55	24	15	16	76	53

C1: (0) None
C2: (4) 71-72, 77-78, 79-80, 84-85
C3: (6) 74-75, 76-77, 80-81, 82-83, 87-88, 91-92

Dnepr Dnepropetrovsk (Ukraine) C3

Founded as Stal Dnepropetrovsk. Known from 1946 until 1961 as Metallurg Dnepropetrovsk. Soviet champions twice and once Cup winners. European debut as a Soviet representative in the 1984-85 Champions' Cup when they reached the quarter finals, a feat repeated in 1989-90. In the last three seasons of the Soviet League finished 2nd, 6th and 9th, also winning the third place play-off in the Ukrainian League and runners-up in 1993.

Full Name: Dnepr Dnepropetrovsk   **Founded:** 1936
Address: Ul Kirova 12, Dnepropetrovsk
Phone: 910526
Stadium: Meteor   **Capacity:** 30,000
Colours: Red, Red, Red

Euro Record

	P	W	D	L	F	A
C1	12	5	3	4	15	13
C2	0	0	0	0	0	0
C3	12	3	4	5	12	15
Total	24	8	7	9	27	28

C1: (2) 84-85, 89-90
C2: (0) None
C3: (4) 85-86, 86-87, 88-89, 90-91

Dudelange (Luxembourg) C2

Just two years old Dudelange were promoted from the Second Division as runners-up in the playoffs in 1992. Finished 5th last season. No European experience.

Full Name: F91 Dudelange   **Founded:** 1991
Address: 146 Rue RPJ Thiel, 3572 Dudelange, Luxembourg
Phone: 518468
Stadium: Jos Nosbaum   **Capacity:** 4,000

Euro Record	P	W	D	L	F	A
C1	0	0	0	0	0	0
C2	0	0	0	0	0	0
C3	0	0	0	0	0	0
Total	0	0	0	0	0	0

C1: (0)   None
C2: (0)   None
C3: (0)   None

Dundee United (Scotland) C3

Founded as Dundee Hibernian. Joined the League in 1910-11 but led a precarious existence until adopting current name (though nearly becoming Dundee City) in 1923. Promoted to the top division for the last time in 1960. One League championship, 1982-83. Six times Cup runners-up, all since 1974. Their European debut came in the 1966-67 Fairs Cup. Reached the Champions' Cup semi-finals in 1983-84.

Full Name: Dundee United FC   **Founded:** 1909
Address: Tannadice Park, Dundee DD3 7JW
Phone: 0382-833166
Stadium: Tannadice Park   **Capacity:** 20,862
Colours: Tangerine/Black, Black/Tangerine/White, Tangerine/Black

Euro Record	P	W	D	L	F	A
C1	8	5	1	2	14	5
C2	8	2	3	3	5	5
C3	86	39	22	25	130	88
Total	102	46	26	30	149	98

C1: (1)   83-84
C2: (2)   74-75, 88-89
C3: (17)   66-67, 67-68, 69-70, 70-71, 75-76, 77-78, 78-79, 79-80, 80-81, 81-82, 82-83, 84-85, 85-86, 86-87, 87-88, 89-90, 90-91

Dynamo Kiev (Ukraine) C1

The capital city club have in the past been USSR representatives in Europe.
13 times Soviet champions and nine times Cup winners. In the last three
seasons of an all-Soviet League they were 3rd, 1st and 5th, also being
Championship play-off runners-up in the Ukrainian League in 1992. Ukraine
League champions and Cup winners 1993.

Full Name: Dynamo Kiev   **Founded:** 1927
Address: Ul. Kirova 3, Kiev, Ukraine
Phone: 299520
Stadium: Republican   **Capacity:** 100,169
Colours: White, White, White

Euro Record	P	W	D	L	F	A
C1	62	33	12	17	81	55
C2	30	20	6	4	72	27
C3	28	12	8	8	34	25
Total	120	65	26	29	187	107

C1: (11) 67-68, 69-70, 72-73, 75-76, 76-77, 78-79, 81-82, 82-83, 86-87, 87-88, 91-92
C2: (4) 65-66, 74-75, 85-86, 90-91
C3: (7) 73-74, 77-78, 79-80, 80-81, 83-84, 89-90, 92-93

Eintracht Frankfurt (Germany) C3

West German champions just once, in 1959. Bundesliga founder members in
1963 but never finished higher than 3rd. Four times West German Cup
winners. Took part in first Fairs Cup competition, 1956-58. In the last four
seasons they have finished 3rd and 4th in the West German League, 3rd and
3rd yet again.

Full Name: SH Eintracht Frankfurt   **Founded:** 1899
Address: Am Erlenburch 25, 6000 Frankfurt am Main 60, Germany
Phone: 69-4209700
Stadium: Waldstadion   **Capacity:** 61,146
Colours: Red/Black, Black, Black

Euro Record	P	W	D	L	F	A
C1	7	4	2	1	23	15
C2	24	14	3	7	41	23
C3	58	28	10	20	117	78
Total	89	46	15	28	181	116

C1: (1) 59-60
C2: (4) 74-75, 75-76, 81-82, 88-89
C3: (12) 56-58, 64-65, 66-67, 67-68, 68-69, 72-73, 77-78, 79-80, 80-81, 90-91, 91-92, 92-93

Ekranas Panevezys (Lithuania)   C1

Third in the Baltic League in 1990 and 4th in the Spring 1991 Lithuanian League. Champions in 1992. No European experience.

Full Name: **Founded:**
Address:
Phone:
Stadium: **Capacity:**

Euro Record	P	W	D	L	F	A
C1	0	0	0	0	0	0
C2	0	0	0	0	0	0
C3	0	0	0	0	0	0
Total	0	0	0	0	0	0

C1: (0)   None
C2: (0)   None
C3: (0)   None

FC Aarau (Switzerland)   C1

Twice national champions before the First World War when regional champions took part in a mini-league, but not again until 1993. Cup winners once, in 1985, this bringing them their European debut in the following season's Cup-Winners' Cup. Frequently fighting relegation in the 1950's, they reverted to amateur status for a short period. In 1990 they survived the relegation play-offs and in the subsequent seasons finished 10th, 11th and 1st.

Full Name: FC Aarau   **Founded:** 1902
Address: Postfach 2738, 5001 Aarau , Switzerland
Phone: 64-247561
Stadium: Brugglifield   **Capacity:** 14,000

Euro Record	P	W	D	L	F	A
C1	0	0	0	0	0	0
C2	2	0	1	1	2	4
C3	2	0	0	2	0	7
Total	4	0	1	3	2	11

C1: (0)   None
C2: (1)   85-86
C3: (1)   88-89

FC Copenhagen (Denmark)   C1

Created on the amalgamation of KB and B1903, founded in 1876 and 1903 respectively and with over 20 League titles between them as well as many European campaigns. Took B1903's UEFA Cup place for 1992-93 as League runners-up.

Full Name: FC Copenhagen   **Founded:** 1992
Address: Baunegardsvej 7L, 2820 Gentofte, Copenhagen, Denmark
Phone: 31-656055
Stadium: Gentofte Stadion   **Capacity:** 18,000

Euro Record	P	W	D	L	F	A
C1	0	0	0	0	0	0
C2	0	0	0	0	0	0
C3	4	2	0	2	11	7
Total	4	2	0	2	11	7

C1: (0) None
C2: (0) None
C3: (1) 92-93

FC Lugano (Switzerland)   C2

National League founder members. Three times League champions and twice Cup winners. European debut in the 1968-69 Cup-Winners' Cup. In the last four seasons they have finished 5th, 5th, 10th and 3rd.

Full Name: FC Lugano   **Founded:** 1908
Address: Casella Postale 96, 6904 Lugano, Switzerland
Phone: 91-519447
Stadium: Comunale di Cornaredo   **Capacity:** 25,200

Euro Record	P	W	D	L	F	A
C1	0	0	0	0	0	0
C2	2	0	1	1	1	3
C3	2	0	1	1	1	3
Total	4	0	2	2	2	6

C1: (0) None
C2: (1) 68-69
C3: (1) 71-72

FC Nantes (France) C3

Six times League champions and Cup winners once. They reached the Cup-Winners' Cup semi-finals in 1980. In the last four seasons in the League they have finished 7th, 15th, 9th and 5th.

Full Name: Football Club de Nantes **Founded:** 1943
Address: Centre Sportif Jose-Arribas, route de la Chapelle,
44240 La Chapelle-sur-Erdre, France
Phone: 40-291559
Stadium: La Beajoire **Capacity:** 38,000

Euro Record		P	W	D	L	F	A
	C1	18	5	6	7	25	28
	C2	12	7	0	5	28	21
	C3	22	6	9	7	25	28
	Total	52	18	15	19	78	77

C1: (6) 65-66, 66-67, 73-74, 77-78, 80-81, 83-84
C2: (2) 70-71, 79-80
C3: (6) 71-72, 74-75, 78-79, 81-82, 85-86, 86-87

FC Porto (Portugal) C1

First Cup winners, 1922, and founder members and first champions of the Portuguese League, 1935. Now 13 times League champions, including six times in the last decade, and 11 times Cup winners. World Club champions in 1986.

Full Name: Futebol Clube do Porto **Founded:** 1906
Address: Estadio dos Antas, Avenida Fernao de Magalhaes, 4300 Porto
Phone: 2-481738
Stadium: Das Antas **Capacity:** 72,500
Colours: Blue/White, Blue, White

Euro Record		P	W	D	L	F	A
	C1	47	24	7	16	89	59
	C2	35	17	7	11	48	41
	C3	50	23	8	19	70	61
	Total	132	64	22	46	207	161

C1: (9) 56-57, 59-60, 78-79, 79-80, 85-86, 86-87, 87-88, 88-89, 90-91
C2: (8) 64-65, 68-69, 77-78, 81-82, 83-84, 84-85, 91-92, 92-93
C3: (14) 62-63, 63-64, 65-66, 66-67, 67-68, 69-70, 71-72, 72-73, 74-75, 75-76, 76-77, 80-81, 82-83, 89-90

FC Tirol-Innsbruck (Austria) C2

Known as Swarovski-Tirol Innsbruck 1986-92. Seven times League champions and six times Cup winners. Their European debut came in the 1968-69 Fairs Cup. They reached the semi-finals of the UEFA Cup in 1987.

Full Name: FC Swarovski Tirol   **Founded:** 1914
Address: Resselstrasse 18/11, A-6020 Innsbruck, Austria
Phone: 5222-478800
Stadium: Tivoli
Colours: White, White, White   **Capacity:** 17,200

Euro Record		P	W	D	L	F	A
	C1	22	7	3	12	34	46
	C2	14	6	6	2	18	26
	C3	30	11	4	15	35	47
	Total	66	24	13	29	87	119

C1: (7)   71-72, 72-73, 73-74, 75-76, 77-78, 89-90, 90-91
C2: (5)   70-71, 78-79, 79-80, 83-84, 87-88
C3: (8)   68-69, 74-75, 76-77, 84-85, 85-86, 86-87, 91-92, 92-93

FC Twente (Holland) C3

Founded on the amalgamation of Enschede (founded 1910 and national champions once) and Enschede Boys. Present club has one domestic honour, 1977 Cup winners. Spent some of the 1980s in the Second Division. In the last four seasons they have finished 3rd, 6th, 6th and 5th.

Full Name: FC Twente   **Founded:** 1965
Address: JJ Van Deinselaan 30, 7541 PE Enschede, Netherlands
Phone: 53-310080
Stadium: Het Diekman   **Capacity:** 18,000
Colours: White/Red, Red, Red

Euro Record		P	W	D	L	F	A
	C1	0	0	0	0	0	0
	C2	10	6	1	3	17	9
	C3	48	20	11	17	86	60
	Total	58	26	12	20	103	69

C1: (0)   None
C2: (2)   77-78, 79-80
C3: (9)   69-70, 70-71, 72-73, 73-74, 74-75, 78-79, 80-81, 89-90, 90-91

Ferencvaros (Hungary)

Generally known as FTC (Ferencvaros Torna (ie gymnastics) Club) until the early 1950s. They played as Kinizsi (the name of a national hero) for a handful of seasons before emerging under their familiar name, a district of the country's capital, in the late 1950s. League founder members 1901 when they finished third. A record 24 times champions and 16 times Cup winners. Were Hungary's representative in the first Cup-Winners' Cup, 1960-61. Between-the-wars Cup winners of the Mitropa Cup twice.

Full Name: Ferencvaros Torna Club   **Founded:** 1899
Address: Ulloi ut 129, 1091 Budapest IX
Phone: 1-1136025   **Stadium:** Ulloi   **Capacity:** 20,000
Colours: Green, Green, Green

Euro Record	P	W	D	L	F	A
C1	20	9	3	8	40	37
C2	27	12	6	9	49	35
C3	67	31	11	25	109	79
Total	114	52	20	42	198	151

C1: (6)   63-64, 65-66, 69-70, 76-77, 81-82, 92-93
C2: (6)   60-61, 72-73, 74-75, 78-79, 89-90, 91-92
C3: (12)   62-63, 64-65, 66-67, 67-68, 70-71, 71-72, 73-74, 77-78, 79-80, 82-83, 83-84, 90-91

Feyenoord (Holland)

Founded by the head of a mining company and known as Stadionklub Rotterdam. Twelve times League champions and eight times Cup winners. World Club champions 1970. In the last four seasons they have finished 11th, 8th, 3rd and 2nd.

Full Name: Feyenoord   **Founded:** 1908
Address: Olympiaweg 50, 3077 AL Rotterdam, Netherlands
Phone: (010) 4929400
Stadium: Feyenoord   **Capacity:** 55,000

Euro Record	P	W	D	L	F	A
C1	39	20	10	9	90	41
C2	22	10	6	6	30	21
C3	58	31	9	18	112	69
Total	119	61	25	33	232	131

C1: (8)   61-62, 62-63, 65-66, 69-70, 70-71, 71-72, 74-75, 84-85
C2: (3)   80-81, 91-92, 92-93
C3: (12)   68-69, 72-73, 73-74, 75-76, 76-77, 79-80, 81-82, 83-84, 85-86, 86-87, 87-88, 89-90

Floriana (Malta) C1

Founder members of the League and its first champions, 1910. First Cup runners-up, 1935. Twenty five League titles and 17 Cup wins. First Maltese club to play in the Cup-Winners' Cup in 1961-62.

Full Name: Floriana FC **Founded:** 1900
Address: 28 St. Anne Street, Floriana, Malta
Phone: 238864/220559
Stadium: National, Ta'Qali **Capacity:** 35,000

Euro Record		P	W	D	L	F	A
	C1	12	0	2	10	3	49
	C2	16	1	2	13	10	69
	C3	6	1	1	4	3	16
	Total	34	2	5	27	16	134

C1: (6) 62-63, 68-69, 70-71, 73-74, 75-76, 77-78
C2: (9) 61-62, 65-66, 66-67, 67-68, 72-73, 76-77, 78-79, 81-82, 88-89
C3: (3) 69-70, 91-92, 92-93

Galatasaray (Turkey) C1

League founder members and first runners-up, 1959, and nine times winners since then. Cup winners ten times, including the first four competitions, 1963-66. First Turkish participants in the Champions' Cup, 1956-57. Champions' Cup semi-finalists 1968-69.

Full Name: Galatasaray Spor Kulubu **Founded:** 1905
Address: Hasnun Galip Sokak 7-11, Beyoglu, Istanbul, Turkey
Phone: 1-1511707
Stadium: Al Sami Yen **Capacity:** 34,000

Euro Record		P	W	D	L	F	A
	C1	35	12	8	15	42	53
	C2	28	9	7	12	33	49
	C3	18	5	4	9	19	30
	Total	81	26	19	36	94	132

C1: (9) 56-57, 62-63, 63-64, 69-70, 71-72, 72-73, 73-74, 87-88, 88-89
C2: (7) 64-65, 65-66, 66-67, 76-77, 82-83, 85-86, 91-92
C3: (6) 75-76, 78-79, 79-80, 86-87, 89-90, 92-93

GKS Katowice (Poland) C2

Gorniczy Klub Katowice was founded in 1964. Three times League runners-up, the first in 1988, twice Cup winners. Made their European debut in the 1970-71 Fairs Cup.

Full Name: Garniczy Klub Sportowy Katowice   **Founded:** 1964
Address: Al.Korfantego 117a, 40-157 Katowice
Phone: 32-581271
Stadium: GKS   **Capacity:** 14,000
Colours: Yellow, Black, Black

Euro Record	P	W	D	L	F	A
C1	0	0	0	0	0	0
C2	8	3	1	4	9	12
C3	14	2	2	10	12	22
Total	22	5	3	14	21	34

C1: (0)   None
C2: (2)   86-87, 91-92
C3: (6)   70-71, 87-88, 88-89, 89-90, 90-91, 92-93

Gloria Bistrita (Romania) C3

No domestic League or Cup honours or European experience.

Full Name: Gloria Bistrita   **Founded:** 1926
Address: Str. Parcului nr. 3, 4400 Bistrita, Romania
Phone: 90-12998
Stadium: Gloria   **Capacity:** 10,000

Euro Record	P	W	D	L	F	A
C1	0	0	0	0	0	0
C2	0	0	0	0	0	0
C3	0	0	0	0	0	0
Total	0	0	0	0	0	0

C1: (0)   None
C2: (0)   None
C3: (0)   None

Hajduk Split (Croatia)

Nine times Yugoslavian League champions, the last time in 1979, and nine times Cup winners, Croatian League champions 1992.

Full Name: NK Hajduk   **Founded:** 1911
Address: Stadion Poljud, P. Box 218, 58000 Split
Phone: 58-41755
Stadium: Poljud   **Capacity:** 50,000

Euro Record	P	W	D	L	F	A
C1	18	12	2	4	41	18
C2	28	9	3	16	30	40
C3	42	23	5	14	74	46
Total	88	44	10	34	145	104

C1: (4) 71-72, 74-75, 75-76, 79-80
C2: (7) 67-68, 72-73, 76-77, 77-78, 84-85, 87-88, 91-92
C3: (7) 70-71, 78-79, 81-82, 82-83, 83-84, 85-86, 86-87

Havnar HB (Faeroe Islands)

Fourteen times League champions, the first in 1955. The Club from the capital have won the Cup more than any other club, with 11 wins. No European experience.

Full Name: **Founded:**
Address:
Stadium:

Euro Record	P	W	D	L	F	A
C1	0	0	0	0	0	0
C2	0	0	0	0	0	0
C3	0	0	0	0	0	0
Total	0	0	0	0	0	0

C1: (0) None
C2: (0) None
C3: (0) None

Heart of Midlothian (Scotland)   C3

Founder members of the League 1890-91 and sixth in the first season. Four times League champions, the last in 1960, and never relegated. Five times Cup winners. Their European debut came in the 1958-59 Champions' Cup.

Full Name: Heart of Midlothian FC   **Founded:** 1874
Address: Tynecastle Park, Gorgie Road, Edinburgh, EH11 2NL
Phone: 031-3376132
Stadium: Tynecastle Park   **Capacity:** 25,605
Colours: Maroon, White, Maroon

Euro Record	P	W	D	L	F	A
C1	4	1	0	3	4	11
C2	4	1	0	3	8	11
C3	32	13	7	12	47	46
Total	40	15	7	18	59	68

C1: (2) 58-59, 60-61
C2: (1) 76-77
C3: (8) 61-62, 63-64, 65-66, 84-85, 86-87, 88-89, 90-91, 92-93

HJK Helsinki (Finland)   C1

Eighteen League titles and three Cup wins. European debut in the 1965-66 Champions' Cup. In the last four seasons in the League they have finished 5th, 2nd, 5th and 1st.

Full Name: Helsingin Jalkapalloklubi   **Founded:** 1907
Address: Stadion, 00250 Helsinki, Finland
Phone: 90-448693
Stadium: Olympiastadion   **Capacity:** 50,000
Colours:

Euro Record	P	W	D	L	F	A
C1	20	5	0	15	17	53
C2	6	3	0	3	9	18
C3	6	0	0	6	2	23
Total	32	8	0	24	28	94

C1: (8) 65-66, 74-75, 79-80, 82-83, 86-87, 88-89, 89-90, 91-92
C2: (2) 67-68, 85-86
C3: (3) 75-76, 83-84, 84-85

Honved (Hungary) C1

Kispest, a district of the country's capital, founded 1909 had one Cup win and a League runners-up spot before the war. Absorbed into the new Ministry of Sports team Honved in 1949. Mitropa Cup winners in 1959. Took present name in 1991. All told, 13 times League champions and four times Cup winners. Their European debut came in the 1956-57 Champions' Cup.

Full Name: Kispest-Honved Futball Club **Founded:** 1909
Address: Ujtemeto utca 1, 1194 Budapest
Phone: 1-2671602/2671614
Stadium: Jozsef Bozsik **Capacity:** 15,000

Euro Record

	P	W	D	L	F	A
C1	26	12	3	11	41	45
C2	12	5	1	6	25	17
C3	36	19	5	12	66	55
Total	74	36	9	29	132	117

C1: (7) 56-57, 80-81, 84-85, 85-86, 86-87, 88-89, 89-90
C2: (3) 64-65, 65-66, 70-71
C3: (7) 72-73, 73-74, 75-76, 76-77, 78-79, 83-84, 87-88

IA Akranes (Iceland) C1

First club from outside the capital to win the League, and they now have 13 titles and five Cup wins. Relegated in 1991, but promoted as champions at first attempt. Their European debut came in the 1970-71 Fairs Cup. Reached the 2nd round of the Champions' Cup 1975-76.

Full Name: Knattspyrnufelag Ithrottabandalags **Founded:** 1946
Address: Postholf 30, 300 Akranes
Phone: 3-12188
Stadium: Akranesvollur **Capacity:** 3,000

Euro Record

	P	W	D	L	F	A
C1	14	1	3	10	14	36
C2	8	0	2	6	2	15
C3	10	0	1	9	2	48
Total	32	1	6	25	18	99

C1: (6) 71-72, 75-76, 76-77, 78-79, 84-85, 85-86
C2: (4) 77-78, 79-80, 83-84, 87-88
C3: (5) 70-71, 80-81, 86-87, 88-89, 89-90

Iberya Tbilisi (Georgia)

Better known as Dynamo Tbilisi. Twice Soviet Champions and twice Soviet Cup winners. European debut came in the 1972-73 UEFA Cup.

Full Name: Iberya Tbilisi **Founded:** 1925
Address:
Stadium: Dynamo **Capacity:** 50,000
Colours: White/Blue

Euro Record	P	W	D	L	F	A
C1	4	1	0	3	7	8
C2	21	11	3	7	30	17
C3	26	13	5	8	39	32
Total	51	25	8	18	76	57

C1: (1) 79-80
C2: (3) 76-77, 80-81, 81-82
C3: (6) 72-73, 73-74, 77-78, 78-79, 82-83, 87-88

IFK Norrkoping (Sweden)

Twelve times League champions, the 11th in 1963, the 12th in 1989. Five times Cup winners. European debut in the 1956-57 Champions' Cup. In the last four seasons in the League they have finished 2nd on each occasion.

Full Name: Idrottsforeningen Kamraterna Norrkoping **Founded:** 1897
Address: Box 12067, 600 12 Norrkoping, Sweden
Phone: 11-132225
Stadium: Norrkopings Idrottsparken **Capacity:** 18,000
Colours: White, Blue, White

Euro Record	P	W	D	L	F	A
C1	12	2	5	5	14	20
C2	14	6	2	6	23	17
C3	14	4	5	5	13	17
Total	40	12	12	16	50	54

C1: (4) 56-57, 57-58, 62-63, 63-64
C2: (4) 68-69, 69-70, 88-89, 91-92
C3: (5) 72-73, 78-79, 82-83, 90-91, 92-93

Internazionale (Italy)   C3

Founded as an off-shoot of AC Milan. Merged with US Milanese in 1928 to
become Ambrosiana-Internazionale who were the first League champions in
1928-29 and Mitropa Cup finalists in 1933. As from 1945 known as
Internazionale again. 13 times League champions and three times Cup
winners. Took part in the first Fairs Cup competition, 1956-58. World Club
champions 1964 and 1965.

Full Name: FC Internazionale Milano SpA   **Founded:** 1908
Address: Piazza Eleonora Duse 1, 20122 Milan, Italy **Phone:** 2-782531
Stadium: Giuseppe Meazza   **Capacity:** 75,510
Colours: Blue/ Black, Black, Black/Blue

Euro Record		P	W	D	L	F	A
	C1	51	27	14	10	74	38
	C2	12	6	2	4	22	9
	C3	117	54	26	37	188	116
	Total	180	87	42	51	284	163

C1: (7) 63-64, 64-65, 65-66, 66-67, 71-72, 80-81, 89-90
C2: (2) 78-79, 82-83
C3: (21) 56-58, 58-60, 60-61, 61-62, 69-70, 70-71, 72-73, 73-74, 74-75, 76-77, 77-78,
79-80, 81-82, 83-84, 84-85, 85-86, 86-87, 87-88, 88-89, 90-91, 91-92

Juventus (Italy)   C3

Founded by students and British residents. Became Sport Club Juventus in
1899. During World War One adopted by the owners of Fiat. Founder
members of the League in 1928-29 when finished third. Never relegated and
now won the championship a record 22 times. Also won the Cup a record
number of times, eight. Their European debut came in the 1958-59
Champions' Cup.

Full Name: Juventus FC SpA   **Founded:** 1897
Address: Piazza Crimea 7, 10147 Torino   **Phone:** 11-6509706
Stadium: Delle Alpi   **Capacity:** 70,012
Colours: White/Black, White, White/Black

Euro Record		P	W	D	L	F	A
	C1	77	41	15	21	124	70
	C2	27	17	5	5	53	19
	C3	116	74	17	25	122	93
	Total	220	132	37	51	299	182

C1: (14) 58-59, 60-61, 61-62, 67-68, 72-73, 73-74, 75-76, 77-78, 78-79, 81-82,
82-83, 84-85, 85-86, 86-87
C2: (4) 65-66, 79-80, 83-84, 90-91
C3: (14) 63-64, 64-65, 66-67, 68-69, 69-70, 70-71, 71-72, 74-75, 76-77, 80-81,
87-88, 88-89, 89-90, 92-93

Karlsruher SC (Germany) C3

Merged with Mulberg and Phonex '94 (German champions in 1909) in 1952. West German League runners-up in 1956. No other League honours, but have won Cup twice. In the last four seasons they have finished 10th and 13th in the West German League, 8th and 6th. No European experience.

Full Name: Karlsruher Sportclub   **Founded:** 1894
Address: Adenauering 17, 7500 Karlsruhe
Phone: 721-60107/8
Stadium: Wildparkstadion   **Capacity:** 46,000

Euro Record		P	W	D	L	F	A
	C1	0	0	0	0	0	0
	C2	0	0	0	0	0	0
	C3	0	0	0	0	0	0
	Total	0	0	0	0	0	0

C1: (0)   None
C2: (0)   None
C3: (0)   None

Karpaty Lvov (Ukraine) C2

Soviet Cup winners once, 1969, and European debut as Soviet representatives in the 1970-71 Cup-Winners' Cup. Sixth in their Ukrainian League First Division group in 1992, and 6th in 1993.

Full Name: SKA Karpati Lvov   **Founded:** 1963
Address:
Stadium: Druzjba
Colours: Green/White

Euro Record		P	W	D	L	F	A
	C1	0	0	0	0	0	0
	C2	2	0	1	1	3	4
	C3	0	0	0	0	0	0
	Total	2	0	1	1	3	4

C1: (0)   None
C2: (1)   70-71
C3: (0)   None

Kocaelispor Kulubu (Turkey)   C3

Second Division Group A runners-up in 1991-92 and champions 1992-93. No top division honours. No European experience.

Full Name: Kocaelispor Kulubu   **Founded:** 1966
Address: Izmit
Phone: 211-15969
Stadium: Ispetpasa   **Capacity:** 20,000
Euro Record

	P	W	D	L	F	A
C1	0	0	0	0	0	0
C2	0	0	0	0	0	0
C3	0	0	0	0	0	0
Total	0	0	0	0	0	0

C1: (0)   None
C2: (0)   None
C3: (0)   None

Kongsvinger IL (Norway)   C3

No major domestic honours but third in the League three times before reaching their highest finishing position of 2nd in the season finishing in late 1992. In the last four seasons they have finished 5th, 8th, 8th and 2nd. No European experience.

Full Name: Kongsvinger Idrettslag   **Founded:** 1892
Address: Boks 682, 2201 Kongsvinger
Phone: 66-16882/16226
Stadium: Gjemselund   **Capacity:** 8,000
Euro Record

	P	W	D	L	F	A
C1	0	0	0	0	0	0
C2	0	0	0	0	0	0
C3	0	0	0	0	0	0
Total	0	0	0	0	0	0

C1: (0)   None
C2: (0)   None
C3: (0)   None

KR Reykjavik (Iceland) C3

A record 20 League championships, having been founders and first title
winners in 1912 having won the play-offs. First team from Iceland to play in
the Champions' Cup, in 1964-65.

Full Name: Knattspyrnufelag Reykjavikur (KR) **Founded:** 1899
Address: Knattspyrnudeild,, Frostaskfol 2, 107 Reykjavik
Phone: 1- 27181
Stadium: KR-vollur   **Capacity:** 2,500
Colours:

Euro Record		P	W	D	L	F	A
	C1	6	0	0	6	7	35
	C2	6	0	0	6	3	24
	C3	4	0	0	4	1	15
	Total	16	0	0	16	11	74

C1: (3) 64-65, 66-67, 69-70
C2: (3) 65-66, 67-68, 68-69
C3: (2) 84-85, 91-92

KSV Waregem (Belgium) C3

Founded 1946 by the amalgamation of Red Star and Sportief. Belgian Cup
winners once, 1974. In the last four seasons they have finished 16th, 13th,
10th and 4th. Reached the UEFA Cup semi-final in 1985-86, their furthest
ever progress in Europe.

Full Name: KSV Waregem   **Founded:** 1946
Address: Ragenboogstraat, 8190 Waregem
Phone: 56-603607
Stadium: Regenboogstadion   **Capacity:** 19,000

Euro Record		P	W	D	L	F	A
	C1	0	0	0	0	0	0
	C2	2	1	0	1	3	5
	C3	18	9	3	6	27	24
	Total	20	10	3	7	30	29

C1: (0) None
C2: (1) 74-75
C3: (3) 68-69, 85-86, 88-89

Kuusysi Lahti (Finland) C3

Founded following a sequence of mergers having previously played as Upon Pallo and Lahti '69. Five championship wins and two Cup wins all since being promoted to the top division for the first time in 1981. They finished 5th in 1990, were promoted as Division One champions in 1991 and were 4th in the season finishing in October 1992. Champions' Cup quarter-finalists 1985-86.

Full Name: FC Kuusysi   **Founded:** 1974
Address: Vesijarvenkatu 15, 15140 Lahti
Phone: 18-512505
Stadium: Keskusurheilukentta   **Capacity:** 10,000
Colours: White, White, White

Euro Record

	P	W	D	L	F	A
C1	14	5	1	8	12	25
C2	6	0	2	4	3	11
C3	4	1	1	2	3	9
Total	24	6	4	14	18	45

C1: (5)   83-84, 85-86, 87-88, 90-91, 92-93
C2: (3)   82-83, 84-85, 88-89
C3: (2)   89-90, 91-92

KV Mechelen (Belgium) C3

Founded by students from the local universities. Also known by their French name, Malinous. Four times national champions and once Cup winners, all in the post-war period. After several promotions and relegations, were last promoted to the top division in 1983. In the last four seasons they have finished 3rd, 2nd, 4th and 3rd.

Full Name: KV Mechelen   **Founded:** 1904
Address: Liersesteenweg 34, 2800 Mechelen
Phone: 15-218230
Stadium: Achter de Kazerne   **Capacity:** 20,000
Colours: Red/Yellow, Black, Black

Euro Record

	P	W	D	L	F	A
C1	6	2	3	1	9	3
C2	17	13	3	1	26	8
C3	8	1	3	4	5	8
Total	31	16	9	6	40	19

C1: (1)   89-90
C2: (2)   87-88, 88-89
C3: (3)   90-91, 91-92, 92-93

Lazio (Italy) C3

Founded as SP Lazio and took current name in 1925. Mitropa Cup finalists 1937. Won League title for the only time in 1973-74. Their only Cup win came in 1957-58. Their European debut came in the 1970-71 UEFA Cup.

Full Name: Societa Sportiva Lazio SpA   **Founded:** 1900
Address: Via Margutta 54, 00187 Roma
Phone: 6-6781843
Stadium: Olimpico   **Capacity:** 82,656
Colours: Sky Blue, Sky Blue, Sky Blue

Euro Record		P	W	D	L	F	A
	C1	0	0	0	0	0	0
	C2	0	0	0	0	0	0
	C3	14	5	1	8	20	28
	Total	14	5	1	8	20	28

C1: (0)   None
C2: (0)   None
C3: (4)   70-71, 73-74, 75-76, 77-78

Lech Poznan (Poland) C1

Founded and known as Kolejarz from 1947 until 1956. Four League championships and three Cup wins. European debut in the 1978-79 UEFA Cup.

Full Name: Kolejowy Klub Sportowy Lech Poznan
Founded: 1922
Address: Ul. Bulgarska 5/7, 61-875 Poznan
Phone: 6-676512
Stadium: Lech   **Capacity:** 23,734
Colours: Blue, White, Blue

Euro Record		P	W	D	L	F	A
	C1	12	5	1	6	13	22
	C2	8	4	2	2	10	7
	C3	4	0	1	3	3	13
	Total	24	9	4	11	26	42

C1: (4)   83-84, 84-85, 90-91, 92-93
C2: (2)   82-83, 88-89
C3: (2)   78-79, 85-86

Levski Sofia (Bulgaria) C1

Founded by teenagers as Levski and subsequently drew players from Government ministries. Amalgamated with Spartak Sofia in 1969 and became Levski-Spartak. Following disbanding in 1985, reformed as Vitosha (the name of a nearby mountain), but became Levski Sofia in 1989. 18 times League champions, six times winners of the Bulgarian Cup. UEFA Cup quarter-finalists 1975-76. In the last four seasons in the League they have finished 2nd, 6th, 2nd and 1st.

Full Name: FC Levski   **Founded:** 1914
Address: Todorini Kukli 47, Sofia
Phone: 2-453162
Stadium: Georgi Asparuchov   **Capacity:** 60,000

Euro Record	P	W	D	L	F	A
C1	20	4	4	12	30	40
C2	28	12	3	13	57	49
C3	30	10	7	13	44	57
Total	78	26	14	38	131	146

C1: (7) 65-66, 70-71, 74-75, 77-78, 79-80, 84-85, 88-89
C2: (8) 67-68, 69-70, 71-72, 76-77, 86-87, 88-87, 91-92, 92-93
C3: (8) 72-73, 75-76, 78-79, 80-81, 81-82, 82-83, 83-84, 89-90

Lillestrom SK (Norway) C2

Five times League champions and four times Cup winners, all since 1959. Reached the second round of the Champions' Cup in 1978-79. In the last four seasons they have finished 1st, 10th, 3rd and 4th.

Full Name: Lillestrom Sportsklubb   **Founded:** 1917
Address: Postboks 196, 2001 Lillestrom
Phone: 6-812341
Stadium: Arasen   **Capacity:** 12,000
Colours: Yellow, Black, Yellow

Euro Record	P	W	D	L	F	A
C1	12	3	5	4	10	15
C2	6	0	0	6	1	14
C3	4	1	0	3	4	12
Total	22	4	5	13	15	41

C1: (4) 77-78, 78-79, 87-88, 90-91
C2: (3) 79-80, 82-83, 86-87
C3: (2) 84-85, 89-90

Linfield (Northern Ireland) C1

Founded by workers from the Linfield Spinning Mills. A record 41 times winners of the All-Ireland and Northern Ireland championship and 31 times winners of the All-Ireland and Northern Ireland Cup. Founder members and first champions of the All-Ireland League, 1891, and first winners of the Northern Ireland Cup, 1922. Their European debut came in the Champions' Cup 1959-60. Reached the Champions' Cup quarter-final stage 1966-67.

Full Name: Linfield FC   **Founded:** 1886
Address: Windsor Park, Donegal Ave, Belfast, BT12 6LW
Phone: 0232- 244196
Stadium: Windsor Park   **Capacity:** 25,000

Euro Record	P	W	D	L	F	A
C1	39	4	12	23	43	83
C2	4	2	0	2	5	6
C3	8	1	2	5	4	20
Total	51	7	14	30	52	109

C1: (17) 59-60, 61-62, 62-63, 66-67, 69-70, 71-72, 75-76, 78-79, 79-80, 80-81, 82-83, 83-84, 84-85, 85-86, 86-87, 87-88, 89-90

C2: (2) 63-64, 70-71

C3: (4) 67-68, 68-69, 81-82, 88-89

Lokomotiv Moscow (Russia) C3

Founded as Kor, becoming Lokomotive in 1936. Soviet League runners-up in 1959, their highest finishing position. Twice Soviet Cup winners, including the first competition in 1936. No European experience.

Full Name: Lokomotiv Moskva   **Founded:** 1923
Address: 125 A/B Cherkizovskaja Str., Moscow 107553, Russia
Phone: 7095-1619704
Stadium: Lokomotiv   **Capacity:** 24,093

Euro Record	P	W	D	L	F	A
C1	0	0	0	0	0	0
C2	0	0	0	0	0	0
C3	0	0	0	0	0	0
Total	0	0	0	0	0	0

C1: (0) None
C2: (0) None
C3: (0) None

Lokomotiv Plovdiv (Bulgaria)　　　C3

Played under various names including Slavia and Torpedo. Bulgaria's first entrant in the Fairs Cup in 1963-64. In the last four seasons in the League they have finished 13th, 11th, 3rd and 4th.

Full Name: FC Lokomotiv　　　　　　　　**Founded:** 1936
Address:　Sport Komplex Lokomotiv, Park K. Blagoev
Phone:　　32-26551
Stadium:　Lokomotiv　　　　　　　　**Capacity:** 25,500

Euro Record		P	W	D	L	F	A
	C1	0	0	0	0	0	0
	C2	0	0	0	0	0	0
	C3	32	10	7	15	43	59
	Total	32	10	7	15	43	59

C1: (0)　None
C2: (0)　None
C3: (11)　63-64, 64-65, 65-66, 67-68, 69-70, 71-72, 73-74, 74-75, 76-77, 83-84, 92-93

Maccabi Haifa (Israel)　　　　　C2

Four times League champions and three times Cup winners. No European experience.

Full Name:　　　　　　　　　　**Founded:** 1924
Address:
Stadium:

Euro Record		P	W	D	L	F	A
	C1	0	0	0	0	0	0
	C2	0	0	0	0	0	0
	C3	0	0	0	0	0	0
	Total	0	0	0	0	0	0

C1: (0)　None
C2: (0)　None
C3: (0)　None

Manchester United (England)　C1

Original club formed by railwaymen in 1878 as Newton Heath Cricket and
Football Club. Newton Heath joined the League in 1892 and Manchester
United were a new company created on their bankruptcy in 1902. Last
promoted to the top division in 1975. Eight League championships, the
seventh in 1966-67, the eighth (the first season as the Premier League) in
1992-93. Seven times Cup winners. England's first Champions' Cup entrant,
1956-57, and first winner, 1967-68.

Full Name: Manchester United FC　　　　**Founded:** 1887
Address:　Old Trafford, Manchester, M16 ORA
Phone:　　061-8721661
Stadium:　Old Trafford　　　　　　　　**Capacity:** 50,276
Colours:　Red, White, Black

Euro Record		P	W	D	L	F	A
	C1	41	26	7	8	100	45
	C2	31	16	9	6	55	35
	C3	29	12	11	6	46	24
	Total	101	54	27	20	201	104

C1: (5)　56-57, 57-58, 65-66, 67-68, 68-69
C2: (5)　63-64, 77-78, 83-84, 90-91, 91-92
C3: (6)　64-65, 76-77, 80-81, 82-83, 84-85, 92-93

Maribor Branik (Slovenia)　C3

No Yugoslavian League honours before 1991, finishing 7th in Division Three
(North) in their final season. Slovenian League members and runners up in
the first season, 1991-92. Cup winners that season, winning a penalty shoot-
out. This gave them their European debut in the 1992-93 Cup-Winners' Cup
as the first Slovenian representative in that competition.

Full Name:　　　　　　　　　　　　**Founded:**
Address:
Stadium:

Euro Record		P	W	D	L	F	A
	C1	0	0	0	0	0	0
	C2	4	1	0	3	6	11
	C3	0	0	0	0	0	0
	Total	4	1	0	3	6	11

C1: (0)　None
C2: (1)　92-93
C3: (0)　None

Maritimo (Portugal) C3

One pre-war Cup win to their name, but otherwise no domestic honours or European experience. 10th, 11th, 7th and 5th in last four seasons.

Full Name: Clube Sport Maritimo   **Founded:** 1910
Address: Rua D. Carlos I 17, 9000 Funchal
Phone: 91-23679/33063
Stadium: Barreiros   **Capacity:** 13,000

Euro Record	P	W	D	L	F	A
C1	0	0	0	0	0	0
C2	0	0	0	0	0	0
C3	0	0	0	0	0	0
Total	0	0	0	0	0	0

C1: (0) None
C2: (0) None
C3: (0) None

Marseille (France) C1

Reigning Champions' Cup holders. Nine times League champions, including each of the last five seasons. Promoted from Division 2(A) as champions 1984. Ten times Cup winners.

Full Name: Olympique de Marseille   **Founded:** 1898
Address: 441 Avenue du Prado, BP 124, 13257 Marseille Cedex 08
Phone: 91-765609
Stadium: Velodrome   **Capacity:** 46,000
Colours: White, White, White

Euro Record	P	W	D	L	F	A
C1	38	22	10	6	78	32
C2	14	8	2	4	19	13
C3	12	6	0	6	21	19
Total	64	36	12	16	118	64

C1: (6) 71-72, 72-73, 89-90, 90-91, 91-92, 92-93
C2: (3) 69-70, 76-77, 87-88
C3: (5) 62-63, 68-69, 70-71, 73-74, 75-76

Milan (Italy) C1

Founded as Milan Cricket and Football Club by Englishmen. Became Milan Associazione Sportiva in 1930 and Milan Associazione Calcio in 1939. 13 times League champions and four times Cup winners, they took part in the first Champions' Cup in 1955-56. World Club champions 1969, 1989 and 1990.

Full Name: Milan Associazione Calcio   **Founded:** 1899
Address: Via Turati 3, 20121 Milan, Italy
Phone: 2-6559016
Stadium: Giuseppe Meazza   **Capacity:** 75,510
Colours: Red/Black, White, White

Euro Record		P	W	D	L	F	A
	C1	79	48	13	18	182	72
	C2	30	17	10	3	47	20
	C3	53	22	12	19	71	57
	Total	162	87	35	40	300	149

C1: (12) 55-56, 57-58, 59-60, 62-63, 63-64, 68-69, 69-70, 79-80, 88-89, 89-90, 90-91, 92-93
C2: (4) 67-68, 72-73, 73-74, 77-78
C3: (9) 61-62, 64-65, 65-66, 71-72, 75-76, 76-77, 78-79, 85-86, 87-88

Monaco (France) C3

League champions and Cup winners on five occasions each. Promoted from Division 2(A) as champions in 1977 and in the top division ever since. In the last four seasons they have finished 3rd, 2nd, 2nd and 3rd.

Full Name: Association Sportive de Monaco   **Founded:** 1924
Address: 7 Avenue des Castellans, MC 98000 Monaco, France
Phone: 93-304529
Stadium: Louis II   **Capacity:** 20,000
Colours: Red/White, Red, White

Euro Record		P	W	D	L	F	A
	C1	18	4	4	10	25	23
	C2	27	8	13	6	32	27
	C3	14	6	2	6	23	23
	Total	59	18	19	22	80	73

C1: (5) 61-62, 63-64, 78-79, 82-83, 88-89
C2: (6) 74-75, 80-81, 85-86, 89-90, 91-92, 92-93
C3: (4) 79-80, 81-82, 84-85, 90-91

MTK-VM (Hungary) C3

Founded as the football section of the Hungarian Athletic Club (Magyar Testyarkorlok Kore) and joined the League in 1903. Known as Hungaria for a period before the war, later playing under various titles including Voros Lobogo before settling back as MTK in 1956. Joined with VM Egyetertes in 1975 to produce their current name. First winners of the Cup in 1910. 19 times League champions and nine times Cup winners. Were Hungary's representative in the first Champions' Cup, 1955-56.

Full Name: Magyar Testgyakorlok Kore   **Founded:** 1902
Address: Salgotarjani u. 12-14, 1087 Budapest
Phone: 1-1338368
Stadium: MTK   **Capacity:** 24,000
Colours: Blue, White, Blue

Euro Record	P	W	D	L	F	A
C1	10	5	1	4	26	22
C2	19	8	5	6	27	22
C3	15	7	1	7	32	30
Total	44	20	7	17	85	74

C1: (3) 55-56, 58-59, 87-88
C2: (3) 63-64, 69-70, 76-77
C3: (4) 61-62, 78-79, 89-90, 90-91

MyPa (Finland) C2

Promoted as champions of the First Division in 1991. Cup winners in 1992. No European experience.

Full Name: Myllykosken Pallo-47   **Founded:** 1947
Address: Myllykoski Oy c/o Oksanen, 46800 Anjalankoski
Phone: 951-50352
Stadium: Saviniemi   **Capacity:** 10,000

Euro Record	P	W	D	L	F	A
C1	0	0	0	0	0	0
C2	0	0	0	0	0	0
C3	0	0	0	0	0	0
Total	0	0	0	0	0	0

C1: (0) None
C2: (0) None
C3: (0) None

Neman Grodno (Bielorussia) C2

No European experience.

Full Name: **Founded:**
Address:
Stadium:
Euro Record

	P	W	D	L	F	A
C1	0	0	0	0	0	0
C2	0	0	0	0	0	0
C3	0	0	0	0	0	0
Total	0	0	0	0	0	0

C1: (0) None
C2: (0) None
C3: (0) None

Nikol Tallinn (Estonia) C2

No European experience.

Full Name: **Founded:**
Address:
Stadium:
Euro Record

	P	W	D	L	F	A
C1	0	0	0	0	0	0
C2	0	0	0	0	0	0
C3	0	0	0	0	0	0
Total	0	0	0	0	0	0

C1: (0) None
C2: (0) None
C3: (0) None

Norma Tallinn (Estonia) C1

The club from the capital were League champions in 1992 and appeared in the 1992-93 Champions' Cup competition as Estonia's first representative.

Full Name: **Founded:**
Address:
Stadium:

Euro Record		P	W	D	L	F	A
	C1	2	0	0	2	0	5
	C2	0	0	0	0	0	0
	C3	0	0	0	0	0	0
	Total	2	0	0	2	0	5

C1: (1)   92-93
C2: (0)   None
C3: (0)   None

Norwich City (England) C3

Founded by local schoolteachers. Joined League in 1920 and reached top division for the first time in 1972. Highest finishing position third in 1992-93. Technically qualified for Europe in 1985 (as League Cup winners) but excluded because of ban on English clubs. No Cup wins but losing semi-finalists three times. No European experience.

Full Name: Norwich City FC   **Founded:** 1902
Address: Carrow Road, Norwich, NR1 1JE
Phone: 0603-612131
Stadium: Carrow Road   **Capacity:** 24,284
Colours: Yellow and Green

Euro Record		P	W	D	L	F	A
	C1	0	0	0	0	0	0
	C2	0	0	0	0	0	0
	C3	0	0	0	0	0	0
	Total	0	0	0	0	0	0

C1: (0)   None
C2: (0)   None
C3: (0)   None

OB Odense (Denmark) C2

Three League championships and two Cup wins to their credit, all since 1977. Survived relegation play-offs in 1991. Their European debut came in the 1968-69 Fairs Cup.

Full Name: Odense Boldklub   **Founded:** 1887
Address: Sdr. Boulevard172, 5000 Odense C, Denmark
Phone: 66-121703
Stadium: Odense Stadion   **Capacity:** 24,362
Colours: Blue/White, Blue, White

Euro Record	P	W	D	L	F	A
C1	4	0	1	3	3	10
C2	2	0	0	2	1	4
C3	4	0	0	4	4	11
Total	10	0	1	9	8	25

C1: (2)   78-79, 83-84
C2: (1)   91-92
C3: (2)   68-69, 84-85

OFI Crete (Greece) C3

Highest League finishing position as runners-up achieved in 1986. Cup winners once. Their European debut came in the 1986-87 UEFA Cup. In the last four seasons in the League they have finished 6th, 8th, 6th and 4th.

Full Name: OFI   **Founded:** 1925
Address: 25 Avgoustou 16-18, 71202 Iraklion, Crete
Phone: 81-283920
Stadium: Irakiou   **Capacity:** 14,250

Euro Record	P	W	D	L	F	A
C1	0	0	0	0	0	0
C2	4	2	0	2	4	4
C3	2	1	0	1	1	4
Total	6	3	0	3	5	8

C1: (0)   None
C2: (1)   87-88
C3: (1)   86-87

Olimpija Ljubljana (Slovenia) C1

Merged with Erotnost and Odred in 1962. Yugoslavian Cup runners-up 1970, but no League honours before formation of Slovenian League which they have won twice. They were first club to represent Slovenia in Europe, in the Champions' Cup 1992-93. Domestic Cup winners 1993. Their European debut for Yugoslavia came in the 1966-67 Cup-Winners' Cup.

Full Name: NK Olimpija **Founded:** 1960
Address: Vodovodna 20, 61000 Ljubljana
Phone: 61-348397/341847
Stadium: Bezigrad **Capacity:** 18,000

Euro Record

	P	W	D	L	F	A
C1	4	2	0	2	5	7
C2	2	0	1	1	2	9
C3	4	0	1	3	4	11
Total	10	2	2	6	11	27

C1: (1) 92-93
C2: (1) 70-71
C3: (2) 66-67, 68-69

Olympiakos (Greece) C3

Founded out of Union Piraeus, 1920. 26 times League champions and 19 times Cup winners. First Greek entrant in the Cup-Winners' Cup, 1961-62. In the last four seasons in the League they have finished 4th, 2nd, 2nd and 3rd.

Full Name: Olympiakos **Founded:** 1925
Address: Vassileos Yeoryiou & Kountouriotou 138, 18532 Piraeus
Phone: 1-4128323
Stadium: Karaiskakis **Capacity:** 34,023
Colours: Red/White, White, White

Euro Record

	P	W	D	L	F	A
C1	28	7	6	15	25	43
C2	33	14	6	13	43	47
C3	22	9	5	8	24	31
Total	83	30	17	36	92	121

C1: (11) 59-60, 66-67, 67-68, 73-74, 74-75, 75-76, 80-81, 81-82, 82-83, 83-84, 87-88
C2: (9) 61-62, 63-64, 65-66, 68-69, 69-70, 71-72, 86-87, 90-91, 92-93
C3: (7) 72-73, 76-77, 77-78, 78-79, 79-80, 84-85, 89-90

Omonia Nicosia (Cyprus)　　　C1

Seventeen times League champions, nine times Cup winners. In the
Champions' Cup they have reached the 2nd round four times, 1988 being the
last occasion. Their European debut was in the 1965-66 Cup-Winners' Cup.
In the last four seasons in the League they have finished 2nd, 4th, 4th and 1st.

Full Name: Omonia FC　　　　　　　　　　**Founded:** 1948
Address:　PO Box 617, Nicosia
Phone:　　2-444544
Stadium:　Makarion　　　　　　　　　　**Capacity:** 20,000
Colours:　White, White, White

Euro Record	P	W	D	L	F	A
C1	36	11	2	23	44	87
C2	8	0	2	6	2	14
C3	6	1	2	3	7	10
Total	50	12	6	32	53	111

C1: (14) 66-67, 72-73, 75-76, 76-77, 77-78, 78-79, 79-80, 81-82, 82-83, 83-84,
84-85, 85-86, 87-88, 89-90
C2: (4) 65-66, 80-81, 88-89, 91-92
C3: (2) 86-87, 90-91

Osters IF (Sweden)　　　C3

League champions four times, including 1968, their debut season in the top
division. Cup winners once. European debut in the 1969-70 Champions' Cup.
Fourth in the League in 1990, they survived relegation play-offs in 1991 and
were third in the season finishing in late 1992.

Full Name: Osters Idrottsforening　　　　　**Founded:** 1930
Address:　Tipshallen, Varendsvallen Hejaregatan, 352 46 Vaxjo
Phone:　　471-19020/1
Stadium: Varendsvallen　　　　　　　　**Capacity:** 21,000

Euro Record	P	W	D	L	F	A
C1	8	1	1	6	3	14
C2	2	0	2	0	2	2
C3	20	6	1	13	25	36
Total	30	7	4	19	30	52

C1: (2) 69-70, 86-87
C2: (1) 77-78
C3: (7) 73-74, 74-75, 75-76, 76-77, 84-85, 88-89, 91-92

Panathinaikos (Greece)　C2

Founded as Panhellenic by Englishmen and known until 1980 as PAO (Panathinaikos Athletikos Omilos). Sixteen times League champions and 13 times Cup winners. In the last four seasons they have finished 1st, 1st, 3rd and 2nd.

Full Name: FC Panathinaikos　　　　　**Founded:** 1908
Address:　Armatolon & Klefton 47, Ampelokipi, 11471 Athens
Phone:　　1-6445322
Stadium:　OAKA 'Spiros Louis'　　　　**Capacity:** 74,433
Colours:　Green, Green, Green

Euro Record		P	W	D	L	F	A
	C1	53	13	19	21	60	71
	C2	14	4	2	8	13	28
	C3	28	9	4	15	40	41
	Total	95	26	25	44	113	140

C1: (13) 60-61, 61-62, 62-63, 64-65, 65-66, 69-70, 70-71, 72-73, 77-78, 84-85, 86-87, 90-91, 91-92
C2: (5) 67-68, 75-76, 82-83, 88-89, 89-90
C3: (9) 68-69, 73-74, 74-75, 78-79, 80-81, 81-82, 85-86, 87-88, 92-93

Paris Saint-Germain (France)　C2

Paris FC founded in 1970 as an attempt to bring top football back to the capital were joined by local amateurs Saint-Germain in the Second Division. The venture failed and the two split, Paris St. Germain coming into being as a Division Three side in 1973. Promoted in successive seasons, they have never been relegated. Three times Cup winners, their European debut was in the 1982-83 Cup-Winners' Cup. In the last four seasons in the League they have finished 5th, 9th, 3rd and 2nd.

Full Name: Paris Saint-Germain　　　　**Founded:** 1973
Address:　30 Avenue du Parc des Princes, 75016 Paris
Phone:　　40-719191
Stadium:　Parc des Princes　　　　　　**Capacity:** 48,725

Euro Record		P	W	D	L	F	A
	C1	2	0	1	1	2	3
	C2	10	6	2	2	16	9
	C3	18	6	5	7	25	20
	Total	30	12	8	10	43	32

C1: (1) 86-87
C2: (2) 82-83, 83-84
C3: (3) 84-85, 89-90, 92-93

Parma (Italy) C2

First Cup win came in 1992 which gave them European entry for the first time, their Cup-Winners' Cup campaign ending in victory. No domestic League honours, promoted from Division Two, 1989-90.

Full Name: Parma Associazione Calcio   **Founded:** 1913
Address: Via Furlotti 8, 43100 Parma
Phone: 521-240019/240007
Stadium: Ennio Tardijni   **Capacity:** 20,480
Colours: White, White, White

Euro Record		P	W	D	L	F	A
	C1	0	0	0	0	0	0
	C2	9	5	3	1	11	4
	C3	2	0	2	0	1	1
	Total	11	5	5	1	12	5

C1: (0) None
C2: (1) 92-93
C3: (1) 91-92

Partizani Tirana (Albania) C1

Sixteen League titles and 12 Cup wins. First club from Albania to play in the Champions' Cup, 1962-63. Reached the 2nd round of the Cup-Winners' Cup 1970-71.

Full Name: Klubi Sportiv Partizani   **Founded:** 1946
Address: Rruga Frosina Plaku 31, Tirana
Phone: 42-23933
Stadium: Qemal Stafa   **Capacity:** 20,000
Colours: Red, Red, Red

Euro Record		P	W	D	L	F	A
	C1	13	3	2	8	7	23
	C2	10	2	3	5	8	11
	C3	2	0	0	2	0	2
	Total	25	5	5	15	15	36

C1: (7) 62-63, 63-64, 64-65, 71-72, 79-80, 81-82, 87-88
C2: (4) 68-69, 70-71, 80-81, 91-92
C3: (1) 90-91

PSV Eindhoven (Holland)　　　　　C3

Philips Sport Vereniging (PSV) have been League champions 13 times and Cup winners six times. Took part in first Champions' Cup, 1955-56. In the last four seasons in the League they have finished 2nd, 1st, 1st and 1st again.

Full Name: Philips Sport Vereniging　　　　**Founded:** 1913
Address:　Frederiklaan 10 A, 5616 NH Eindhoven
Phone:　　40-511917
Stadium:　Philips Stadion　　　　　　**Capacity:** 29,700
Colours:　Red/ White, White, White

Euro Record	P	W	D	L	F	A
C1	59	23	15	21	97	60
C2	22	13	3	6	45	17
C3	42	21	6	15	73	48
Total	123	57	24	42	215	125

C1: (11)　55-56, 63-64, 75-76, 76-77, 78-79, 86-87, 87-88, 88-89, 89-90, 91-92, 92-93
C2: (4)　69-70, 70-71, 74-75, 90-91
C3: (9)　71-72, 77-78, 79-80, 80-81, 81-82, 82-83, 83-84, 84-85, 85-86

Publikum Celje (Slovenia)　　　　C2

No Yugoslavian League honours before 1991. Slovenian League members and Cup runners-up 1993. No European experience.

Full Name:　　　　　　　　　　**Founded:**
Address:
Stadium:

Euro Record	P	W	D	L	F	A
C1	0	0	0	0	0	0
C2	0	0	0	0	0	0
C3	0	0	0	0	0	0
Total	0	0	0	0	0	0

C1: (0)　None
C2: (0)　None
C3: (0)　None

RAF Jelgava (Latvia)   C2

Eighth in the Baltic League in 1990. Latvian runners-up in 1992. No European experience.

Full Name: **Founded:**
Address:
Stadium: **Capacity:**

Euro Record		P	W	D	L	F	A
	C1	0	0	0	0	0	0
	C2	0	0	0	0	0	0
	C3	0	0	0	0	0	0
	Total	0	0	0	0	0	0

C1: (0)   None
C2: (0)   None
C3: (0)   None

Rangers (Scotland)   C1

Founded by a family of brothers and their friends from Gareloch. Early members of the English FA and Cup semi-finalists in the 1880s. Founder members and joint champions of the Scottish League in 1890-91. A record 41 times champions and never relegated. Twenty-six times Cup winners. First club from Scotland to play in the Cup-Winners' Cup, 1960-61, having had their European debut in the 1956-57 Champions' Cup.

Full Name: Rangers FC   **Founded:** 1872
Address: Ibrox Stadium, Edminston Drive, Glasgow, G51 2XD
Phone: 041-427 8500
Stadium: Ibrox Stadium   **Capacity:** 45,407
Colours: Royal Blue, White, Royal Blue

Euro Record		P	W	D	L	F	A
	C1	67	32	12	23	108	99
	C2	54	27	11	16	100	62
	C3	38	18	8	12	53	41
	Total	159	77	31	51	261	202

C1: (14) 56-57, 57-58, 59-60, 61-62, 63-64, 64-65, 75-76, 76-77, 78-79, 87-88, 89-90, 90-91, 91-92, 92-93
C2: (10) 60-61, 62-63, 66-67, 69-70, 71-72, 73-74, 77-78, 79-80, 81-82, 83-84
C3: (8) 67-68, 68-69, 70-71, 82-83, 84-85, 85-86, 86-87, 88-89

Rapid Bucharest (Romania) C3

Founded as Casa Ferovarilul Rapid. In 1936 became Rapid, but changed back in 1946. Reached Mitropa Cup semi-finals in 1938. In 1950 became Locomotive then Rapid again in 1958. League champions for the only time in 1967, though have been runners-up since. Nine times Cup winners, their European debut came in the 1967-68 Champions' Cup.

Full Name: Rapid Bucharest   **Founded:** 1923
Address: Calea Giulesti 18, Bucharest, Romania
Phone: 0-170301
Stadium: Giulesti   **Capacity:** 18,000

Euro Record	P	W	D	L	F	A
C1	4	1	1	2	3	3
C2	8	3	1	4	9	13
C3	10	3	0	7	12	22
Total	22	7	2	13	24	38

C1: (1)   67-68
C2: (2)   72-73, 75-76
C3: (3)   68-69, 69-70, 71-72

Real Madrid (Spain) C2

Formed by students in the late 1890s, and formalised as Madrid FC in 1902. In 1920 King Alfonso XIII allowed the club to add Real (Royal) to the title. Spanish League founder members and first runners-up 1929. Now has 25 League titles and 17 Cup wins. Spain's first European representative by taking part in the Champions' Cup, 1955-56. World Club champions 1960.

Full Name: Real Madrid Club de Futbol   **Founded:** 1902
Address: Avda. Concha Espina 1, 28038 Madrid
Phone: 1-2500600
Stadium: Santiago Bernabeu   **Capacity:** 90,200
Colours: White, White, White

Euro Record	P	W	D	L	F	A
C1	170	101	25	44	401	187
C2	25	13	7	5	46	20
C3	58	30	9	19	100	67
Total	253	144	41	68	547	274

C1: (26) 55-56, 56-57, 57-58, 58-59, 59-60, 60-61, 61-62, 62-63, 63-64, 64-65, 65-66, 66-67, 67-68, 68-69, 69-70, 72-73, 75-76, 76-77, 78-79, 79-80, 80-81, 86-87, 87-88, 88-89, 89-90, 90-91
C2: (3)   70-71, 74-75, 82-83
C3: (8)   71-72, 73-74, 81-82, 83-84, 84-85, 85-86, 91-92, 92-93

Rosenborg BK (Norway) C1

Based in Trondheim they have won the League championship seven times, all since 1967. They have won the Cup five times, the first time in 1960, the year they reached the top division for the first time. Reached the 2nd round of the UEFA Cup in 1971-72 and of the Champions' Cup in 1986-87. In the last four seasons they have finished 2nd, 1st, 2nd and 1st.

Full Name: Rosenborg Ballklub   **Founded:** 1917
Address: Boks 4126, 7002 Trondheim
Phone: 7-940240
Stadium: Lerkendal   **Capacity:** 28,455
Colours: White, White, White

Euro Record	P	W	D	L	F	A
C1	14	1	3	10	10	38
C2	4	2	0	2	7	8
C3	12	6	0	6	18	27
Total	30	9	3	18	35	73

C1: (6) 68-69, 70-71, 72-73, 86-87, 89-90, 91-92
C2: (1) 65-66
C3: (5) 69-70, 71-72, 74-75, 90-91, 92-93

Royal Antwerp FC (Belgium) C3

Founded by English dock workers. Four times national champions, the last in 1957, and once Cup winners. Reached the Cup-Winners' Cup final at first attempt but lost to Parma (1992-93). In the last four seasons they have finished 4th, 7th, 5th and 5th.

Full Name: Royal Antwerp FC   **Founded:** 1880
Address: Oude Basuilbaan 54/a, 2100 Deurne, Antwerp, Belgium
Phone: 3-3246270
Stadium: Bosuil   **Capacity:** 35,000
Colours: Red/White, Red, Red

Euro Record	P	W	D	L	F	A
C1	2	0	0	2	1	8
C2	9	2	4	3	14	14
C3	38	14	8	16	53	55
Total	49	16	12	21	68	77

C1: (1) 57-58
C2: (1) 92-93
C3: (10) 64-65, 65-66, 66-67, 67-68, 74-75, 75-76, 83-84, 88-89, 89-90, 90-91

RSC Anderlecht (Belgium)   C1

Founded 1908 as SC (Sporting Club) Anderlecht, the Brussels club reached
the first division for the first time in 1921. Became Royal Sporting Club
(RSC) Anderlecht in 1933. They have now won the national championship 22
times, all in the post-war period, and the Cup seven times. Took part in the
first Champions' Cup, 1955-56. In the last four seasons in the League they
have finished 2nd, 1st, 2nd and 1st.

Full Name: Royal Sporting Club Anderlecht   **Founded:** 1908
Address: Avenue Theo Verbeek 2, 1070 Brussels
Phone: 2-5229400
Stadium: Constant Vanden Stock   **Capacity:** 36,000
Colours: White, White, White

Euro Record

	P	W	D	L	F	A
C1	80	35	16	29	135	125
C2	44	29	3	12	86	34
C3	68	37	15	16	140	81
Total	192	101	34	57	361	240

C1: (16) 55-56, 56-57, 59-60, 62-63, 64-65, 65-66, 66-67, 67-68, 68-69,
72-73, 74-75, 81-82, 85-86, 86-87, 87-88, 91-92

C2: (7) 73-74, 75-76, 76-77, 77-78, 78-79, 88-89, 89-90

C3: (10) 69-70, 70-71, 71-72, 79-80, 80-81, 82-83, 83-84, 84-85, 90-91,
92-93

Servette (Switzerland)   C3

Founded 1890 and played mostly rugby before joining the Swiss FA in 1900.
First champions of the National League, 1934, and champions 15 times all
told. Took part in first Champions' Cup, 1955-56. Cup-Winners' Cup quarter-
finalists twice. They survived the League relegation play-offs in 1990 and in
subsequent seasons finished 7th, 5th and 4th.

Full Name: Servette FC   **Founded:** 1890
Address: Case Postale 12, 1219 Chatelaine, Geneva
Phone: 22-7890922
Stadium: Charmiles   **Capacity:** 30,000

Euro Record

	P	W	D	L	F	A
C1	17	6	4	7	27	30
C2	24	11	4	9	36	25
C3	26	8	6	12	34	48
Total	67	25	14	28	97	103

C1: (5) 55-56, 61-62, 62-63, 79-80, 85-86

C2: (6) 66-67, 71-72, 76-77, 78-79, 83-84, 84-85

C3: (9) 63-64, 64-65, 65-66, 67-68, 74-75, 77-78, 80-81, 82-83, 88-89

Shelbourne (Rep. Ireland)   C2

Known as Reds United for a couple of seasons in the 1930s. Eight times
League champions, the seventh in 1962, the eighth in 1992. Three times
winners of the All-Ireland Cup, and four times winners of the Republic of
Ireland Cup, the third in 1962-63, the fourth in 1992-93. Their European
debut came in the 1962-63 Champions' Cup. Reached the 2nd round of the
Fairs Cup 1964-65.

Full Name: Shelbourne FC   **Founded:** 1895
Address: Tolka Park, Richmond Road, Dublin 3
Phone: 1-375754/375538
Stadium: Tolka Park   **Capacity:** 15,000

Euro Record		P	W	D	L	F	A
	C1	4	0	1	3	2	9
	C2	2	0	0	2	1	5
	C3	7	1	3	3	4	6
	Total	13	1	4	8	7	20

C1: (2)   62-63, 92-93
C2: (1)   63-64
C3: (2)   64-65, 71-72

Skonto Riga (Latvia)   C1

The Club from the capital were Latvian champions in 1991 and, following a
play-off, in 1992. They took part in the 1992-93 Champions' Cup as Latvia's
first representative.

Full Name: **Founded:**
Address:
Stadium:

Euro Record		P	W	D	L	F	A
	C1	4	2	1	1	6	3
	C2	0	0	0	0	0	0
	C3	0	0	0	0	0	0
	Total	4	2	1	1	6	3

C1: (1)   92-93
C2: (0)   None
C3: (0)   None

Slavia Prague (Czech) C3

Founded 1893 (Prague was then in Bohemia) from part of a sports club, ACOS Prague, already ten years old. Czechoslovakian League founder members and first champions, 1925. Nine times League champions, the last time in 1947. Known as Dymano Slavia 1951-65. Their European debut was in the 1967-68 Fairs Cup. In the last four seasons in the League they have finished 10th, 9th, 4th and 2nd.

Full Name: SK Slavia Praha Ips   **Founded:** 1893
Address: Stadion dr. V. Vacka, 100 05 Prague 10
Phone: 2-743725/746519
Stadium: Dr. Vacka   **Capacity:** 35,000

Euro Record	P	W	D	L	F	A
C1	0	0	0	0	0	0
C2	2	1	0	1	1	1
C3	14	6	1	7	20	23
Total	16	7	1	8	21	24

C1: (0) None
C2: (1) 74-75
C3: (6) 67-68, 68-69, 76-77, 77-78, 85-86, 92-93

Sliema Wanderers (Malta) C2

Founder members of the League and its first runners-up, 1910. First Cup winners, 1935. 22 League titles and 17 Cup wins. European debut in the 1963-64 Cup-Winners' Cup. Reached the 2nd round of the Cup-Winners' Cup in 1968-69 and the Champions' Cup in 1971-72.

Full Name: Sliema Wanderers FC   **Founded:** 1909
Address: 21 Tower Road, Sliema
Phone: 332033
Stadium: National, Ta'Qali   **Capacity:** 35,000
Colours: Blue/Light Blue, Black, Blue

Euro Record	P	W	D	L	F	A
C1	16	4	1	11	11	41
C2	18	4	1	13	10	57
C3	14	0	1	13	7	42
Total	48	8	3	37	28	140

C1: (7) 64-65, 65-66, 66-67, 71-72, 72-73, 76-77, 89-90
C2: (8) 63-64, 68-69, 69-70, 74-75, 79-80, 82-83, 87-88, 90-91
C3: (7) 70-71, 73-74, 75-76, 77-78, 80-81, 81-82, 88-89

Slovan Bratislava (Slovakia) C3

Founded 1919 as SK Bratislava and for many years backed by the city's chemical works. Eight times League champions and five times Cup winners, all in the post-war period. First Czechoslovakian entrant in the Champions' Cup, 1956-57. In the last four seasons in the League they have finished 5th, 2nd, 1st and 3rd.

Full Name: Slovan SK Bratislava   **Founded:** 1919
Address: Junacka 2, 832 15 Bratislava
Stadium: Tehelne Poli   **Capacity:** 48,000

Euro Record

	P	W	D	L	F	A
C1	16	7	1	8	23	30
C2	25	14	3	8	41	29
C3	10	4	3	3	25	15
Total	51	25	7	19	89	74

C1: (5) 56-57, 70-71, 74-75, 75-76, 92-93
C2: (6) 62-63, 63-64, 68-69, 69-70, 82-83, 89-90
C3: (3) 72-73, 76-77, 91-92

Sparta Prague (Czech) C1

Founded 1893 (Prague was then in Bohemia) as Athletic Club Vinohrady. The next year they became AC Sparta and, after 1948, played under several names before taking on the current one in 1965. Czechoslovakian League founder members and first runners-up, 1925. 19 times League champions and eight times national Cup winners. They reached the Cup-Winners' Cup semi-finals in 1972-73. In the last four seasons in the League they have finished 1st, 1st, 2nd and 1st.

Full Name: AC Sparta Prague   **Founded:** 1893
Address: Trida Obrancu miru 98, 170 82 Prague 7
Phone: (02) 372119/382441
Stadium: Letna   **Capacity:** 36,000
Colours: Dark Red, White, Black

Euro Record

	P	W	D	L	F	A
C1	42	19	9	14	67	60
C2	24	13	3	8	50	22
C3	20	8	4	8	31	33
Total	86	40	16	30	148	115

C1: (9) 65-66, 67-68, 84-85, 85-86, 87-88, 88-89, 89-90, 90-91, 91-92
C2: (5) 64-65, 72-73, 76-77, 80-81, 92-93
C3: (6) 66-67, 69-70, 70-71, 81-82, 83-84, 86-87

Spartak Moscow (Russia) C1

Founded as the team of the Soviet Producers' Co-operative, Klub Sparta.
Became Spartak in 1935. Twelve times Soviet champions, including the first
title winners in 1937, and a record ten times Soviet Cup winners. Russian
League champions once. Their European debut came in the 1966-67 Cup-
Winners' Cup, while they were the first Soviet club to take part in the UEFA
Cup, 1971-72. Reached the Champions' Cup semi-final in 1990-91 and the
Cup-Winners' Cup semi-finals in 1992-93.

Full Name: Spartak Moscow   **Founded:** 1922
Address: Ul. Verhniaia Krasnoselskaia 38/19, Moscow
Phone: 95-2088736
Stadium: Lenin   **Capacity:** 100,360
Colours: Red, White, White

Euro Record	P	W	D	L	F	A
C1	20	8	5	7	29	20
C2	18	10	4	4	31	17
C3	60	34	11	15	97	65
Total	98	52	20	26	157	102

C1: (4)   70-71, 80-81, 88-89, 90-91
C2: (3)   66-67, 72-73, 92-93
C3: (12)   71-72, 74-75, 75-76, 81-82, 82-83, 83-84, 84-85, 85-86, 86-87, 87-88,
            89-90, 91-92

Spartak Vladikavkaz (Russia) C3

Runners-up in the first Russian League. No European experience.
Full Name: Spartak Vladikavkaz   **Founded:** 1937
Address: Spartak Stadion, Vladikavka, Russia
Stadium: Spartak   **Capacity:** 27,500

Euro Record	P	W	D	L	F	A
C1	0	0	0	0	0	0
C2	0	0	0	0	0	0
C3	0	0	0	0	0	0
Total	0	0	0	0	0	0

C1: (0)   None
C2: (0)   None
C3: (0)   None

Sporting Lisbon (Portugal)   C3

Founded 1906. League founder members 1935 and first runners-up. Had also
been first runners-up in the Cup competition, 1922. Now has 16 League titles
and 15 Cup wins. Were Portugal's first representative in European football
when took part in 1955-56 Champions' Cup.

Full Name: Sporting Clube de Portugal   **Founded:** 1906
Address: Estadio Jose de Alvalade, Apartado 4120, 1503 Lisbon Codex
Phone: 1-7589021
Stadium: Jose Alvalade   **Capacity:** 70,000
Colours: Green/White, Black, Green/White

Euro Record		P	W	D	L	F	A
	C1	28	9	5	14	41	48
	C2	36	16	8	12	76	45
	C3	75	34	19	22	130	73
	Total	139	59	32	48	247	166

C1: (9) 55-56, 58-59, 61-62, 62-63, 66-67, 70-71, 74-75, 80-81, 82-83
C2: (7) 63-64, 64-65, 71-72, 72-73, 73-74, 78-79, 87-88
C3: (16) 65-66, 67-68, 68-69, 69-70, 75-76, 77-78, 79-80, 81-82, 83-84, 84-85,
85-86, 86-87, 88-89, 89-90, 90-91, 92-93

Standard Liege (Belgium)   C2

Eight times national champions and five times Cup winners, all in the post-
war period. In the last four seasons they have finished 3rd, 2nd, 4th and 3rd.

Full Name: R. Standard de Liege   **Founded:** 1898
Address: 2 Rue de la Centrale, 4020 Sclessin-Liege
Phone: 41-522122
Stadium: Sclessin   **Capacity:** 30,500

Euro Record		P	W	D	L	F	A
	C1	40	23	3	14	72	47
	C2	32	17	5	10	60	36
	C3	46	20	12	14	71	55
	Total	118	60	20	38	203	138

C1: (8) 58-59, 61-62, 63-64, 69-70, 70-71, 71-72, 82-83, 83-84
C2: (5) 65-66, 66-67, 67-68, 72-73, 81-82
C3: (9) 68-69, 73-74, 77-78, 78-79, 79-80, 80-81, 84-85, 86-87, 92-93

Steaua Bucharest (Romania) C1

Founded as Armata, the army team. Changed to CSCA in 1948 and to CCA in 1950. Became Steaua in 1961. Fifteen times League champions and 18 times Cup winners. Their European debut came in the 1957-58 Champions' Cup.

Full Name: Steaua Bucharest   **Founded:** 1947
Address: 35 Boul. Ghencia, Bucharest
Phone: 0-497727
Stadium: Steaua   **Capacity:** 30,000
Colours: Red, Red, Red/Blue

Euro Record		P	W	D	L	F	A
	C1	43	20	8	15	68	55
	C2	40	14	12	14	51	48
	C3	10	2	3	5	11	18
	Total	93	36	23	34	130	121

C1: (10) 57-58, 61-62, 68-69, 76-77, 78-79, 85-86, 86-87, 87-88, 88-89, 89-90

C2: (11) 62-63, 64-65, 66-67, 67-68, 69-70, 70-71, 71-72, 79-80, 84-85, 90-91, 92-93

C3: (3) 77-78, 80-81, 91-92

SV Casino Salzburg (Austria) C3

Founded by the amalgamation of Hertha and Rapid Salzburg. League runners-up in 1971 and 1992. Three times Cup runners-up. Their European debut came in the 1971-72 UEFA Cup.

Full Name: SV Casino Salzburg   **Founded:** 1933
Address: Schumacherstrasse 14, 5020 Salzburg
Phone: 662-33332
Stadium: Lehen   **Capacity:** 20,000

Euro Record		P	W	D	L	F	A
	C1	0	0	0	0	0	0
	C2	2	0	0	2	0	8
	C3	8	3	0	5	12	15
	Total	10	3	0	7	12	23

C1: (0) None
C2: (1) 80-81
C3: (2) 71-72, 76-77

Tenerife (Spain)　　　　　　　　　　　　C3

No League or Cup honours, or any European experience.

Full Name: Club Deportivo Tenerife　**Founded:** 1910
Address:　　Vieray Clavijo 2, 38003 Santa Cruz de Tenerife
Phone:　　　22- 205500
Stadium:　　Heliodoro Rodriguez　　　**Capacity:** 24,000

Euro Record	P	W	D	L	F	A
C1	0	0	0	0	0	0
C2	0	0	0	0	0	0
C3	0	0	0	0	0	0
Total	0	0	0	0	0	0

C1: (0)　None
C2: (0)　None
C3: (0)　None

Tofta B68 (Faeroe Islands)　　　　C1

Three times League champions. the first in 1984. No European experience.

Full Name:　　　　　　　　　　　　**Founded:**
Address:
Stadium:

Euro Record	P	W	D	L	F	A
C1	0	0	0	0	0	0
C2	0	0	0	0	0	0
C3	0	0	0	0	0	0
Total	0	0	0	0	0	0

C1: (0)　None
C2: (0)　None
C3: (0)　None

Torino (Italy) C2

Founded by a Swiss trader formerly associated with Juventus. Origins, however, with FC Torinese, founded 1894 and League runners-up in 1900, who had merged with Internazionale Torino (runners-up in the first two League championships, 1898 and 1899) in 1900. Eight times League champions, the last in 1978, and five times Cup winners, their European debut came in the 1964-65 Cup-Winners' Cup. Promoted from Division Two in 1989-90.

Full Name: Torino Calcio   **Founded:** 1906
Address: Corso Vittorio Emanuele 11 77, 10128 Torino
Phone: 11-513941
Stadium: Delle Alpi   **Capacity:** 70,012

Euro Record	P	W	D	L	F	A
C1	4	1	2	1	4	4
C2	19	9	4	6	28	17
C3	52	21	14	17	74	56
Total	75	31	20	24	106	77

C1: (1) 76-77
C2: (3) 64-65, 68-69, 71-72
C3: (12) 65-66, 72-73, 73-74, 74-75, 77-78, 78-79, 79-80, 80-81, 85-86, 86-87, 91-92, 92-93

Torpedo Moscow (Russia) C2

Founded as Proletarskkaja Kuznica and was associated with the Likhatchev car works. Founder members of the Soviet League Second Division and promoted at first attempt. Became Torpedo in 1936. Three times Soviet champions and six times Cup winners. They were the first Soviet club to take part in the Champions' Cup, 1966-67, their European debut. Reached the UEFA Cup quarter finals in 1990-91.

Full Name: Torpedo Moscow   **Founded:** 1924
Address: Avtozavodskaia ul. 23, Moscow
Phone: 95-2778800   **Stadium:** Torpedo
Capacity: 16,000   **Colours:** White, Black, White

Euro Record	P	W	D	L	F	A
C1	4	0	3	1	0	1
C2	23	10	8	5	32	20
C3	28	14	6	8	49	36
Total	55	24	17	14	81	57

C1: (2) 66-67, 77-78
C2: (6) 67-68, 69-70, 73-74, 82-83, 86-87, 89-90
C3: (6) 75-76, 78-79, 88-89, 90-91, 91-92, 92-93

Trabzonspor (Turkey) C3

Six times League champions and four times Cup winners. Their European debut came in the 1976-77 Champions' Cup.

Full Name: Trabzonspor Kulubu   **Founded:** 1967
Address: PK 27 Havaalani alti, Trabzon
Phone: 31-50967
Stadium: Avni Aker   **Capacity:** 27,500
Colours: Claret Red/Blue, Blue, Claret Red

Euro Record		P	W	D	L	F	A
	C1	14	6	1	7	12	19
	C2	8	3	3	2	10	12
	C3	10	4	2	4	14	17
	Total	32	13	6	13	36	48

C1: (6) 76-77, 77-78, 79-80, 80-81, 81-82, 84-85
C2: (2) 90-91, 92-93
C3: (3) 82-83, 83-84, 91-92

Universitatea Craiova (Romania) C2

Known as Stiinta between 1950 and 1966. Reached the first Division in 1964 and since 1974 have won the League championship four times and won the Cup five times. Their European debut came in the 1970-71 UEFA Cup. Reached the UEFA Cup semi-finals in 1982-83.

Full Name: Universitatea Craiova   **Founded:** 1948
Address: Str. Libertrati 9, 1100 Craiova
Phone: 41-324804
Stadium: Central   **Capacity:** 40,000
Colours: White, Blue, White

Euro Record		P	W	D	L	F	A
	C1	12	4	2	6	14	17
	C2	10	4	2	4	19	15
	C3	44	21	6	17	45	43
	Total	66	29	10	27	78	75

C1: (4) 74-75, 80-81, 81-82, 91-92
C2: (3) 77-78, 78-79, 85-86
C3: (11) 70-71, 73-74, 75-76, 79-80, 82-83, 83-84, 84-85, 86-87, 87-88, 90-91, 92-93

US Luxembourg (Luxembourg)　C3

Founded as Union Sportive Hollerich, taking on their current name in 1925 when merging with Jeunesse Sportive Verlorenkost. Eleven times League champions and nine times Cup winners. Their European debut came in the 1962-63 Champions' Cup. In the last four seasons in the League they have finished 1st three times and, last season, 2nd.

Full Name: FC Union Sportive Luxembourg　　**Founded:** 1908
Address: BP 1614, 1016 Luxembourg
Phone: 493548
Stadium: Achille-Hammerel　　**Capacity:** 6,000
Colours: White, Blue, White

Euro Record		P	W	D	L	F	A
	C1	10	0	0	10	3	43
	C2	16	2	2	12	8	48
	C3	8	0	0	8	2	42
	Total	34	2	2	30	13	133

C1: (5)　62-63, 71-72, 90-91, 91-92, 92-93
C2: (8)　63-64, 64-65, 69-70, 70-71, 78-79, 84-85, 86-87, 89-90
C3: (4)　65-66, 66-67, 73-74, 88-89

Vac FC Samsung (Hungary)　C3

Founded 1899 in the town to the north of the capital. Known as Vaci Izzo MTE until 1992. League champions, League runners-up and twice Cup winners, all in the 1990s, achievements not previously recorded. Their European debut came in the 1991-92 UEFA Cup.

Full Name: Vac FC Samsung　　**Founded:** 1889
Address: Stadion Utca 2, 2600 Vac
Phone: 27-10324
Stadium: Varosi　　**Capacity:** 12,000

Euro Record		P	W	D	L	F	A
	C1	0	0	0	0	0	0
	C2	0	0	0	0	0	0
	C3	6	2	1	3	5	11
	Total	6	2	1	3	5	11

C1: (0)　None
C2: (0)　None
C3: (2)　91-92, 92-93

Valencia (Spain)

Founded in the early 1900s by foreign residents and local students but reconstituted as a Spanish Club in 1919. Reached the First Division for the first time in 1931. Has now won the championship four times, the last in 1971, and the Cup five times. European debut was in the 1961-62 Fairs Cup, a competition they won. Won the Cup-Winners' Cup in 1979-80.

Full Name: Valencia Club de Futbol   **Founded:** 1919
Address: Artes Graficas 44, 46410 Valencia
Phone: 6-3600550
Stadium: Luis Casanova   **Capacity:** 49,291
Colours: White, White, White

Euro Record	P	W	D	L	F	A
C1	6	2	2	2	6	5
C2	19	10	5	4	39	20
C3	88	42	19	27	161	117
Total	113	54	26	33	206	142

C1: (1) 71-72
C2: (3) 67-68, 79-80, 80-81
C3: (16) 61-62, 62-63, 63-64, 64-65, 65-66, 66-67, 68-69, 69-70, 70-71, 72-73, 78-79, 81-82, 82-83, 89-90, 90-91, 92-93

Valletta (Malta)

Founded as Valletta United, their name until 1939. 14 League titles and six Cup wins. European debut in the 1963-64 Champions' Cup.

Full Name: Valletta FC   **Founded:** 1904
Address: 126 St. Lucia Street, Valletta
Phone: 224939
Stadium: National, Ta'Qali   **Capacity:** 35,000
Colours: White, White, White

Euro Record	P	W	D	L	F	A
C1	14	1	0	13	6	57
C2	10	0	1	9	2	45
C3	8	0	0	8	2	28
Total	32	1	1	30	10	130

C1: (7) 63-64, 74-75, 78-79, 80-81, 84-85, 90-91, 92-93
C2: (5) 64-65, 75-76, 77-78, 83-84, 91-92
C3: (4) 72-73, 79-80, 87-88, 89-90

Valur (Iceland) C2

Nineteen League titles and seven Cup wins. Their European debut came in the 1966-67 Cup-Winners' Cup and were the first team from Iceland in the Fairs Cup, 1969-70. Reached the 2nd round of the Champions' Cup 1967-68.

Full Name: Knattspyrnufelagid Valur **Founded:** 1911
Address: Knattspyrnudeild, Hildarenda v/Laufasveg, 101 Reykjavik
Phone: 1-12187
Stadium: Valur **Capacity:** 3,500

Euro Record		P	W	D	L	F	A
	C1	16	2	3	11	9	50
	C2	12	0	4	8	6	32
	C3	8	1	3	4	4	15
	Total	36	3	10	23	19	97

C1: (7) 67-68, 68-69, 77-78, 79-80, 81-82, 86-87, 88-89
C2: (6) 66-67, 75-76, 78-79, 89-90, 91-92, 92-93
C3: (4) 69-70, 74-75, 85-86, 87-88

Vitesse Arnhem (Holland) C3

Runners-up in first League championship and four times more before the First World War, though not since. Three times Cup runners-up. Their European debut came in the 1990-91 UEFA Cup. In the last four seasons in the League they have finished 4th, 5th, 4th and 4th again.

Full Name: Vitesse Arnhem **Founded:** 1892
Address: Postbus 366, 6800 AJ Arnhem
Phone: 85-425402
Stadium: Monnikenhuize **Capacity:** 13,000
Colours: Yellow/Black, White, White

Euro Record		P	W	D	L	F	A
	C1	0	0	0	0	0	0
	C2	0	0	0	0	0	0
	C3	12	7	1	4	14	7
	Total	12	7	1	4	14	7

C1: (0) None
C2: (0) None
C3: (2) 90-91, 92-93

VSS Kosice (Slovakia) C2

Founded in 1952 as Spartak Kosice. In 1956 became Jednota Kosice, 1962 became VSS Kosice, 1979 ZTS Kosice, 1990 Jednota VSS Kosice. Czechoslovakian League runners-up 1971 and Czechoslovakian Cup runners-up three times. First represented Czechoslovakia in the 1971-72 UEFA Cup.

Full Name: Jednota VSS Kosice   **Founded:** 1952
Address:
Stadium:

Euro Record		P	W	D	L	F	A
	C1	0	0	0	0	0	0
	C2	0	0	0	0	0	0
	C3	4	2	0	2	5	8
	Total	4	2	0	2	5	8

C1: (0) None
C2: (0) None
C3: (1) 71/72

Werder Bremen (Germany) C1

Twice West German League champions, German champions in 1993, and once West German Cup winners. In the last four seasons they have finished 7th and 3rd in the West German League, 9th and 1st.

Full Name: SV Werder Bremen   **Founded:** 1899
Address: Weserstadion, 2800 Bremen 1
Phone: 421-498106
Stadium: Weserstadion   **Capacity:** 40,640

Euro Record		P	W	D	L	F	A
	C1	10	5	2	3	5	5
	C2	17	10	2	5	34	17
	C3	36	17	8	11	65	42
	Total	63	32	12	19	104	64

C1: (2) 65-66, 88-89
C2: (3) 61-62, 91-92, 92-93
C3: (7) 82-83, 83-84, 84-85, 85-86, 86-87, 87-88, 89-90

Young Boys (Switzerland)   C3

Eleven times national champions (six before the formation of the nationwide League) and six times Cup winners. Champions' Cup semi-finalists 1958-59. In the last four seasons in the League they have finished 6th, 6th, 4th and 2nd.

Full Name: BSC Young Boys   **Founded:** 1898
Address: Papiermuhlestrasse 71, 3014 Berne
Phone: 31-4218484
Stadium: Wankdorf   **Capacity:** 48,000

Euro Record		P	W	D	L	F	A
	C1	17	7	5	5	29	31
	C2	10	2	2	6	10	18
	C3	2	0	1	1	2	4
	Total	29	9	8	12	41	53

C1: (5)   57-58, 58-59, 59-60, 60-61, 86-87
C2: (3)   77-78, 79-80, 87-88
C3: (1)   75-76

Zhalgiris Vilnius (Lithuania)   C2

Founded as Dinamo, and were known from 1948 until 1962 as Sparkak. The club from the capital spent a handful of early post-war seasons in the top division and third place in the Soviet League in 1987 brought them their European debut in the UEFA Cup 1988-89 competition. Withdrew from the 1990 Soviet League and were champions of the Baltic League and then the Spring 1991 Lithuanian League, the latter bringing them a Champions' Cup place as the country's first representative.

Full Name: Zhalgiris Vilnius   **Founded:** 1947
Address:
Stadium: Zhalgiris   **Capacity:** 15,000
Colours: Green and White stripes, White, White

Euro Record		P	W	D	L	F	A
	C1	2	0	0	2	0	8
	C2	0	0	0	0	0	0
	C3	6	2	0	4	7	11
	Total	8	2	0	6	7	19

C1: (1)   92-93
C2: (0)   None
C3: (2)   88-89, 89-90

Zimbru Kishinev (Moldavia) C1

Nineteenth in the 22-club Soviet Supreme League Second Division 1992. No European experience.

Full Name: **Founded:**
Address:
Stadium:

Euro Record	P	W	D	L	F	A
C1	0	0	0	0	0	0
C2	0	0	0	0	0	0
C3	0	0	0	0	0	0
Total	0	0	0	0	0	0

C1: (0)   None
C2: (0)   None
C3: (0)   None

COUNTRY by COUNTRY

For many years, the number of UEFA's member associations remained fairly constant at 30, the same as it had been when the European Football Union came into being in 1954. At the time of its 25th anniversary in 1979, just four new members had joined UEFA: Turkey (1955), Malta (1960), Cyprus (1964) and Liechtenstein (1976). San Marino (1988) and the Faeroe Islands (1990) subsequently increased the total membership to 36.

However, it was after 1989 and the political opening-up of Eastern Europe that the membership boom really began. Estonia, Lithuania and Latvia set the ball rolling by becoming full members; Azerbaijan and Moldavia were also granted associate membership status in 1992. Then, in 1993, the associations from Armenia, Bielorussia, Georgia, Croatia, Russia, Slovenia, the Ukraine, the Czech Republic and Slovakia all joined the throng. UEFA therefore now totals 45 member associations and two associate members. This figure takes into account the merging of the two German associations plus the end of the USSR and Czechoslovakia. Israel should also not be forgotten, although not a member of UEFA they still take part in certain European competitions.

This section of Playfair lists details of nearly all of these associations, in particular those who are due to have clubs competing in the European club competitions for 1993-94. Each country is arranged alphabetically and the information supplied throughout is consistent as possible. Certain information about some of the newer member associations is a little sparse at the time of going to press and I hope to be able to enlarge on this in future editions. Czechoslovakia, who started the season as a single country, finished competing as the RCS – the Representation of Czechs and Slovaks – and this is how they are referred to in this annual.

ALBANIA

Full Name: Federata Shqipatre Futbollit   **Founded:** 1930
Address: Rruga Dervish Hima #31, Tirana, Albania
Phone: (010 355) 42 7556   **Fax:** (010 355) 42 28198
UEFA Affiliation: 1954   **FIFA Affiliation:** 1932
National Stadium: Qemal Stafa   **Capacity:** 24,000
Colours: Red, Red, Red   **Change:** White, White, White

National League Final Table 1992-93

	P	W	D	L	F	A	Pts
Partizani Tirana	30	17	9	4	53	22	43
SK Teuta	30	15	8	7	32	21	38
Besa Kavaje	30	14	9	7	42	22	37
Vllaznia Shkoder	30	15	7	8	44	26	37
Elbasani	30	12	7	11	36	32	31
Dinamo Tirana	30	10	9	11	32	33	29
Apolonia	30	9	10	11	41	43	28
Lushnja	30	10	8	12	30	35	28
Albpetrol	30	10	8	12	38	48	28
Laci	30	11	6	13	26	37	28
FK Tirana	30	7	13	10	24	28	27
Sopoti	30	9	9	12	36	41	27
Flamurtari Vlore	30	8	11	11	28	34	27
Kastrioti	30	8	10	12	29	32	26
Tomori	30	11	3	16	28	53	25
Pogradeci	30	8	5	17	26	38	21

5-Year One, Two, Three Records

	1st....................pts	2nd....................pts	3rd....................pts
1988-89	17 Nentori Tirana 48	Partizani Tirana ..45	Dinamo Tirana....42
1989-90	Dinamo Tirana....50	Partizani Tirana ..49	Flamurtari Vlore.39
1990-91	Flamurtari Vlore .54	Partizani Tirana ..48	Vllaznia Shkoder 45
1991-92	Vllaznia Shkoder 44	Partizani Tirana ..38	Teuta Durres 33
1992-93	Partizani Tirana ..43	SK Teuta..............38	Besa Kavaje........37

5-Year Cup Final Results

1989	Dinamo Tirana	3-1	Partizani Tirana	after 0-0 draw
1990	Dinamo Tirana	1-1	Flamurtari Vlore	4-2 on pens
1991	Partizani Tirana	1-1	Flamurtari Vlore	5-3 on pens
1992	Elbasani	2-1	Besa Kavaje	
1993	Partizani Tirana	1-0	Albpetrol	

International Results 1992-93

Date	Opponents	Result	Venue	Comp.	Scorers
09/09	N. Ireland	0-3	Belfast	WCQ3	
11/11	Latvia	1-1	Tirana	WCQ3	Kepa (67)
17/02	N. Ireland	1-2	Tirana	WCQ3	Rraki (89)
14/04	Lithuania	1-3	Vilnius	WCQ5	Demollari (86)
15/05	Latvia	0-0	Riga	WCQ3	
26/05	Rep. Ireland	1-2	Tirana	WCQ3	Kushta (7)
02/06	Denmark	0-4	Copenhagen	WCQ3	

National Record	P	W	D	L	F	A
EC	33	3	4	26	14	77
WC (Finals)	Never qualified					
WC (Qualify)	42	4	5	33	23	91

(Includes Group 3 match v Denmark 2/6/93)

AUSTRIA

Full Name: Osterreichischer Fussball-Bund   **Founded:** 1904
Address: Praterstadion, Sektor A/F, Meierestrasse, Postfach 340, A-1020
         Vienna, Austria
Phone: (010 43) 1 217180   **Fax:** (010 43) 1 2181632
UEFA Affiliation: 1954   **FIFA Affiliation:** 1905
National Staduim: Wiener Stadion (Prater)   **Capacity:** 62,000
Colours: White, Black, Black   **Change:** Red, White, Red

National League Final Table 1992-93

	P	W	D	L	F	A	Pts
FK Austria	36	22	6	8	81	35	36
Salzburg	36	20	10	6	69	33	36
Admira Wacker	36	17	6	13	72	54	28
Rapid Vienna	36	15	10	11	53	51	27
Innsbruck	36	14	12	10	63	43	26
St Pollen	36	9	16	11	51	61	23
Sportclub	36	14	8	14	47	67	23
Vorwarts Sleyr	36	10	9	17	37	53	18

5-Year One,Two, Three Records

	1st	Pts	2nd	Pts	3rd	Pts
1988-89	FC Tirol	39	Admira Wacker	33	FK Austria	39
1989-90	FC Tirol	38	FK Austria	31	Admira Wacker	29
1990-91	FK Austria	36	FC Tirol	35	Sturm Graz	32
1991-92	FK Austria	33	Salzburg	33	FC Tirol	33
1992-93	FK Austria	36	Salzburg	36	Admira Wacker	28

5-Year Cup Final Results

1989	FC Tirol	0-2	6-2	Admira Wacker	6-4 on agg
1990	FK Austria		3-1	Rapid Vienna	
1991	SV Stockerau		2-1	Rapid Vienna	
1992	FK Austria		1-0	Admira Wacker	
1993	FC Tirol		3-1	Rapid Vienna	

International Results 1992-93

Date	Opponents	Result	Venue	Comp.	Scorers
19/08	RCS	2-2	Bratislava	Frdly	Stoger (17), Pfeifenberger (22)
02/09	Portugal	1-1	Linz	Frdly	Polster (37)
14/10	France	0-2	Paris	WCQ6	
28/10	Israel	5-2	Vienna	WCQ6	Herzog (41, 46), Polster (49), Stoger (56), Orgris (87)
18/11	Germany	0-0	Nuremberg	Frdly	
10/03	Greece	2-1	Vienna	Frdly	Pfeifenberger (3), Baier (13)
27/03	France	0-1	Vienna	WCQ6	
14/04	Bulgaria	3-1	Vienna	WCQ6	Pfeifenberger (11), Kuhbauer (25), Polster (89)
13/05	Finland	1-3	Pori	WCQ6	Zisser (89)
19/05	Sweden	0-1	Stockholm	WCQ6	

National Record	P	W	D	L	F	A
EC	54	21	11	22	88	77
WC (Finals)	26	12	2	12	40	43
WC (Qualify)	59	29	12	18	116	63

(Includes Group 6 match v Sweden 19/5/93)

BELGIUM

Full Name: Union Royal Belge de Societes de Football-Association
Founded: 1895
Address: Avenue Houba de Strooper #145, B-1020 Brussels, Belgium
Phone: (010 32) 2 477 1211   **Fax:** (010 322) 2 478 2391
UEFA Affiliation: 1954   **FIFA Affiliation:** 1904
National Stadium: Stade du Heysel   **Capacity:** 35,000
Colours: Red, Red, Red   **Change:** White, White, White

National League Final Table 1992-93

	P	W	D	L	F	A	Pts
RSC Anderlecht 34	26	6	2	80	24	58
Standard Liege 34	18	9	7	69	43	45
KV Mechelen 34	18	6	10	53	33	42
Waregem......................34	17	7	10	76	46	41
Royal Antwerp...............34	17	7	10	61	42	41
Club Bruges 34	16	8	10	49	32	40
Charleroi 34	16	8	10	58	46	40
Beveren 34	15	7	12	46	41	37
Gent............................34	12	10	12	51	51	34
RWD Molenbeek 34	10	11	13	39	45	31
Lierse..........................34	12	7	15	41	51	31
Cercle Bruges................34	9	10	15	65	73	28
RFC Liege.....................34	10	8	16	48	71	28
Ekeren.........................34	10	7	17	56	66	27
Genk...........................34	8	11	15	37	50	27
Lommel........................34	10	3	21	43	77	23
Lokeren........................34	4	12	18	32	58	20
Boom...........................34	6	7	21	40	95	19

5-Year One, Two, Three Records

	1st ....Pts		2nd............Pts		3rd.................Pts
1988-89	KV Mechelen 57	RSC Anderlecht..53	RFC Liege 46
1989-90	Club Bruges........57	RSC Anderlecht..53	KV Mechelen 50
1990-91	RSC Anderlecht..53	KV Mechelen 50	Club Bruges........47
1991-92	Club Bruges........53	RSC Anderlecht..49	Standard Liege....46
1992-93	RSC Anderlecht..58	Standard Liege....45	KV Mechelen 42

5-Year Cup Final Results

1989	RSC Anderlecht	2-0	Standard CL	
1990	RFC Liege	2-1	Ekeren	
1991	Club Brugge	3-1	KV Mechelen	
1992	Royal Antwerp	2-2	KV Mechelen	5-4 on pens
1993	Standard Liege	2-0	Charleroi	

International Results 1992-93

Date	Opponents	Result	Venue	Comp.	Scorers
02/09	RCS	2-1	Prague	WCQ4	Chovanecof (og 44), Czemiatynski (83)
14/10	Romania	1-0	Brussels	WCQ4	Smidts (27)
18/11	Wales	2-0	Brussels	WCQ4	Staelens (53), Degryse (58)
13/02	Cyprus	3-0	Nicosia	WCQ4	Scifo (2, 4), Albert (87)

31/03	Wales	0-2	Cardiff	WCQ4	
22/05	Faeroe Islands	3-0	Brussels	WCQ4	Wilmots (32, 75), Scifo (50 pen)

National Record	P	W	D	L	F	A
EC	61	27	16	18	91	69
WC (Finals)	25	7	4	14	33	49
WC (Qualify)	71	40	14	17	136	79

(Includes Group 4 match v Faeroe Islands 22/5/93)

BULGARIA

Full Name: Bulgarski Futbolen Soius   **Founded:** 1923
Address: Gotcho Gopin #19, 1000 Sofia, Bulgaria
Phone: (010 359) 2 877490   **Fax:** (010 359) 2 803237
UEFA Affiliation: 1954   **FIFA Affiliation:** 1924
National Stadium: Stadion Vasilij Levski   **Capacity:** 55,000
Colours: White, Green, Red   **Change:** Red, Green, White

National League Final Table 1992-93

	P	W	D	L	F	A	Pts
Levski Sofia	30	22	6	2	76	28	50
CSKA Sofia	30	17	8	5	66	31	42
Botev Plovdiv	30	16	6	8	53	33	38
Lokomotiv Plovdiv	30	16	5	9	57	29	37
Lokomotiv Sofia	30	11	13	6	52	39	35
Pirin	30	13	7	10	33	32	33
Etur	30	12	9	9	36	40	33
Lokomotiv Gorna	30	11	9	10	35	36	31
Chernomorets	30	11	8	11	34	31	30
Beroe	30	10	8	12	29	35	28
Yantra	30	10	6	14	38	51	26
Spartak	30	8	8	14	30	48	24
Dobrudja	30	9	4	17	31	56	22
Slavia Sofia	30	8	5	17	39	56	21
Haskovo	30	6	5	19	32	65	17
Sliven	30	6	1	23	26	57	13

5-Year One, Two, Three Records

	1st	Pts	2nd	Pts	3rd	Pts
1988-89	CFKA Sredets	48	Vitosha Sofia	39	Etur	34
1989-90	CSKA Sofia	47	Levski Spartak	36	Slavia Sofia	36
1990-91	Etur	44	Slavia Sofia	37	CSKA Sofia	37

| 1991-92 | CSKA Sofia........47 | Levski Sofia........45 | Botev Plovdiv.....37 |
| 1992-93 | Levski Sofia........50 | CSKA Sofia........42 | Botev Plovdiv.....38 |

5-Year Cup Final Results

1989	CFKA Sredets	3-0	Chernomorets
1990	Sliven	2-0	CSKA Sofia
1991	Levski Sofia	2-1	Botev Plovdiv
1992	Levski Sofia	5-0	Pirin
1993	CSKA Sofia	1-0	Botev Plovdiv

International Results 1992-93

Date	Opponents	Result	Venue	Comp.	Scorers
19/08	Mexico	1-1	Sofia	Frdly	Stoichkov (36)
26/08	Turkey	2-3	Trabzon	Frdly	Stoilov (11,39)
09/09	France	2-0	Sofia	WCQ6	Stoichkov (21 pen), Balakov (29)
07/10	Sweden	0-2	Stockholm	WCQ6	
11/11	Portugal	1-2	Paris	Frdly	Balakov (29)
02/12	Israel	2-0	Tel-Aviv	WCQ6	Sirakov (55), Penev (83)
10/01	Tunisia	0-3	Beja	Frdly	
18/02	UAE	0-1	Dubai	Frdly	
14/04	Austria	1-3	Vienna	WCQ6	Ivanov (54)
12/05	Israel	2-2	Sofia	WCQ6	Stoichkov (35 pen), Sirakov (60)

National Record	P	W	D	L	F	A
EC	57	24	13	20	84	66
WC (Finals)	16	0	6	10	11	35
WC (Qualify)	68	33	11	24	108	91

(Includes Group 6 match v Israel 12/5/93)

BIELORUSSIA

International Results 1992-93

Date	Opponents	Result	Venue	Comp.	Scorers
28/10	Ukraine	1-1	Minsk	Frdly	Gotsmanov (47)
27/01	Ecuador	1-1	Guayaquil	Frdly	Khtokouich (70)
30/01	Peru	1-1	Lima	Frdly	Orlevski
12/05	Moldavia	0-1	Minsk	Frdly	

CROATIA

Full Name: Croation Football Federation   **Founded:**
Address: Illica 21/11, CRO-41000, Zagreb, Croatia
Phone: 38-41/42 46 47   **Fax:** 38-41/42 46 39

National League Final Table 1992-93

	P	W	D	L	F	A	Pts
Croatia Zagreb	30	21	7	2	84	27	49
Hajduk Split	30	15	11	4	52	27	41
Zagreb	30	15	10	5	51	28	40
Rijeka	30	14	11	4	41	24	39
Vinkoveci	30	11	9	10	31	30	31
Osijek	30	11	7	12	40	42	29
Varteks	30	10	9	11	38	47	29
Istra Pola	30	12	4	14	32	35	28
Inker	30	9	9	12	35	31	27
Segesta Sisak	30	10	5	15	31	44	25
Pazinka Pisino	30	7	11	12	20	28	25
Zandar	30	9	7	14	30	48	25
Radnik	30	9	7	14	30	52	25
Dubrovnik	30	9	7	14	24	37	25
Belisce	30	8	9	13	34	50	25
Sibenik	30	4	8	18	21	45	16

Cup Final

| 1993 | Hajduk Split | 4-1 | 1-2 | Croatia Zagreb | 5-3 on agg. |

International Results 1992-93

Date	Opponents	Result	Venue	Comp.	Scorers
22/10	Mexico	3-0	Zagreb	Frdly	Suker (44, 89), Racunica (85)

CYPRUS

Full Name: Cyprus Football Association   **Founded:** 1934
Address: Stasinos Str # 1, Engomi 152, PO Box 5071, Nicosia, Cyprus
Phone: (010 357) 2 445341   **Fax:** (010 357) 2 472544
UEFA Affiliation: 1954   **FIFA Affiliation:** 1948
National Stadium: Makarion Athletic Centre   **Capacity:** 20,000
Colours: Blue, White, Blue   **Change:** White, Blue, White

National League Final Table 1992-93

	P	W	D	L	F	A	Pts
Omonia	26	18	5	3	75	30	59
Apollon	26	17	6	3	66	25	57
Salamina	26	15	3	8	44	28	48
Apoel	26	12	7	7	52	39	43
Anorthosis	26	11	6	9	32	33	39
Pezoporikos	26	8	10	8	46	39	34
AEL	26	9	6	11	42	40	33
Paralimni	26	10	3	13	46	48	33
Ethnikos	26	10	3	13	46	49	33
EPA	26	8	8	10	40	48	32
Olympiakos	26	8	7	11	34	52	31
Evagoras	26	8	6	12	39	45	30
Aris	26	8	6	12	33	52	30
Apop	26	1	2	23	17	84	5

5-Year One, Two, Three Records

	1st	Pts	2nd	Pts	3rd	Pts
1988-89	Omonia	43	Apollon	40	Apoel	34
1989-90	Apoel	41	Omonia	35	Pezoporikos	31
1990-91	Apollon	44	Anorthosis	41	Apoel	35
1991-92	Apoel	60	Anorthosis	58	Apollon	53
1992-93	Omonia	59	Apollon	57	Salamina	48

5-Year Cup Final Results

1989	AEL	3-2	Aris
1990	Salamina	3-2	Omonia
1991	Omonia	1-0	Olympiakos
1992	Apollon	1-0	Omonia
1993	Apoel	4-1	Apollon

International Results 1992-93

Date	Opponents	Result	Venue	Comp.	Scorers
18/06	Faeroe Islands	2-0	Toftir	WCQ4	Sotiriou (30), Papavasilou (58)
02/09	Greece	3-2	Salonika	Frdly	Charalambous (5), Sotiriou (37), Anonis (85 pen)
07/10	Malta	3-1	Limassol	Frdly	Hadjilukas (52), Costa (60), D. Ioannou (74)
14/10	Wales	0-1	Nicosia	WCQ4	

18/11	Slovenia	1-1	Larnaca	Frdly	Savvides (50)
29/11	Romania	1-4	Larnaca	WCQ4	Pittas (39 pen)
31/01	Poland	0-0	Nicosia	Frdly	
13/02	Belgium	0-3	Nicosia	WCQ4	
24/03	RCS	1-1	Limassol	WCQ4	Sotiriou (47)
14/04	Romania	1-2	Bucharest	WCQ4	Sotiriou (23)
25/04	Faeroe Islands	3-1	Limassol	WCQ4	Xiuruppas (7), Sotiriou (43), Y. Ioannou (75)

National Record	P	W	D	L	F	A
EC	48	1	4	43	16	148
WC (Finals)	Never qualified					
WC (Qualify)	54	3	3	48	29	179

(Includes Group 4 match v Faeroe Isles 25/4/93)

DENMARK

Full Name: Dansk Boldspil-Union   **Founded:** 1889
Address: Ved Amagerbanen #15, DK- 2300 Copenhagen S, Denmark
Phone: (010 45) 31950511   **Fax:** (010 45) 31950588
UEFA Affiliation: 1954   **FIFA Affiliation:** 1904
National Stadium: Idraetspark, Copenhagen   **Capacity:** 48,000
Colours: Red, White, Red   **Change:** White, White, Red

National League Final Table 1992-93

	P	W	D	L	F	A	Pts
FC Copenhagen	14	8	3	3	31	23	32
Odense	14	8	3	3	19	15	31
Brondby	14	8	3	3	29	16	30
AaB Aalborg	14	5	5	4	24	22	26
Silkeborg	14	4	5	5	17	17	23
AGF Aarhus	14	4	3	7	24	29	21
Lyngby BK	14	4	2	8	22	22	18
Navestved	14	1	4	9	16	36	14

5-Year One, Two, Three Records

	1st	Pts	2nd	Pts	3rd	Pts
1988-89	OB Odense	41	Brondby	38	Lyngby BK	38
1989-90	Brondby	42	B1903	31	Ikast BK	30
1990-91	Brondby	26	Lyngby BK	24	Frem	19
1991-92	Lyngby BK	32	Apollon	29	Frem	26
1992-93	FC Copenhagen	32	Odense	31	Brondby	30

5-Year Cup Final Results

1989	Brondby	6-3	Ikast BK		
1990	Lyngby BK	6-1	AGF Aarhus	after 0-0 draw	
1991	OB Odense	0-0	AaB Aalborg	after 0-0 draw	4-3 on pens
1992	AGF Aarhus	3-0	B1903		
1993	Odense	2-0	AaB Aalborg		

International Results 1992-93

Date	Opponents	Result	Venue	Comp.	Scorers
11/06	England	0-0	Malmo	EC Grp 1	
14/06	Sweden	0-1	Stockholm	EC Grp 1	
17/06	France	2-1	Malmo	EC Grp 1	Larsen (7), Elstrup (78)
22/06	Holland	2-2	Gothenburg	EC SF	Larsen (5, 32)
26/06	Germany	2-0	Gothenburg	EC F	Jensen (18), Vilfort (78)
26/08	Latvia	0-0	Riga	WCQ3	
09/09	Germany	1-2	Copenhagen	Frdly	Elstrup
23/09	Lithuania	0-0	Vilnius	WCQ3	
14/10	Rep. Ireland	0-0	Copenhagen	WCQ3	
18/11	N. Ireland	1-0	Belfast	WCQ3	Larsen (51)
30/01	United States	2-2	Tempe Arizona	Fdly	Strudal (29), Kjeldberg (85)
06/02	El Salvador	2-1	Los Angeles	Frdly	B. Nielsen (26), Elstrup (60)
24/02	Argentina	1-1	Mar del Plata	FT	Craviotto (12 og)
31/03	Spain	1-0	Copenhagen	WCQ3	Povisen (20)
14/04	Latvia	2-0	Copenhagen	WCQ3	Vilfort (23), Strudal (76)
28/04	Rep. Ireland	1-1	Dublin	WCQ3	Vilfort (27)
02/06	Albania	4-0	Copenhagen	WCQ3	Jensen (11), Pingel (20, 40), Moller (28)

National Record	P	W	D	L	F	A
EC	71	26	14	31	103	108
WC (Finals)	4	3	0	1	10	6
WC (Qualify)	56	21	10	25	87	90

(Includes Group 3 match v Albania 2/6/93)

ENGLAND

Full Name: The Football Association   **Founded:** 1863
Address: 16 Lancaster Gate, London, W2 3LW
Phone: (010 44) 71 2624542   **Fax:** (010 44) 71 4020486
UEFA Affiliation: 1954   **FIFA Affiliation:** 1905-1920, 1924-1928, 1946
National Stadium: Empire Stadium, Wembley   **Capacity:** 80,000
Colours: White, Blue, White   **Change:** Red, White, Red

National League Final Table 1992-93

	P	W	D	L	F	A	Pts
Manchester United	42	24	12	6	67	31	84
Aston Villa	42	21	11	10	57	40	74
Norwich City	42	21	9	12	61	65	72
Blackburn Rovers	42	20	11	11	68	46	71
Queens Park Rangers	42	17	12	13	63	55	63
Liverpool	42	16	11	15	62	55	59
Sheffield Wednesday	42	15	14	13	55	51	59
Tottenham Hotspur	42	16	11	15	60	66	59
Manchester City	42	15	12	15	56	51	57
Arsenal	42	15	11	16	40	38	56
Chelsea	42	14	14	14	51	54	56
Wimbledon	42	14	12	16	56	55	54
Everton	42	15	8	19	53	55	53
Sheffield United	42	14	10	18	54	53	52
Coventry City	42	13	13	16	52	57	52
Ipswich Town	42	12	16	14	50	55	52
Leeds United	42	12	15	15	57	62	51
Southampton	42	13	11	18	54	61	50
Oldham Athletic	42	13	10	19	63	74	49
Crystal Palace	42	11	16	15	48	61	49
Middlesbrough	42	11	11	20	54	75	44
Nottingham Forest	42	10	10	22	41	62	40

5-Year One, Two, Three Records

	1st	Pts	2nd	Pts	3rd	Pts
1988-89	Arsenal	76	Liverpool	76	Nottingham F.	64
1989-90	Liverpool	79	Aston Villa	70	Tottenham H.	63
1990-91	Arsenal	83	Liverpool	76	Crystal Palace	69
1991-92	Leeds United	82	Manchester Utd	78	Sheffield Wed.	75
1992-93	Manchester Utd	84	Aston Villa	74	Norwich	72

5-Year Cup Final Results

1989	Liverpool	3-2	Everton	
1990	Manchester Utd	1-0	Crystal Palace	after 3-3 draw
1991	Tottenham H.	2-1	Nottingham Forest	
1992	Liverpool	2-0	Sunderland	
1993	Arsenal	2-1	Sheffield Wed	after 1-1 draw

International Results 1992-93

Date	Opponents	Result	Venue	Comp.	Scorers
11/06	Denmark	0-0	Malmo	EC Grp 1	
14/06	France	0-0	Malmo	EC Grp 1	
17/06	Sweden	1-2	Stockholm	EC Grp 1	Platt (3)
09/09	Spain	0-1	Santander	Frdly	
14/10	Norway	1-1	Wembley	WCQ2	Platt (55)
18/11	Turkey	4-0	Wembley	WCQ2	Gascoigne (16, 61), Shearer (28), Pearce (60)
17/02	San Marino	6-0	Wembley	WCQ2	Platt (13, 24, 67, 83) Palmer (78), Ferdinand (86)
31/03	Turkey	2-0	Izmir	WCQ2	Platt (6), Gascoigne (44)
28/04	Holland	2-2	Wembley	WCQ2	Barnes (2), Platt (23)
29/05	Poland	1-1	Chorzow	WCQ2	Wright (84)
02/06	Norway	0-2	Oslo	WCQ2	
09/06	USA	0-2	Foxboro	US Cup	
13/06	Brazil	1-1	Washington	US Cup	Platt (47)
19/06	Germany	1-2	Pontiac	US Cup	Platt (31)

National Record	P	W	D	L	F	A
EC	62	35	16	11	123	43
WC (Finals)	41	18	12	11	55	38
WC (Qualify)	53	32	15	6	134	38

(Includes Group 2 match v Norway 2/6/93)

ESTONIA

Full Name: Estonian Football Association
Address: Refati PTI 1-376, 200103 Tallinn
Phone: 7-0142-238253   Fax:7-0142-238387/238355

International Results 1992-93

Date	Opponents	Result	Venue	Comp.	Scorers
03/06	Slovenia	1-1	Tallinn	Frdly	Pustov (10)
15/07	Latvia	1-2	Liapaya	Baltic Cup	Olumets (65)
16/07	Lithuania	1-1	Liapaya	Baltic Cup	Olumets (64)
16/08	Switzerland	0-6	Tallinn	WCQ1	
25/10	Malta	0-0	Valletta	WCQ1	
07/04	Slovenia	0-2	Ljubljana	Frdly	
14/04	Italy	0-2	Trieste	WCQ1	
12/05	Malta	0-1	Tallinn	WCQ1	
19/05	Scotland	0-3	Tallinn	WCQ1	
02/06	Scotland	1-3	Aberdeen	WCQ1	Bragin (57)

National Record	P	W	D	L	F	A
EC	Never participated					
WC (Finals)	Never qualified					
WC (Qualify)	4	1	0	3	6	17
WC (Qualify) †	6	0	1	5	1	15

† Post War (Includes Group 1 match v Scotland 2/6/93)

FAEROE ISLANDS

Full Name: Fotboltssambund Foroya, The Faeroes' Football Association
Founded: 1979
Address: Gundadular, PO Box 1028, FR-110 Torshavn, Faeroe Islands
Phone: (010 298) 16707   **Fax:** (010 298) 19079
UEFA Affiliation: 1988   **FIFA Affiliation:** 1988
National Stadium: Gundadulur   **Capacity:** 8,000
Colours: White, Blue, White

National League Final Table 1992-93

	P	W	D	L	F	A	Pts
B68	18	11	5	2	35	18	27
GI	18	11	3	4	33	20	25
HB	18	8	7	3	35	21	23
KI	18	7	8	3	30	17	22
TB	17	8	4	5	28	27	20

B36	18	5	8	5	30	30	18
VB	18	4	9	5	20	24	17
B71	17	2	7	8	25	29	11
SIF	18	3	5	10	27	41	11
NSI	18	1	2	15	14	50	4

5-Year Cup Finals

1987	HB Thorshavn 2-3	3-0	IF Fuglafjordur		5-3 on agg
1988	HB Thorshavn 1-0		NSI Runavik		
1989	HB Thorshavn 1-1	2-0	B71		3-1 on agg
1990	KL Klaksvik 6-1		GI Gotu		
1991	B36 Thorshavn 1-0		HB Thorshavn		

International Results 1992-93

Date	Opponents	Result	Venue	Comp.	Scorers
18/06	Cyprus	0-2	Toftir	WCQ4	
09/09	Wales	0-6	Cardiff	WCQ4	
23/09	RCS	0-4	Kosice	WCQ4	
25/04	Cyprus	1-3	Limassol	WCQ4	Arge (82)
22/05	Belgium	0-3	Brussels	WCQ4	
06/06	Wales	0-3	Toftir	WCQ4	
16/06	RCS	0-3	Toftir	WCQ4	

National Record	P	W	D	L	F	A
EC	8	1	1	6	3	26
WC (Finals)	Never qualified					
WC (Qualify)	9	0	0	9	1	34

(Includes Group 4 match v RCS 16/6/93)

FINLAND

Full Name: Suomen Palloliito Finlands Bollfoerbund **Founded:** 1907
Address: Kuparitie #1, PO Box 29, SF-00441 Helsinki, Finland
Phone: (010 358) 0 905626233 **Fax:** (010 358) 0 5626413
UEFA Affiliation: 1954 **FIFA Affiliation:** 1908
National Stadium: Olympiastadion **Capacity:** 50,000
Colours: White, Blue, White **Change:** Blue, White, Blue

National League Final Table 1992-93

	P	W	D	L	F	A	Pts
HJK Helsinki	33	20	6	7	59	35	66
Kuusysi Lahti	33	19	6	8	61	38	63
Jazz Pori	33	18	9	6	62	42	63
MyPa	33	16	8	9	57	29	56

Jaro	33	14	8	11	49	37	50
Haka	33	15	5	13	42	51	50
RoPS	33	12	6	15	55	49	42
TPS Turku	33	9	8	16	29	45	35
Ilves	33	10	5	18	43	54	35
MP Mikkeli	33	10	3	20	34	60	33
Oulu	33	9	5	19	42	68	32
Kups	33	8	7	18	33	56	31

5-Year One, Two, Three Records

	1st	Pts	2nd	Pts	3rd	Pts
1987-88	HJK Helsinki	43	Kuusysi Lahti	34	RoPS	31
1988-89	Kuusysi Lahti	41	TPS Turku	39	RoPS	34
1989-90	HJK Helsinki	1-1	1-0 Kuusysi Lahti		2-1 on agg	
1990-91	Kuusysi Lahti	59	MP Mikkeli	58	Haka	54
1992-93	HJK Helsinki	66	Kuusysi Lahti	63	Jazz Pori	63

5-Year Cup Final Results

1988	Haka Valkeakoski	1-0	OTP Oulu	
1989	KuPS Kuopio	3-2	Haka Valkeakoski	
1990	Ilves Tampere	2-1	HJK Helsinki	
1991	TPS Turku	0-0	Kuusysi Lahti	5-3 on pens
1992	MyPa	2-0	Jaro	

International Results 1992-93

Date	Opponents	Result	Venue	Comp.	Scorers
26/08	Poland	0-0	Jakobstad	Frdly	
09/09	Sweden	0-1	Helsinki	WCQ6	
04/11	Tunisia	1-1	Tunis	Frdly	Chihi (23 og)
14/11	France	1-2	Paris	WCQ6	Jarvinen (54)
13/04	Poland	1-2	Radom	Frdly	Heikkinen (42)
13/05	Austria	3-1	Pori	WCQ6	Paatelainen (17), Rajamaki (20), Hjelm (50)
16/06	Israel	0-0	Lahti	WCQ6	

National Record	P	W	D	L	F	A
EC	44	4	12	28	31	88
WC (Finals)	Never qualified					
WC (Qualify)	69	11	8	50	56	204

(Includes Group 6 match v Israel 16/6/93)

FRANCE

Full Name: Federation Francaise de Football   **Founded:** 1918
Address: 60 bis, Avenue d'Iena, F-75783 Paris Cedex 16, France
Phone: (010 33) 1 44317300   **Fax:** (010 33) 1 47208296
UEFA Affiliation: 1954   **FIFA Affiliation:** 1904
National Stadium: Parc des Princes **Capacity:** 49,000
Colours: Blue, White, Red   **Change:** White, Blue, Red

National League Final Table 1992-93

	P	W	D	L	F	A	Pts
Marseille	38	23	9	6	72	36	55
Paris Saint-Germain	38	20	11	7	61	29	51
Monaco	38	21	9	8	56	29	51
Bordeaux	38	18	12	8	42	25	48
Nantes	38	17	11	10	54	39	45
Auxerre	38	18	7	13	57	44	43
Saint Etienne	38	13	17	8	34	26	43
Strasbourg	38	12	16	10	58	57	40
Lens	38	12	16	10	36	41	40
Montpellier	38	12	12	14	36	41	36
Caen	38	13	9	16	55	54	35
Metz	38	11	13	14	44	45	35
Toulouse	38	9	16	13	36	45	34
Lyon	38	9	15	14	40	45	33
Le Havre	38	11	11	16	42	53	33
Sochaux	38	11	10	17	33	50	32
Lille	38	7	16	15	26	48	30
Valenciennes	38	9	11	18	42	57	29
Toulon	38	6	13	19	31	57	25
Nimes	38	3	16	19	32	66	22

Leading Scorers

23 Boksic (Marseille); 20 Gravelaine (Caen); 19 Klinsmann (Monaco); 18
Voller (Marseille); 14 Tiehi (Le Harve), Weah (Paris Saint-Germain); 13
Quodec (Nantes), Ferrer (Toulouse).

5-Year One, Two, Three Records

	1st	Pts	2nd	Pts	3rd	Pts
1988-89	Marseille	73	Paris S-Germain	.70	Monaco	.68
1989-90	Marseille	53	Bordeaux	51	Monaco	.46
1990-91	Marseille	55	Monaco	51	Auxerre	.48
1991-92	Marseille	58	Monaco	52	Paris S-Germain	.47
1992-93	Marseille	55	Paris S-Germain	51	Monaco	51

5-Year Cup Final Results

1989	Marseille	4-3	Monaco
1990	Montpellier	2-1	Racing Club Paris
1991	Monaco	1-0	Marseille
1992	Competition cancelled in memory of Bastia disaster		
1993	Paris S-Germain	3-0	Nantes

International Results 1992-93

Date	Opponents	Result	Venue	Comp.	Scorers
10/06	Sweden	1-1	Stockholm	EC Grp 1	Papin (58)
14/06	England	0-0	Malmo	EC Grp 1	
17/06	Denmark	1-2	Malmo	EC Grp 1	Papin (58)
26/08	Brazil	0-1	Paris	Frdly	
09/09	Bulgaria	0-2	Sofia	WCQ6	
14/10	Austria	2-0	Paris	WCQ6	Papin (3), Cantona (77)
14/11	Finland	2-1	Paris	WCQ6	Papin (17), Cantona (31)
17/02	Israel	4-0	Tel Aviv	WCQ6	Cantona (28), Blanc (62, 84), Roche (89)
27/03	Austria	1-0	Vienna	WCQ6	Papin (58)
28/04	Sweden	2-1	Paris	WCQ6	Cantona (43 pen, 82)

National Record	P	W	D	L	F	A
EC	62	31	15	16	118	76
WC (Finals)	34	15	5	14	71	56
WC (Qualify)	65	39	9	17	140	56

(Includes Group 6 match v Sweden 28/4/93)

GEORGIA

Full Name: Football Federation of Georgia
Address: 5 Shota Iamanidze Stret, Tbillisi 380012, Georgia.
Phone: 8883 34 0744

GERMANY

Full Name: Deutscher Fussball-Bund
Founded: 1900 (1948 for East German DFB)
Address: Otto-Fleck-Schneise 6, Postfach 710265, D-6000,
Frankfurt am Main, Germany
Phone: (010 49) 69 67880   **Fax:** (010 49) 69 6788266
UEFA Affiliation: 1954   **FIFA Affiliation:** 1904-1946, 1950
(1952-90 for the East German DFB)
National Stadium: Olympiastadion, Munich   **Capacity:** 73,000
Colours: White, Black, White   **Change:** Green, White, White

National League Final Table 1992-93

	P	W	D	L	F	A	Pts
Werder Bremen	34	19	10	5	63	30	48
Bayern Munich	34	18	11	5	74	45	47
Eintracht Frankfurt	34	15	12	7	56	39	42
Borussia Dortmund	34	18	5	11	61	43	41
Bayer Leverkusen	34	14	12	8	64	45	40
Karlsruhe	34	14	11	9	60	54	39
VfB Stuttgart	34	12	12	10	56	50	36
Kaiserslautern	34	13	9	12	50	40	35
Bor. Monchengladbach	34	13	9	12	59	59	35
Schalke	34	11	12	11	42	43	34
Hamburg	34	8	15	11	42	44	31
Cologne	34	12	4	18	41	51	28
Nuremberg	34	10	8	16	30	47	28
Wattenscheid	34	10	8	16	46	67	28
Dynamo Dresden	34	7	13	14	32	49	27
Bochum	34	8	10	16	45	52	26
Uerdingen	34	7	10	17	35	64	24
Saarbrucken	34	5	13	16	37	71	23

Leading Scorers
20 Yeboah (Eintracht Frankfurt), Kirsten (Bayer Leverkusen).

5-Year One, Two, Three Records

	1st	Pts	2nd	Pts	3rd	Pts
1988-89	Bayern Munich	50	Cologne	45	Werder Bremen	44
1989-90	Bayern Munich	49	Cologne	43	Eint. Frankfurt	43
1990-91	Kaiserslautern	48	Bayern Munich	45	Werder Bremen	42
1991-92	VfB Stuttgart	52	Bor. Dortmund	52	Eint. Frankfurt	50
1992-93	Werder Breman	48	Bayern Munich	47	Eint. Frankfurt	42

5-Year Cup Final Results

1989	Borussia Dortmund	4-1	Werder Bremen	
1990	Kaiserslautern	3-2	Werder Bremen	
1991	Werder Bremen	1-1	Cologne	4-3 on pens
1992	Hannover 96	0-0	B. Monchengladbach	4-3 on pens
1993	Bayer Leverkusen	1-0	Hertha Berlin	

International Results 1992-93

Date	Opponents	Result	Venue	Comp.	Scorers
12/06	CIS	1-1	Norrkoping	EC Grp 2	Hassler (89)
15/06	Scotland	2-0	Norrkoping	EC Grp 2	Riedle (30), Effenberg (47)
18/06	Holland	1-3	Gothenburg	EC Grp 2	Klinsmann (53)
21/06	Sweden	3-2	Stockholm	EC SF	Hassler (10), Riedle (58, 88)
26/06	Denmark	0-2	Gothenburg	EC Final	
09/09	Denmark	2-1	Copenhagen	Frdly	Riedle (47), Effenberg (85)
14/10	Mexico	1-1	Dresden	Frdly	Voller (58)
18/11	Austria	0-0	Lumberg	Frdly	
16/12	Brazil	1-3	Porto Alegre	Frdly	Sammer (84)
20/12	Uruguay	4-1	Montevideo	Frdly	Buchwald (42), Moller (60), Hassler (69), Klinsmann (76)
24/03	Scotland	1-0	Ibrox	Frdly	Riedle (19)
14/04	Ghana	6-1	Bochum	Frdly	Kirsten (69), Effenberg (70,82), Klinsmann (71,86), Moller (88)
10/06	Brazil	3-3	Washington	US Cup	Klinsmann (66, 89), Moller (80)
13/06	USA	4-3	Chicago	US Cup	Klinsmann (14), Riedle (34, 39, 59)
19/06	England	2-1	Pontiac	US Cup	Effenberg (26), Klinsmann (55)

National Record	P	W	D	L	F	A
Pre-War Record						
WC (Finals)	6	3	1	2	14	13
WC (Qualify)	4	4	0	0	20	2
East Germany – Complete record						
	P	W	D	L	F	A
EC	46	20	12	14	76	57
WC (Finals)	6	2	2	2	5	5
WC (Qualify)	47	22	8	17	87	65

West Germany – Complete record

	P	W	D	L	F	A
EC	50	30	15	5	99	31
WC (Finals)	62	36	14	12	131	77
WC (Qualify)	40	31	8	1	122	28

Germany – Post-reunification

	P	W	D	L	F	A
EC	10	6	1	3	17	10

(Germany qualify for 1994 WC as holders)

GREECE

Full Name: Elliniki Podosfairiki Omnospondia   **Founded:** 1926
Address: Singrou Avenue #137, Athens, Greece
Phone: (010 30) 1 9338850   **Fax:** (010 33) 1 9359666
UEFA Affiliation: 1954   **FIFI Affiliation:** 1927
National Stadium: OAKA Spiros Louis Athens   **Capacity:** 74,000
Colours: White, Blue, White   **Change:** Blue, White, Blue

National League Final Table 1992-93

	P	W	D	L	F	A	Pts
AEK Athens	34	24	6	4	78	27	78
Panathinaikos	34	24	5	5	85	21	77
Olympiakos	34	20	8	6	68	31	68
OFI Crete	34	19	9	6	64	32	66
PAOK Salonika	34	17	6	11	52	38	57
Heraklis	34	16	6	10	51	41	56
Larissa	34	11	10	13	36	42	43
Xanthi	34	11	9	14	56	66	42
Aris	34	12	6	16	40	54	42
Panahaiki	34	10	9	15	41	50	39
Athinaikos	34	9	12	13	27	37	39
Kalamaria	34	8	13	13	28	42	37
Apollon	34	10	7	17	27	49	37
Doxa	34	9	9	16	34	57	36
Edessaikos	34	9	7	18	36	60	34
Pierikos	34	9	7	18	35	62	34
Ionikos	34	9	6	19	33	49	33
Corinthos	34	6	9	19	28	65	27

5-Year One, Two, Three Records

	1st	Pts	2nd	Pts	3rd	Pts
1988-89	AEK Athens	44	Olympiakos	41	Panathinaikos	37

1989-90	Panathinaikos 53	AEK Athens 50	PAOK Salonika ..46
1990-91	Panathinaikos 54	Olympiakos 46	AEK Athens 42
1991-92	AEK Athens 54	Olympiakos 51	Panathinaikos 48
1992-93	AEK Athens 78	Panathinaikos 77	Olympiakos 68

5-Year Cup Final Results

1989	Panathinaikos	3-1		Panionios	
1990	Olympiakos	4-2		OFI Crete	
1991	Panathinaikos	3-0	2-1	Athinaikos	5-1 on agg
1992	Olympiakos	1-1	2-0	PAOK Salonica	3-1 on agg
1993	Panathinaikos	1-0		Olympiakos	

International Results 1992-93

Date	Opponents	Result	Venue	Comp.	Scorers
02/09	Cyprus	2-3	Salonika	Frdly	Tsaluhidis (22), Donis (78)
07/10	Iceland	1-0	Reykjavik	WCQ5	Tsaluhidis (61)
11/11	Hungary	0-0	Salonika	WCQ5	
17/02	Luxembourg	2-0	Athens	WCQ5	Dootroados (30 pen), Mitropulos (65)
10/03	Austria	1-2	Vienna	Frdly	Machlas (38)
31/03	Hungary	1-0	Budapest	WCQ5	Apostolakis (70)
20/05	Russia	1-1	Moscow	WCQ5	Mitropoulos (45)

National Record	P	W	D	L	F	A
EC	53	18	14	21	70	77
WC (Finals)	Never qualified					
WC (Qualify)	62	19	13	30	67	114

(Includes Group 5 match v Russia 20/5/93)

HOLLAND

Full Name: Koninklijke Nederlandsche Voetbalbond   **Founded:** 1889
Address: Woudenbergseweg #56, Postbus 515,
          NL-3700 Am Zeist, Netherlands
Phone: (010 31) 34399211   **Fax:** (010 31) 34391397
UEFA Affiliation: 1954   **FIFA Affiliation:** 1904
National Stadium: Olympisch Stadion Amsterdam   **Capacity:** 59,000
Colours: Orange, White, Orange   **Change:** White, White, White

National League Final Table 1992-93

	P	W	D	L	F	A	Pts
Feyenoord	34	22	9	3	82	32	53
PSV Eindhoven	34	22	7	5	81	34	51
Ajax	34	20	9	5	87	30	49

Vitesse Arnhem	34	16	14	4	58	29	46
FC Twente	34	17	8	9	64	39	42
FC Volendam	34	12	13	9	51	34	37
MW Maastricht	34	15	7	12	49	47	37
FC Utrecht	34	12	11	11	44	40	35
RKC	34	12	9	13	49	57	33
Willem II	34	12	8	14	41	38	32
Roda JC	34	11	7	16	51	59	29
FC Groningen	34	9	11	14	31	49	29
Sparta	34	8	11	15	36	65	27
Cambuur	34	6	13	15	39	58	25
Go Ahead Eagles	34	8	9	17	36	64	25
Fortuna Sittard	34	7	7	20	34	76	21
Den Bosch	34	6	9	19	35	79	21
SW/Dordrecht	34	5	10	19	30	68	20

5-Year One, Two, Three, Records

	1st	Pts	2nd	Pts	3rd	Pts
1988-89	PSV Eindhoven	53	Ajax	50	FC Twente	40
1989-90	Ajax	49	PSV Eindhoven	48	FC Twente	42
1990-91	PSV Eindhoven	53	Ajax	53	FC Groningen	46
1991-92	PSV Eindhoven	58	Ajax	55	Feyenoord	49
1992-93	Feyenoord	53	PSV Eindhoven	51	Ajax	49

5-Year Cup Final Results

1989	PSV Eindhoven	4-1	FC Groningen
1990	PSV Eindhoven	1-0	Vitesse Arnhem
1991	Feyenoord	1-0	Den Bosch
1992	Feyenoord	3-0	Roda JC
1993	Ajax	6-2	Heerenveen

International Results 1992-93

Date	Opponents	Result	Venue	Comp.	Scorers
12/06	Scotland	1-0	Gothenburg	EC Grp 2	Bergkamp (76)
15/06	Russia	0-0	Gothenburg	EC Grp 2	
18/06	Germany	3-1	Gothenburg	EC Grp 2	Rijkaard (2), Witschge (14), Bergkamp (71)
22/06	Denmark	2-2	Gothenburg	EC SF	Bergkamp (23), Rijkaard (85)
09/09	Italy	2-3	Eindhoven	Frdly	Bergkamp (4, 21)
23/09	Norway	1-2	Oslo	WCQ2	
14/10	Poland	2-2	Rotterdam	WCQ2	Van Vossen (43, 46)
16/12	Turkey	3-1	Istanbul	WCQ2	Van Vossen (57, 87), Gullit (59)

24/02	Turkey	3-1	Utrecht	WCQ2	Overmars (4), Witschge (37, 57)
24/03	San Marino	6-0	Utrecht	WCQ2	Van den Brom (2), Canti (29 og), De Wolf (52, 85), de Boer (68 pen), Van Vossen (78)
28/04	England	2-2	Wembley	WCQ2	Bergkamp (34), Van Vossen (85 pen)
09/06	Norway	0-0	Rotterdam	WCQ2	

National Record	P	W	D	L	F	A
EC	70	44	12	14	152	61
WC (Finals)	20	8	6	6	35	23
WC (Qualify)	64	34	17	13	129	57

(Includes Group 2 match v Norway 9/6/93)

HUNGARY

Full Name: Magyar Labdarugo Szovetseg   **Founded:** 1901
Address: Nepstadion, Toronyepulet, Tower Bldg, Istvanm. ut 3-5, H1146 Budapest, Hungary
Phone: (010 36) 1 2529296   **Fax:** (010 36) 1 2529986
UEFA Affiliation: 1954   **FIFA Affiliation:** 1906
National Stadium: Nepstadion, Budapest   **Capacity:** 72,000
Colours: Red, White, Green   **Change:** White, White, White

National League Final Table 1992-93

	P	W	D	L	F	A	Pts
Honved Kipest	30	19	5	6	59	28	43
Vaci Izzo	30	17	8	5	48	28	42
Ferencvaros	30	19	3	8	49	27	41
MTK-VM	30	14	8	8	59	27	36
Bekescsaba	30	12	12	6	42	31	36
Videoton	30	15	5	10	42	34	35
Csepel	30	12	6	12	29	37	30
Siofok	30	11	7	12	36	39	29
Raba Gyor	30	10	9	11	38	43	29
Vasas	30	7	13	10	31	33	27
Pecsi MSC	30	10	7	13	35	39	27
BVSC	30	10	6	14	32	37	26
Diosgyor	30	7	9	14	26	45	23

Ujpest Dozsa	30	4	12	14	29	45	20
Nyiregyhaza	30	3	12	15	17	39	18
Veszprem	30	6	6	18	25	54	18

5-Year One,Two, Three Records

	1st	*Pts*	*2nd*	*Pts*	*3rd*	*Pts*
1988-89	Honved Kipest	61	Ferencvaros	59	MTK-VM	59
1989-90	Ujpest Dozsa	58	MTK-VM	58	Ferencvaros	48
1990-91	Honved	45	Ferencvaros	40	Pecsi MSC	37
1991-92	Ferencvaros	46	Vaci Izzo	45	Honved Kipest	40
1992-93	Honved Kipest	43	Vaci Izzo	42	Ferencvaros	41

5-year Cup Final Results

1989	Honved Kipest	1-0	Ferencvaros
1990	Pecsi MSC	2-0	Honved
1991	Ferencvaros	1-0	Vaci Izzo
1992	Ujpest TE	1-0	Vaci Izzo
1993	Ferencvaros	1-1	Haladas after 1-1 draw. 5-3 on pens

International Results 1992-93

Date	Opponents	Result	Venue	Comp.	Scorers
26/08	Ukraine	2-1	Nyiregyhaza	Frdly	K. Kovacs (82), T. Nagy (89)
09/09	Luxembourg	1-0	Luxembourg	WCQ5	Detari (16), K. Kovacs (52, 79)
23/09	Israel	0-0	Budapest	Frdly	
11/11	Greece	0-0	Salonika	WCQ5	
07/03	Japan	1-0	Fukuoka	Kirin Cup	Kiprich (47)
10/03	United States	0-0	Nagoya	Kirin Cup	
31/03	Greece	0-1	Budapest	WCQ5	
15/04	Sweden	0-2	Budapest	Frdly	
28/04	Russia	0-3	Moscow	WCQ5	
16/06	Iceland	0-2	Reykjavik	WCQ5	

National Record	P	W	D	L	F	A
EC	64	29	13	22	119	89
WC (Finals)	32	15	3	14	87	57
WC (Qualify)	62	34	15	13	131	73

(Includes Group 5 match v Iceland 16/6/93)

ICELAND

Full Name: Knattspyrnusamband Island   **Founded:** 1947
Address: PO Box 8511, IS-104 Reykjavik, Iceland
Phone: (010 354) 1 84444   **Fax:** (010 354) 1 689793
UEFA Affiliation: 1954   **FIFA Affiliation:** 1929
National Stadium: Laugardalsvollur, Reykjavik **Capacity:** 14,000
Colours: Blue, White, Blue   **Change:** White, Blue,White

National League Final Table 1992

	P	W	D	L	F	A	Pts
IA Akranes	18	12	4	2	40	19	40
KR	18	11	4	3	41	17	37
Thor	18	11	4	3	41	17	37
Valur	18	10	5	3	30	14	35
Fram	18	9	4	5	33	27	31
FH	18	5	6	7	24	29	21
Vikingur	18	5	4	9	25	33	19
IBV	18	5	1	12	23	44	16
UBK	18	4	3	11	14	30	15
KA	18	3	4	11	18	33	13

4-Year One, Two, Three Records

	1st	Pts	2nd	Pts	3rd	Pts
1989	KA	34	FH	32	Fram	32
1990	Fram	38	KR	38	IBV	37
1991	Vikingur	37	Fram	37	KR	28
1992	IA Akranes	40	KR	37	Thor	37

5-Year Cup Final Results

1988	Fram	3-1	KR	
1989	Valur	0-0	KR	after 1-1 draw, 5-4 on pens
1990	Valur	2-1	FH	
1991	Valur	1-0	FH	after 1-1 draw
1992	Valur	5-2	KA	

International Results 1992-93

Date	Opponents	Result	Venue	Comp.	Scorers
08/08	Israel	0-2	Reykjavik	Frdly	
07/10	Greece	0-2	Reykjavik	WCQ5	
14/10	Russia	0-1	Moscow	WCQ5	
17/04	United States	1-1	Costa Mesa	Frdly	Stefansson (25)
20/05	Luxembourg	1-1	Luxembourg	WCQ5	Gudjohnsen (40)
02/06	Russia	1-1	Reykjavik	WCQ5	Sverrisson (26)

| 16/06 | Hungary | 2-0 | Reykjavik | WCQ5 | Sverrisson (13), |
| | | | | | Gudjohnsen (77) |

National Record	P	W	D	L	F	A
EC	40	6	6	28	22	71
WC (Finals)	Never qualified					
WC (Qualify)	45	7	8	30	38	115

(Includes Group 5 match v Hungary 16/6/93)

ISRAEL

Full Name: Hitachdut Lekaduregel Beisrael   **Founded:** 1928

Address: Israel Football Association, 12 Carlibach Street, PO Box 20188, Tel Aviv 61201, Israel

Phone: (010 972) 3 5610888   **Fax:** (010 972) 3 5618693

FIFA Affiliation: 1929

National Stadium: Ramat Gan, Tel Aviv   **Capacity:** 55,000

Colours: White, Blue, White   **Change:** Blue, White, White

National League Final Table 1992-93

	P	W	D	L	F	A	Pts
Beitar Jerusalem	33	22	5	6	64	38	71
Maccabi Tel Aviv	33	18	8	7	74	36	62
Bnei Yehoudah	33	17	5	11	66	57	56
Hapoel Beersheba	33	15	9	9	52	36	54
Maccabi Haifa	33	12	11	10	55	46	47
Hapoel Holon	33	13	5	15	49	49	44
Hapoel Haifa	33	11	7	15	42	51	40
Maccabi Netanya	33	11	6	16	35	57	39
Hapoel Tel Aviv	33	10	8	15	52	64	38
Maccabi Petah Tikva	33	9	11	14	43	55	38
Hapoel Petah Tikva	33	10	6	17	41	44	36
Beitar Tel Aviv	33	6	7	20	28	60	25

5-Year League Champions

1989	Maccabi Haifa
1990	Bnei Yehoudah
1991	Maccabi Haifa
1992	Maccabi Tel Aviv
1993	Beitar Jerusalem

5-Year Cup Final Winners

1989	Beitar Jerusalem
1990	Hapoel Kfar Saba
1991	Maccabi Haifa
1992	Hapoel Tel Aviv
1993	Maccabi Haifa

International Results 1992-93

Date	Opponents	Result	Venue	Comp.	Scorers
08/08	Iceland	2-0	Reykjavik	Frdly	Eyal Berkovitz, Shalom Tikva
09/09	Poland	1-1	Mielec	Frdly	Rosenthal (36)
23/09	Hungary	0-0	Budapest	Frdly	
28/10	Austria	2-5	Vienna	WCQ6	Zohar (57,77)
11/11	Sweden	1-3	Tel Aviv	WCQ6	Banin (42)
02/12	Bulgaria	0-2	Tel Aviv	WCQ6	
17/02	France	0-4	Tel Aviv	WCQ6	
03/02	Poland	0-0	Tel Aviv	Frdly	
24/03	Russia	2-2	Haifa	Frdly	Mirahi (64, 69)
12/05	Bulgaria	2-2	Sofia	WCQ6	R. Harazi (52), Rosenthal (53)
02/06	Sweden	0-5	Stockholm	WCQ6	
16/06	Finland	0-0	Lahti	WCQ6	

National Record	P	W	D	L	F	A
EC	Never participated					
WC (Finals)	3	0	2	1	1	3
WC (Qualify)	63	16	15	32	77	92

(Includes Group 6 match v Finland 16/6/93)

ITALY

Full Name: Federazione Italiana Giuoco Calcio   **Founded:** 1898
Address: Via Gregorio Allegri #14, CP 2450, 1-00198, Roma, Italy
Phone: (010 39) 6 84911   **Fax:** (010 39) 6 84912239
UEFA Affiliation: 1954   **FIFA Affiliation:** 1905
National Stadium: Stadio Olimpico, Roma   **Capacity:** 80,000
Colours: Blue, White, Blue   **Change:** White, Blue, Blue

National League Final Table 1992-93

	P	W	D	L	F	A	Pts
Milan	34	18	14	2	65	32	50
Internazionale	34	17	12	5	59	36	46
Parma	34	16	9	9	47	34	41
Juventus	34	15	9	10	59	47	39
Lazio	34	13	12	9	65	51	38
Cagliari	34	14	9	11	45	33	37
Sampdoria	34	12	12	10	50	48	36
Atalanta	34	14	8	12	42	44	36
Torino	34	9	17	8	38	39	35

Roma	34	8	17	9	42	39	33
Napoli	34	10	12	12	49	50	32
Foggia	34	10	12	12	38	53	32
Genoa	34	7	17	10	41	55	31
Fiorentina	34	8	14	12	53	56	30
Udinese	34	10	10	14	42	48	30
Brescia	34	9	12	13	36	44	30
Ancona	34	6	7	21	40	73	19
Pescara	34	6	5	23	45	74	17

Leading Scorers

26 Signori (Lazio); 21 R. Baggio (Juventus), Balbo (Udinese); 20 Sosa (Internazionale); 16 Batistuta (Fiorentina), Fonseca (Napoli); 15 R. Mancini (Sampdoria); 14 Ganz (Atalanta); 13 Raducioiu (Brescia), Papin (Milan), Van Basten (Milan).

5-Year One, Two, Three Records

	1st	Pts	2nd	Pts	3rd	Pts
1988-89	Internazionale	58	Napoli	47	Milan	46
1989-90	Napoli	51	Milan	49	Internazionale	44
1990-91	Sampdoria	51	Milan	46	Internazionale	46
1991-92	Milan	56	Juventus	48	Torino	43
1992-93	Milan	50	Internazionale	46	Parma	41

5-Year Cup Final Results

1989	Sampdoria	0-1	4-0	Napoli	4-1 on agg
1990	Juventus	0-0	1-0	Milan	1-0 on agg'
1991	Roma	3-1	1-1	Sampdoria	4-2 on agg
1992	Parma	0-1	2-0	Juventus	2-1 on agg
1993	Torino	3-0	2-5	Roma	5-5 on agg

Torino win on away goals rule.

International Results 1992-93

Date	Opponents	Result	Venue	Comp.	Scorers
09/09	Holland	3-2	Eindhoven	Frdly	Eranio (29), R. Baggio (40 pen), Vialli (77)
14/10	Switzerland	2-2	Cagliari	WCQ1	R. Baggio (83), Eranio (89)
18/11	Scotland	0-0	Glasgow	WCQ1	
19/12	Malta	2-1	Valletta	WCQ1	Vialli (59), Signori (62)
20/01	Mexico	2-0	Florence	Frdly	R. Baggio (55), Maldini (80)

24/02	Portugal	3-1	Oporto	WCQ1	R. Baggio (2), Casiraghi (24), D. Baggio (75)
24/03	Malta	6-1	Palermo	WCQ1	D. Baggio (19), Signori (38), Vierchwood (48), Mancini (59, 89), Maldini (73)
14/04	Estonia	2-0	Trieste	WCQ1	R. Baggio (21), Signori (86)
01/05	Switzerland	0-1	Bern	WCQ1	

National Record	P	W	D	L	F	A
EC	61	28	22	11	88	44
WC (Finals)	50	30	10	10	84	48
WC (Qualify)	50	33	10	7	115	36

(Includes Group 1 match v Switzerland 1/5/93)

LATVIA

Full Name: The Football Federation of Latvia
Address: 4 Terbatas Str, 226723 Riga
Phone: 7-0132-284206   **Fax:** 7-0132-284412
UEFA Affiliation: 1974   **FIFA Affiliation:** 1974
Colours: Blue, Red, Blue   **Change:** Yellow, Red, Yellow

International Results 1992-93

Date	Opponents	Result	Venue	Comp.	Scorers
15/07	Estonia	2-1	Liapaya	Baltic Cup	Skitik (27), Linards (45)
17/07	Lithuania	2-3	Liapaya	Baltic Cup	not known
12/08	Lithuania	1-2	Riga	WCQ3	Linards (15)
26/08	Denmark	0-0	Riga	WCQ3	
09/09	Rep. Ireland	0-4	Dublin	WCQ3	
23/09	Spain	0-0	Riga	WCQ3	
28/10	Lithuania	1-1	Vilnius	WCQ3	Linards (44)
11/11	Albania	1-1	Tirana	WCQ3	Alexeyenko (3)
18/11	Poland	0-1	Llawa	Frdly	
16/12	Spain	0-5	Seville	WCQ3	
14/04	Denmark	0-2	Copenhagen	WCQ3	
15/05	Albania	0-0	Riga	WCQ3	
02/06	N. Ireland	1-2	Riga	WCQ3	Linards (55)
09/06	Rep. Ireland	0-2	Riga	WCQ3	

National Record	P	W	D	L	F	A
EC	Never participated					
WC (Finals)	Never qualified					
WC (Qualify)	3	2	0	1	10	5
WC (Qualify†)	11	0	5	6	4	19

† Post-War (Includes Group 3 match v Republic of Ireland 9/6/93)

LIECHTENSTEIN

Full Name: Liechtensteiner Fussball-Verband   **Founded:** 1933
Address: Postfach 165, FL-9490 Vaduz, Liechtenstein
Phone: (010 41) 75 23344   **Fax:** (010 41) 75 28265
UEFA Affiliation: 1976   **FIFA Affiliation:** 1974
Colours: Blue, Red, Blue   **Change:** Yellow, Red, Yellow

LITHUANIA

Full Name: Lithuanian Football Federation
Address: 6 Zemaites St, 232675 Vilnius.
Phone: 7-0122-261713   **Fax:** 7-0122-661223

National League Final Table 1992-93

	P	W	D	L	F	A	Pts
Ekranas	27	20	6	1	50	8	46
Zhalgiris	27	18	7	1	54	13	43
Paneris	27	16	4	7	53	29	36
Sirius	27	11	9	7	41	29	31
Banga	27	11	5	11	30	28	27
Romar	27	11	4	12	27	27	26
Aras	27	8	8	11	26	33	24
Gatiajinis Vilkas	27	5	8	14	25	33	18

International Results 1992-93

Date	Opponents	Result	Venue	Comp.	Scorers
16/07	Estonia	1-1	Liapaya	Baltic Cup	Apanovics (30)
17/07	Latvia	3-2	Liapaya	Baltic Cup	not known
12/08	Latvia	2-1	Riga	WCQ3	Poderis (65), Tereskinas (86)
23/09	Denmark	0-0	Vilnius	WCQ3	
28/10	Latvia	1-1	Vilnius	WCQ3	Fridrikas (85)
24/02	Spain	0-5	Seville	WCQ3	
31/03	Poland	1-1		Frdly	Podreis

14/04	Albania	3-1	Vilnius	WCQ3	Baltusnikas (20)
					Sukristovas (25),
					Baranaukas (63)
18/05	Ukraine	1-2	Vilnius	Frdly	Zdancius (4)
25/05	N. Ireland	0-1	Vilnius	WCQ3	
02/06	Spain	0-2	Vilnius	WCQ3	
16/06	Rep. Ireland	0-1	Vilnius	WCQ3	

National Record	P	W	D	L	F	A
EC	Never participated					
WC (Finals)	Never qualified					
WC (Qualify)	3	0	0	3	3	11
WC (Qualify†)	10	2	3	5	8	15

† Post-War (Includes Group 3 match v Republic of Ireland 16/6/93)

LUXEMBOURG

Full Name: Federation Luxembourgeoise de Football   **Founded:** 1908
Address: 50 Rue de Strasbourg, L-2560 Luxembourg
Phone: (010 352) 488665   **Fax:** (010 352) 400201
UEFA Affiliation: 1954   **FIFA Affiliation:** 1910
National Stadium: Stade Municipal   **Capacity:** 10,000
Colours: Red, White, Blue   **Change:** Blue, White, Blue

National League Final Table 1992-93

	P	W	D	L	F	A	Pts
Avenir Beggen	10	7	2	1	31	14	28.5
Union	10	7	1	2	27	10	27.5
Jeunesse Esch	10	4	3	3	23	23	20.5
Grevenmacher	10	3	3	4	12	20	20.5
Dudelange	10	4	1	5	19	21	18
Esch Fola	10	0	0	10	6	30	8.5

5-Year One, Two, Three Records

	1st	Pts	2nd	Pts	3rd	Pts
1988-89	AC Spora	29	Jeunesse Esch	25.5	Union	24
1989-90	Union	29.5	Avenir Beggen	27.5	Jeunesse Esch	26.5
1990-91	Union	28	Jeunesse Esch	25	AC Spora	22.5
1991-92	Avenir Beggen	26	Union	26	Jeunesse Esch	23
1992-93	Avenir Beggen	28.5	Union	27.5	Jeunesse Esch	23

5-Year Cup Final Results

| 1989 | Union | 2-0 | Avenir Beggen | |
| 1990 | Swift Hesperange | 7-1 | AS Differdange | after 3-3 draw |

1991	Union	3-0	Jeunesse Esch
1992	Avenir Beggen	1-0	CS Petange
1993	Avenir Beggen	5-2	Dudelange

International Results 1992-93

Date	Opponents	Result	Venue	Comp.	Scorers
09/09	Hungary	0-3	Luxembourg	WCQ5	
28/10	Russia	0-2	Moscow	WCQ5	
17/02	Greece	0-2	Athens	WCQ5	
14/04	Russia	0-4	Luxembourg	WCQ5	
20/05	Iceland	1-1	Luxembourg	WCQ5	Birgisson (70 og)

National Record	P	W	D	L	F	A
EC	51	1	7	43	28	167
WC (Finals)	Never qualified					
WC (Qualify)	71	2	2	67	38	253

(Includes Group 5 match v Iceland 20/5/93)

MALTA

Full Name: Malta Football Association   **Founded:** 1900
Address: 280 St. Paul Street, Valletta, Malta
Phone: (010 356) 222697   **Fax:** (010 356) 245136
UEFA Affiliation: 1960   **FIFA Affiliation:** 1959
National Stadium: Ta'Qali Stadium   **Capacity:** 30,000
Colours: Red, White, Red   **Change:** White, White, Red

National League Final Table 1992-93

	P	W	D	L	F	A	Pts
Floriana	18	13	3	2	35	13	29
Hamrun Spartans	18	12	2	5	46	23	24
Valletta	18	10	4	4	32	23	24
St. Andrews	18	9	4	5	43	30	22
Hibernians	18	9	3	6	45	30	21
Sliema Wanderers	18	6	3	9	26	31	15
Rabat Ajax	18	6	3	9	30	38	15
Birkirkara	18	5	3	10	22	37	13
St. George's	18	3	4	11	18	44	10
Mellieha	18	2	3	13	14	42	6

5-Year One, Two, Three Records

	1st	Pts	2nd	Pts	3rd	Pts
1988-89	Sliema Wand's	26	Valletta	23	Hamrun Spartans	20
1989-90	Valletta	28	Sliema Wand's	24	Hamrun Spartans	23

1990-91	Hamrun Spartans 24	Valletta 19	Floriana................18
1991-92	Valletta 33	Floriana...............24	Hamrun Spartans 23
1992-93	Floriana...............29	Hamrun Spartans 24	Valletta 24

5-Year Cup Final Results

1989	Hamrun Spartans	1-0	Floriana	
1990	Sliema Wanderers	1-0	Birkirkara	
1991	Valletta	2-1	Sliema Wanderers	
1992	Hamrum Spartans	3-3	Valletta	2-1 on pens
1993	Floriana	5-0	Sliema Wanderers	

International Results 1992-93

Date	Opponents	Result	Venue	Comp.	Scorers
07/10	Cyprus	0-3	Limassol	Frdly	
25/10	Estonia	0-0	Valletta	WCQ1	
18/11	Switzerland	0-3	Bern	WCQ1	
19/12	Italy	1-2	Valletta	WCQ1	Gregory (85)
17/02	Scotland	0-3	Glasgow	WCQ1	
24/01	Portugal	0-1	Valletta	WCQ1	
24/03	Italy	1-6	Palermo	WCQ1	Busuttil (68 pen)
17/04	Switzerland	0-2	Valetta	WCQ1	
12/05	Estonia	1-0	Tallinn	WCQ1	Laferla (16)
19/06	Portugal	0-4	Oporto	WCQ1	

National Record	P	W	D	L	F	A
EC	43	2	5	36	18	146
WC (Finals)	Never qualified					
WC (Qualify)	41	1	4	36	15	126

(Includes Group 1 match v Portugal 19/6/93)

NORTHERN IRELAND

Full Name: Irish Football Association   **Founded:** 1880
Address: 20 Windsor Avenue, Belfast BT9 6EG
Phone: (010 44) 232 669458   **Fax:** (010 44) 232 667620
UEFA Affiliation: 1954   **FIFA Affiliation:**1911-20, 1924-28, 1946
National Stadium: Windsor Park   **Capacity:** 28,000
Colours: Green, White, Green   **Change:** White, Green, Green

National League Final Table 1992-93

	P	W	D	L	F	A	Pts
Linfield 30	20	6	4	49	15	66
Crusaders........................30	21	3	6	53	27	66
Bangor 30	20	4	6	61	32	64

Portadown	30	18	9	3	70	26	63
Distillery	30	20	2	8	60	36	62
Glenavon	30	14	6	10	48	36	48
Glentoran	30	13	8	9	70	40	47
Ards	30	12	9	9	45	45	45
Carrick Rangers	20	12	1	16	50	73	38
Ballymena	30	10	6	14	41	51	36
Cliftonville	30	10	3	17	42	48	33
Omagh	30	9	5	16	38	57	32
Larne	30	9	3	18	41	59	30
Newry	30	5	5	20	30	72	20
Coleraine	30	5	3	22	28	63	18
Ballyclare	30	2	6	22	28	75	12

5-Year One, Two, Three Records

	1st	*Pts*	*2nd*	*Pts*	*3rd*	*Pts*
1988-89	Linfield	65	Glentoran	55	Coleraine	50
1989-90	Portadown	55	Glenavon	54	Glentoran	44
1990-91	Portadown	71	Bangor	61	Glentoran	60
1991-92	Glentoran	77	Portadown	65	Linfield	60
1992-93	Linfield	66	Crusaders	66	Bangor	64

5-Year Cup Final Results

1989	Ballymena United	1-0	Larne
1990	Glentoran	3-0	Portadown
1991	Portadown	2-1	Glenavon
1992	Glenavon	2-1	Linfield
1993	Bangor	1-0	Ards

International Results 1992-93

Date	*Opponents*	*Result*	*Venue*	*Comp.*	*Scorers*
09/09	Albania	3-0	Belfast	WCQ3	Clarke (14), Wilson (31), Magilton (44)
14/10	Spain	0-0	Belfast	WCQ3	
18/11	Denmark	0-1	Belfast	WCQ3	
17/02	Albania	2-1	Tirana	WCQ3	Magilton (14), McDonald (38)
31/03	Rep. Ireland	0-3	Dublin	WCQ3	
28/04	Spain	1-3	Seville	WCQ3	Wilson (11)
25/05	Lithuania	1-0	Vilnius	WCQ3	Dowie (8)
02/06	Latvia	2-1	Riga	WCQ3	Magilton (4), Taggart (15)

National Record

	P	W	D	L	F	A
EC	52	20	10	22	54	61
WC (Finals)	13	3	5	5	13	23
WC (Qualify)	69	25	17	27	80	85

(Includes Group 3 match v Latvia 2/6/93)

NORWAY

Full Name: Norges Fotballforbund   **Founded:** 1902
Address: Ullevaal Stadion, Postboks 3823, Ullevaal Hageby,
           N-0805 Oslo 8, Norway
Phone: (010 47) 2 469830   **Fax:** (010 47) 2 608222
UEFA Affiliation: 1954   **FIFA Affiliation:** 1908
National Stadium: Ullevaal Stadion   **Capacity:** 27,000
Colours: Red, White, Blue   **Change:** Blue, White, Blue

National League Final Table 1992-93

	P	W	D	L	F	A	Pts
Rosenborg	22	14	4	4	58	19	46
Kongsvinger	22	12	4	6	43	27	40
Start	22	11	6	5	38	28	39
Lillestrom	22	11	5	6	48	28	38
Lyn	22	11	4	7	33	29	37
Molde	22	11	3	8	30	30	36
Brann	22	4	12	6	26	30	24
Tromso	22	6	6	10	22	37	24
Viking	22	4	9	9	25	34	21
Hamark	22	5	5	12	30	46	20
Sogndal	22	5	5	12	30	56	20
Mjondalen	22	5	3	14	20	42	18

4-Year One, Two, Three Records

	1st	Pts	2nd	Pts	3rd	Pts
1989-90	Lillestrom	52	Rosenborg	44	Tromso	37
1990-91	Rosenborg	44	Tromso	42	Molde	40
1991-92	Viking	41	Rosenborg	36	Start	34
1992-93	Rosenborg	45	Kongsvinger	40	Start	39

4-Year Cup Final Results

1990	Viking	2-1	Molde	after 2-2 draw
1991	Rosenborg	5-1	Fyllingen	
1992	Stromgodset	3-2	Rosenborg	
1993	Rosenborg	3-2	Lillestrom	

International Results 1992-93

Date	Opponents	Result	Venue	Comp.	Scorers
26/08	Sweden	2-2	Oslo	Frdly	Leonhardsen (18), Nilsen (89)
09/09	San Marino	10-0	Olso	WCQ2	Rekdal (5,79), Galle (6, 51, 69), Sorloth (15, 21), Bukseb (46, 67), Mykland (74)
23/09	Holland	2-1	Oslo	WCQ2	Rekdal (9 pen), Sorloth (78)
07/10	San Marino	2-0	Seravalle	WCQ2	Jakobsen (7), Flo (10)
14/10	England	1-1	Wembley	WCQ2	Rekdal (76)
29/11	Hong Kong	3-3	Hong Kong	CC†	Flo (22, 49), Skammelsrud (88)
02/12	China	1-2	Guanzhou	Frdly	Flo (85)
10/02	Portugal	1-1	Faro	Frdly	Sorloth (87)
30/03	Qatar	6-1	Doha	Frdly	Leonhardsen (6), Flo (26), Fjortoft (43, 51, 59), Jakobsen (74)
02/06	England	2-0	Oslo	WCQ2	Leonhardsen (42), Bohinen (48)
09/06	Holland	0-0	Rotterdam	WCQ2	

† Carlsberg Challenge

National Record	P	W	D	L	F	A
EC	52	7	11	34	48	101
WC (Finals)	1	0	0	1	1	2
WC (Qualify)	65	20	13	32	84	115

(Includes Group 2 match v Holland 9/6/93)

POLAND

Full Name: Polski Zwlazek Pilki Noznej   **Founded:** 1919
Address: Al. Ujazdowskie #22, 00-478 Warsaw, Poland
Phone: (010 48) 22 292489   **Fax:** (010 48) 22 219175
UEFA Affiliation: 1954   **FIFA Affiliation:** 1923
National Stadium: Stadion Slaski, Chorzow   **Capacity:** 70,000
Colours: White, Red, White   **Change:** Red, White, Red

National League Final Table 1992-93

	P	W	D	L	F	A	Pts
Lech Poznan	34	17	13	4	70	29	47†
Legia Warsaw	34	21	7	6	56	26	49†
LKS Lodz	34	19	11	4	60	33	49†
Ruch Chorzow	34	19	6	9	52	27	44
Widzew Lodz	34	16	11	7	60	42	43
Stal Mielec	34	12	15	7	41	28	39
Pogon Szczecin	34	15	9	10	35	33	39
GKS Katowice	34	13	11	10	52	36	37
Gornik Zabrze	34	11	13	10	43	40	35
Wisla Krakow	34	12	10	12	49	43	34
S. Tarnobrzeg	34	11	9	14	39	42	31
Zaglebie Lubin	34	10	10	14	48	41	30
Z. Bydgoszcz	34	12	6	16	41	60	30
Hutnik Krakow	34	6	13	13	40	46	29
Szombierk Bytom	34	8	7	19	31	59	23
Slask Wroclaw	34	9	5	20	33	74	23
Olimpia Poznan	34	7	7	20	28	56	21
Jag. Bialystock	34	2	5	27	28	91	9

† *Lech Poznan declared champions after Legia and LKS found guilty of match-fixing.*

5-Year One, Two, Three Records

	1st		Pts	2nd		Pts	3rd		Pts
1988-89	Ruch Chorzow		52	GKS Katowice		47	Gornik Zabrze		45
1989-90	Lech Poznan		42	Zaglebie Lubin		40	GKS Katowice		40
1990-91	Zaglebie Lubin		44	Gornik Zabrze		40	Wisla Krakow		40
1991-92	Lech Poznan		49	GKS Katowice		44	Widzew Lodz		43
1992-93	Lech Poznan		47	Legia Warsaw		49	LKS Lodz		49

5-Year Cup Final Results

1989	Legia Warsaw	5-2	Jagiellonia Bialystok	
1990	Legia Warsaw	2-0	GKS Katowice	
1991	GKS Katowice	1-0	Legia Warsaw	
1992	Miedz Legnica	1-1	Gornik Zabrze	4-3 on pens
1993	GKS Katowice	1-1	Ruch	5-4 on pens

International Results 1992-93

Date	Opponents	Result	Venue	Comp.	Scorers
26/08	Finland	0-0	Jakobstad	Frdly	
09/09	Israel	1-1	Mielec	Frdly	Szewczyk (24)
23/09	Turkey	1-0	Poznan	WCQ2	Waldoch (33)

14/10	Holland	2-2	Rotterdam	WCQ2	Kosecki (18), Kowalczyk (20)
18/11	Latvia	1-0	Llawa	Frdly	Mielcarski (70)
26/11	Argentina	0-2	Buenos Aires	Frdly	
29/11	Uruguay	1-0	Montevideo	Frdly	Jegor (84)
31/01	Cyprus	0-0	Nicosia	Frdly	
03/02	Isreal	0-0	Tel-Aviv	Frdly	
31/01	Cyprus	0-0	Nicosia	Frdly	
03/02	Israel	0-0	Tel-Aviv	Frdly	
17/03	Brazil	2-2	Riberao Prato	Frdly	Brzeczek (3), K. Warzycha (68)
31/03	Lithuania	1-1		Frdly	Swierczewski
13/04	Finland	2-1	Radom	Frdly	Lesniak (22, 32)
19/05	San Marino	3-0	Serravalle	WCQ2	Lesniak (52, 80), K. Warzycha (56)
29/05	England	1-1	Chorzow	WCQ2	Adamczuk (34)

National Record	P	W	D	L	F	A
EC	50	19	14	17	70	61
WC (Finals)	25	13	5	7	39	29
WC (Qualify)	53	29	10	14	103	17

(Includes Group 2 match v England 29/5/93)

PORTUGAL

Full Name: Federacao Portuguesa de Futebol **Founded:** 1914
Address: Praca de Alegria #25, Apartado 21.100, P-1128 Lisbon Codex,
 Portugal
Phone: (010 351) 1 328207/08/09 **Fax:** (010 351) 1 3467231
UEFA Affiliation: 1954 **FIFA Affiliation:** 1926
National Stadium: Estadio Nacional **Capacity:** 60,000
Colours: Red, Green, Red **Change:** White, Red, White

National League Final Table 1992-93

	P	W	D	L	F	A	Pts
FC Porto	34	24	6	4	59	17	54
Benfica	34	22	8	4	60	18	52
Sporting Lisbon	34	17	11	6	59	30	45
Boavista	34	14	11	9	46	34	39
Maritimo	34	15	7	12	56	48	37
Farense	34	11	13	10	41	36	35
Belenenses	34	11	12	11	42	40	34
Beira Mar	34	10	12	12	24	33	32

Gil Vicente	34	12	7	15	34	42	31
Pacos Ferreira	34	10	11	13	35	44	31
Guimaraes	34	14	3	17	41	53	31
Braga	34	12	6	16	33	34	30
Estoril	34	9	12	13	29	41	30
Famalicao	34	10	10	14	29	48	30
Salgueiros	34	10	9	15	28	44	29
Tirsense	34	10	8	16	27	37	28
Espinho	34	9	10	15	38	55	28
Chaves	34	4	8	22	34	61	16

5-Year One, Two, Three Records

	1st	Pts	2nd	Pts	3rd	Pts
1988-89	Benfica	63	FC Porto	56	Boavista	49
1989-90	FC Porto	59	Benfica	55	Sporting Lisbon	46
1990-91	Benfica	69	FC Porto	67	Sporting Lisbon	56
1991-92	FC Porto	56	Benfica	46	Sporting Lisbon	44
1992-93	FC Porto	54	Benfica	52	Sporting Lisbon	45

5-Year Cup Final Results

1989	Belenenses	2-1	Benfica
1990	Estrela da Amadora	2-0	Farense
1991	FC Porto	3-1	Beira Mar
1992	Boavista	2-1	FC Porto
1993	Benfica	5-2	Boavista

International Results 1992-93

Date	Opponents	Result	Venue	Comp.	Scorers
02/09	Austria	1-1	Linz	Frdly	Helder (56)
14/10	Scotland	0-0	Glasgow	WCQ1	
24/01	Malta	1-0	Valletta	WCQ1	Rui Aguas (58)
10/02	Norway	1-1	Faro	Frdly	Oceano (56)
24/02	Italy	1-3	Oporto	WCQ1	Couto (57)
31/03	Switzerland	1-1	Bern	WCQ1	Semedo (44)
19/06	Malta	4-0	Oporto	WCQ1	Nogueira (2), Rui Costa (9), Joao Pinto II (23), Cadete (87)

National Record	P	W	D	L	F	A
EC	59	28	14	17	75	65
WC (Finals)	9	6	0	3	19	12
WC (Qualify)	69	28	16	25	101	102

(Includes Group 1 match v Malta 19/6/93)

RCS (Representation of Czechs & Slovaks)

Full Name: Ceskoslovensky Fotbalovy Svaz   **Founded:** 1901
Address: NA Porici #12, 11530 Prague 1, Czech Republic
Phone: (010 42) 2 355358   **Fax:** (010 42) 2 352784
UEFA Affiliation: 1954   **FIFA Affiliation:** 1906
National Stadium: The Strahov   **Capacity:** 36,000
Colours: Red, White, Blue   **Change:** White, White, White

All Czech & Slovak League Final Table 1992-93

	P	W	D	L	F	A	Pts
Sparta Prague	30	23	2	5	66	24	48
Slavia Prague	30	18	7	5	70	28	43
Slovan Bratislava	30	17	4	7	61	30	42
Dunajska Streda	30	16	5	9	46	36	37
Sigma Olomouc	30	14	7	9	44	38	35
Internacional ZTS	30	14	3	13	46	42	31
FC Boby Brno	30	13	5	12	40	51	31
Banik Ostrava	30	10	11	9	47	38	31
Tatran Presov	30	9	8	13	42	40	28
Hradec Krelove	30	10	7	13	32	36	27
TJ Vitkovice	30	9	9	12	30	44	27
FC Nitra	30	6	13	10	27	38	25
Budejovice	30	9	5	16	36	39	23
Bohemians Prague	30	5	9	16	23	53	19
Dukla Prague	30	7	5	18	38	74	19
Spartak Trnava	30	3	10	17	24	60	16

5-Year One, Two, Three Records

	1st	Pts	2nd	Pts	3rd	Pts
1988-89	Sparta Prague	45	Banik Ostrava	42	Plastika Nitra	34
1989-90	Sparta Prague	46	Banik Ostrava	41	Internacional ZTS	36
1990-91	Sparta Prague	39	Slovan Bratislava	38	Sigma Olomouc	37
1991-91	Slovan Bratislava	51	Sparta Prague	47	Slavia Prague	43
1992-93	Sparta Prague	50	Slavia Prague	43	Slovan Bratislava	42

5-Year Cup Final Results

1989	Sparta Prague	3-0	Slovan Bratislava	
1990	Dukla Prague	1-1	Internacional ZTS	5-4 on pens
1991	Banik Ostrava	6-1	Spartak Trnava	
1992	Sparta Prague	2-1	Tatran Presov	
1993	Kosice	5-1	Sparta Prague	RCS Cup Final

Sparta Prague	2-0	FC Boby Brno	Czech Cup Final	
Kosice	0-0	Dunajska Streda	Slovak Cup Final	

Kosice win 5-4 on penalties

International Results 1992-93

Date	Opponents	Result	Venue	Comp.	Scorers
19/08	Austria	2-2	Bratislava	Frdly	Chovanec (42), Moravcik (89)
02/09	Belgium	1-2	Prague	WCQ4	M. Kadlec (77)
23/09	Faeroe Islands	4-0	Kosice	WCQ4	Nemecek (24), Kuka (85, 87), Dubovsky (89 pen)
14/11	Romania	1-1	Bucharest	WCQ4	Nemecek (79)
24/03	Cyprus	1-1	Limassol	WCQ4	Moravcik (33)
02/06	Romania	5-2	Kosice	WCQ4	Vrabec (13), Latal (37), Dubovsky (58, 83, 89)
16/06	Faeroe Islands	3-0	Toftir	WCQ4	Hasek (3), Postulka (38, 44)

National Record	P	W	D	L	F	A
EC	64	34	16	14	119	58
WC (Finals)	30	11	5	14	44	45
WC (Qualify)	68	39	14	15	141	61

(Includes Group 4 match v Faeroe Islands 16/6/93)

REPUBLIC OF IRELAND

Full Name: The Football Association of Ireland   **Founded:** 1921
Address: 80 Merrion Square, South Dublin 2, Republic of Ireland
Phone: (010 353) 1 766864   **Fax:** (010 353) 1 610931
UEFA Affiliation: 1954   **FIFA Affiliation:** 1923
National Stadium: Dalymount Park   **Capacity:** 22,000
Colours: Green, White, Green   **Change:** White, Green, White

National League Tables 1992-93

Final Round	P	W	D	L	F	A	Pts
Bohemians	32	13	14	5	46	19	40
Shelbourne	32	15	10	7	53	29	40
Cork City	32	16	8	8	47	34	40
Dundalk	32	13	13	6	35	28	39
Derry City	32	11	15	6	26	23	37
Limerick City	32	6	15	11	27	31	27

Title Round	P	W	D	L	F	A	Pts
Shelbourne	4	1	2	1	3	3	4
Bohemians	4	1	2	1	2	2	4
Cork City	4	1	2	1	2	2	4

Play-offs: Cork City v Bohemians 1-0; Cork City v Shelbourne 3-2; Bohemians v Shelbourne 1-0. Cork City champions.

5-Year One, Two, Three Records

	1st ....Pts	2nd ....Pts	3rd ....Pts
1988-89	Derry City.........53	Dundalk.........51	Limerick City.....45
1989-90	St Patrick's Ath...52	Derry City.........49	Dundalk.........42
1990-91	Dundalk.........52	Cork City.........50	St Patrick's Ath...44
1991-92	Shelbourne.........49	Derry City.........44	Cork City.........43
1992-93	Cork City won play-offs		

5-Year Cup Final Results

1989	Derry City	1-0	Cork City	after 0-0 draw
1990	Bray Wanderers	3-0	St Francis	
1991	Galway United	1-0	Shamrock Rovers	
1992	Bohemians	1-0	Cork City	
1993	Shelbourne	1-0	Dundalk	

International Results 1992-93

Date	Opponents	Result	Venue	Comp.	Scorers
09/09	Latvia	4-0	Dublin	WCQ3	Sheedy (30), Aldridge (59, 82 pen, 86)
14/10	Denmark	0-0	Copenhagen	WCQ3	
18/11	Spain	0-0	Seville	WCQ3	
17/02	Wales	2-1	Dublin	Frdly	Sheedy (75), Coyne (81)
31/03	N. Ireland	3-0	Dublin	WCQ3	Townsend (20), Quinn (22), Staunton (28)
28/04	Denmark	1-1	Dublin	WCQ3	Quinn (75)
26/05	Albania	2-1	Tirana	WCQ3	Staunton (13), Cascarino (77)
09/06	Latvia	2-0	Riga	WCQ3	Aldridge (14), McGrath (42)
16/06	Lithuania	1-0	Vilnius	WCQ3	Staunton (38)

National Record	P	W	D	L	F	A
EC	59	21	17	21	84	77
WC (Finals)	5	0	4	1	2	3
WC (Qualify)	70	25	16	29	91	105

(Includes Group 3 match v Lithuania 16/6/93)

ROMANIA

Full Name: Federatia Romana de Fotbal   **Founded:** 1908
Address: Vasile Conta #16, Bucharest R-70130, Romania
Phone: (010 40) 0 107090   **Fax:** (010 40) 0 117075
UEFA Affiliation: 1954   **FIFA Affiliation:** 1930
National Stadium: Stadionul 23 August, Bucharest   **Capacity:** 65,000
Colours: Yellow, Blue, Red   **Change:** Blue, Yellow, Red

National League Final Table 1992-93

	P	W	D	L	F	A	Pts
Steaua Bucharest	34	25	7	2	84	22	57
Dinamo Bucharest	34	23	7	4	82	40	53
Univ Craiova	34	15	9	10	40	33	39
Gloria	34	15	5	14	45	41	35
Electro Craiova	34	13	9	12	35	32	35
Sportul	34	13	8	13	40	43	34
Inter Sibiu	34	11	11	12	40	46	33
Farul	34	14	4	16	57	66	32
Otelul	34	13	6	15	40	49	32
Cluj	34	14	2	18	43	51	30
Brasov	34	12	6	16	36	45	30
Timisoara	34	8	13	13	34	46	29
Braila	34	10	9	15	36	51	29
Progresul	34	9	11	14	38	53	29
Petrolul	34	12	3	19	47	50	27
Bacau	34	8	9	17	24	44	25
Reista	34	9	3	22	34	73	21

5-Year One, Two, Three Records

	1st	Pts	2nd	Pts	3rd	Pts
1988-89	Steaua Bucharest	65	Dinamo Bucharest	62	Victoria Bucharest	45
1989-90	Dinamo Bucharest	57	Steaua Bucharest	56	Univ Craiova	44
1990-91	Univ Craiova	50	Steaua Bucharest	50	Dinamo Bucharest	43
1991-92	Dinamo Bucharest	55	Steaua Bucharest	48	Electro Craiova	39
1992-93	Steaua Bucharest	48	Dinamo Bucharest	47	Univ Craiova	37

5-Year Cup Final Results

1989	Steaua Bucharest	1-0	Dinamo Bucharest	
1990	Dinamo Bucharest	6-4	Steaua Bucharest	
1991	Univ Craiova	2-1	Bacau	
1992	Steaua Bucharest	1-1	Timisoara	4-3 on pens
1993	Univ Craiova	2-0	Braila	

International Results 1992-93

Date	Opponents	Result	Venue	Comp.	Scorers
26/08	Mexico	2-0	Bucharest	Frdly	Varga (44), Dumitrescu (84)
14/10	Belgium	0-1	Brussels	WCQ4	
14/11	RCS	1-1	Bucharest	WCQ4	Dumitrescu (48)
29/11	Cyprus	4-1	Larnaca	WCQ4	Popescu (4), Raducioiu (36), Hagi (73), Hanganu (86)
31/01	Ecuador	0-3	Guayaquil	Frdly	
03/02	Peru	2-0	Lima	Frdly	Hanganu (44), Dumitrescu (49)
06/02	United States	1-1	Santa Barbara	Frdly	Dumitrescu (39)
10/02	Mexico	0-2	Monterrey	Frdly	
14/04	Cyprus	2-1	Bucharest	WCQ4	Dumitrescu (33, 55)
02/06	RCS	2-5	Kosice	WCQ4	Raducioiu (26, 55)

National Record	P	W	D	L	F	A
EC	58	25	16	17	96	66
WC (Finals)	12	3	3	6	16	19
WC (Qualify)	61	30	14	17	103	64

(Includes Group 4 match v RCS 2/6/93)

RUSSIA (CIS)

Full Name: The Russian Football Federation   **Founded:** 1912
Address: Luzhnetskaja Naberzhnaja #8, 119871 GSP-3 Moscow
Phone: (010 7) 095 2010834   **Fax:** (010 7) 095 2480814
UEFA Affiliation: 1954   **FIFA Affiliation:** 1946
National Stadium: Centralny Stadion **Capacity:** 100,000
Colours: Red, White, Red   **Change:** White, White, White

National League Final Table 1992-93

	P	W	D	L	F	A	Pts
Spartak Moscow	14	10	4	0	36	12	24
Vladikavkaz	14	7	3	4	26	20	17
Dynamo Moscow	14	6	4	4	23	21	16
Lokomotiv Moscow	14	5	5	4	14	15	15
CSKA Moscow	14	5	4	5	25	19	14
Novgorod	14	2	7	5	10	18	11
Asmaral Moscow	14	3	3	8	17	36	9
Rostov	14	1	4	9	9	16	6

4-Year One, Two, Three Records

	1st ....Pts	2nd...............Pts	3rd ....Pts
1989	Spartak Moscow .44	Dnepr Dnep'sk ..42	Dynamo Kiev 38
1990	Dynamo Kiev 34	CSKA Moscow ..31	Dynamo Moscow31
1991	CSKA Moscow ..43	Spartak Moscow.41	Torpedo Moscow36
1992-93	Spartak Moscow.24	Vladikavkaz........17	Dynamo Moscow16

5-Year Cup Final Results

1989	Dnepr Dnepropetrovsk	1-0	Torpedo Moscow	
1990	Dynamo Kiev	6-1	Lokomotiv Moscow	
1991	CSKA Moscow	3-2	Torpedo Moscow	
1992	Spartak Moscow	2-0	CSKA Moscow	
1993	Torpedo Moscow	1-1	CSKA Moscow	5-4 on pens

International Results (Russia) 1992-93

Date	Opponents	Result	Venue	Comp.	Scorers
12/06	Germany	1-1	Norrkoping	EC Grp 2	Dobrovolski (62pen)
15/06	Holland	0-0	Gothenburg	EC Grp 2	
18/06	Scotland	0-3	Norrkoping	EC Grp 2	
17/08	Mexico	2-0	Moscow	Frdly	Karpin (61 pen), Popov (66)
14/10	Iceland	1-0	Moscow	WCQ5	Yuran (64)
28/10	Luxembourg	2-0	Moscow	WCQ5	Yuran (4), Radchenko (23)
13/02	United States	1-0	Orlando	Frdly	Sergeyev (12)
18/02	El Salvador	2-1	Los Angeles	Frdly	Onopko (53), Tedayev (55)
21/02	United States	0-0	Palo Alto	Frdly	
24/03	Israel	2-2	Haifa	Frdly	Popov (50, 61)
14/04	Luxembourg	4-0	Luxembourg	WCQ5	Kiriakov (12, 46), Shalimov (57), Polster (89)
28/04	Hungary	3-0	Moscow	WCQ5	Kanchelskis (55), Kolivanov (60), Yuran (86)
23/05	Greece	1-1	Moscow	WCQ5	Dobrovolski (75 pen)
02/06	Iceland	1-1	Reykjavik	WCQ5	Kiriakov (38)

National Record	P	W	D	L	F	A
(Including record as CIS)						
EC	74	41	20	13	121	57
WC (Finals)	31	15	6	10	53	35
WC (Qualify)	58	39	11	8	112	34

(Includes Group 5 match v Iceland 2/6/93)

SAN MARINO

Full Name: Federazione Sammarinese Giuoco Calcio   **Founded:** 1931
Address: Via Ca dei Lunghi 18, Cailungo, 47031 San Marino
Phone: (010 39) 549 902228   **Fax:** (010 39) 549 906226
UEFA Affiliation: 1988   **FIFA Affiliation:** 1988
National Stadium: Seravalle   **Capacity:** 7,000
Colours: Sky Blue, Sky Blue, Sky Blue

International Results 1992-93

Date	Opponents	Result	Venue	Comp.	Scorers
09/09	Norway	0-10	Oslo	WCQ2	
07/10	Norway	0-2	Serravalle	WCQ2	
28/10	Turkey	1-4	Ankara	WCQ2	Bacciocchi (53)
17/02	England	0-6	Wembley	WCQ2	
10/03	Turkey	0-0	Serravalle	WCQ2	
24/03	Holland	0-6	Utrecht	WCQ2	
19/05	Poland	0-3	Serravalle	WCQ2	

National Record	P	W	D	L	F	A
EC	8	0	0	8	1	33
WC (Finals)	Never qualified					
WC (Qualify)	8	0	1	7	1	32

(Includes Group 2 match v Poland 19/5/93)

SCOTLAND

Full Name: The Scottish Football Association   **Founded:** 1873
Address: 6 Park Gardens, Glasgow, G3 7YF, Scotland
Phone: (010 44) 41 3326372   **Fax:** (010 44) 41 3327559
UEFA Affiliation: 1954   **FIFA Affiliation:** 1910-20, 1924-28, 1946
National Stadium: Hampden Park, Glasgow   **Capacity:** 74,000
Colours: Blue, White, Red   **Change:** White, Blue, Red

National League Final Table 1992-93

	P	W	D	L	F	A	Pts
Rangers	44	33	7	4	97	35	73
Aberdeen	44	27	10	7	87	36	64
Celtic	44	24	12	8	68	41	60
Dundee United	44	19	9	16	56	49	47
Heart of Midlothian	44	15	14	15	46	51	44
St. Johnstone	44	10	20	14	52	66	40
Hibernian	44	12	13	19	54	64	37

Partick Thistle	44	12	12	20	50	71	36
Motherwell	44	11	13,	20	46	62	35
Dundee	44	11	12	21	48	68	34
Falkirk	44	11	7	26	60	86	29
Airdrieonians	44	6	17	21	35	70	29

5-Year One, Two, Three Records

	1st	*Pts*	*2nd*	*Pts*	*3rd*	*Pts*
1988-89	Rangers	56	Aberdeen	50	Celtic	46
1989-90	Rangers	51	Aberdeen	44	Heart of Mid.	44
1990-91	Rangers	55	Aberdeen	53	Celtic	41
1991-92	Rangers	72	Heart of Mid	63	Celtic	62
1992-93	Rangers	73	Aberdeen	64	Celtic	60

5-Year Cup Final Results

1989	Celtic	1-0	Rangers	
1990	Aberdeen	0-0	Celtic	9-8 on pens
1991	Motherwell	4-3	Dundee United	
1992	Rangers	2-1	Airdrieonians	
1993	Rangers	2-1	Aberdeen	

International Results 1992-93

Date	*Opponents*	*Result*	*Venue*	*Comp.*	*Scorers*
12/06	Holland	0-1	Gothenburg	EC Grp 2	
15/06	Germany	0-2	Norrkoping	EC Grp 2	McStay (6),
18/06	Russia	3-0	Norrkoping	EC Grp 2	McClair (17), McAllister (84 pen)
09/09	Switzerland	1-3	Bern	WCQ1	McCoist (15)
14/10	Portugal	0-0	Glasgow	WCQ1	
18/11	Italy	0-0	Glasgow	WCQ1	
17/02	Malta	3-0	Glasgow	WCQ1	McCoist (15, 68), Nevin (84)
24/03	Germany	0-1	Glasgow	Frdly	
19/05	Estonia	3-0	Tallinn	WCQ1	Gallacher (43), Collins (59), Booth (73)
02/06	Estonia	3-1	Aberdeen	WCQ1	McClair (18), Nevin (27, 72 pen)

National Record	*P*	*W*	*D*	*L*	*F*	*A*
EC	48	19	14	15	66	56
WC (Finals)	23	5	6	12	26	38
WC (Qualify)	66	36	12	18	121	81

(Includes Group 1 match v Estonia 19/5/93)

SLOVENIA

Full Name: Nogometna Zveza Slovenije
Address: Tabor 14, PP47. 61004 Ljubljana, Slovenia.
Phone: 38-61/31 18 88   Fax: 28-61/30 23 37

National League Final Table 1992-93

	P	W	D	L	F	A	Pts
Olimpija Ljubljana	34	22	8	4	94	20	52
Branik Maribor	34	18	12	4	49	19	48
Mura	34	19	8	7	60	28	46
Ljubljana	34	16	8	10	44	34	40
Naklo	34	15	10	9	54	47	40
Kompas	34	14	10	10	38	33	38
Studio	34	13	12	9	35	30	38
Koper	34	11	13	10	40	44	35
Rudar	34	13	7	14	45	52	33
Publikum	34	12	8	14	37	47	32
Slovan Mavtica	34	9	13	12	45	43	31
Gorica	34	11	9	14	39	46	31
Isola	34	10	10	14	45	45	30
Potrosnik	34	12	5	17	51	62	29
Zagorje	34	10	8	16	29	40	28
Steklar	34	4	14	16	33	72	22
Zeleznicar	34	6	8	20	30	62	20
Nafta	34	6	7	21	30	64	19

Cup Final Result

1993   Olimpija Ljubljana   2-1   Publikum

International Results 1992-93

Date	Opponents	Result	Venue	Comp.	Scorers
03/06	Estonia	1-1	Tallinn	Frdly	Benedejcic (73)
18/11	Cyprus	1-1	Larnaca	Frdly	Nilosevic (55)

National Record	P	W	D	L	F.	A
EC	Never participated					
WC (Finals)	Never participated					
WC (Qualify)	Never participated					

SPAIN

Full Name: Real Federacion Espanola de Futbol   **Fonded:** 1913
Address: Calle Alberto Bosch #13, Apartado Postal 347, E-28014 Madrid
Phone: (010 34) 1 4201362   **Fax:** (010 34) 1 4202094
UEFA Affiliation: 1954   **FIFA Affiliation:** 1904
Colours: Red, Blue, Black   **Change:** Blue, Blue, Black

National League Final Table 1992-93

	P	W	D	L	F	A	Pts
Barcelona	38	25	8	5	87	34	58
Real Madrid	38	24	9	5	75	28	57
La Coruna	38	22	10	6	67	33	54
Valencia	38	19	10	9	60	33	48
Tenerife	38	15	14	9	59	47	44
Atletico Madrid	38	17	9	12	46	44	43
Sevilla	38	17	9	12	46	44	43
Athletic Bilbao	38	17	6	15	53	49	40
Real Zaragoza	38	11	13	14	37	52	35
Osasuna	38	12	10	16	41	41	34
Celta	38	9	16	13	25	31	34
Real Sociedad	38	13	8	17	46	59	34
Sporting Gijon	38	11	12	15	38	57	34
Rayo Vallecano	38	8	17	13	40	49	33
Logrones	38	11	11	16	32	48	33
Oviedo	38	11	10	17	42	52	32
Albacete	38	11	9	18	54	59	31
Espanol	38	9	11	18	40	56	29
Cadiz	38	4	14	20	29	69	22
Burgos	38	4	14	20	29	69	22

Leading Scorers

30 Bebeto (La Coruna); 27 Zamorano (Real Madrid); 20 Stoichkov
(Barcelona), Penev (Valencia), Luis Garcia (Atletico Madrid); 15 Pizzi
(Tenerife), Beguiristain (Barcelona).

5-Year One, Two Three Records

	1st	Pts	2nd	Pts	3rd	Pts
1988-89	Real Madrid	62	Barcelona	57	Valencia	49
1989-90	Real Madrid	62	Valencia	53	Barcelona	51
1990-91	Barcelona	57	Atletico Madrid	47	Real Madrid	46
1991-92	Barcelona	55	Real Madrid	54	Atletico Madrid	53
1992-93	Barcelona	58	Real Madrid	57	La Coruna	54

5-Year Cup Final Results

1989	Real Madrid	1-0	Valladolid
1990	Barcelona	2-0	Real Madrid
1991	Atletico Madrid	1-0	Mallorca
1992	Atletico Madrid	2-0	Real Madrid
1993	Real Madrid	2-0	Real Zaragoza

International Results 1992-93

Date	Opponents	Result	Venue	Comp.	Scorers
09/09	England	1-0	Santander	Frdly	Fonseca (11)
23/09	Latvia	0-0	Riga	WCQ3	
14/10	N. Ireland	0-0	Belfast	WCQ3	
18/11	Rep. Ireland	0-0	Seville	WCQ3	
16/12	Latvia	5-0	Seville	WCQ3	Bakero (49), Guardiola (51), Alfonso (69), Beguiristain (81, 82)
27/01	Mexico	1-1	Las Palmas	Frdly	Suarez (44)
24/02	Lithuania	5-0	Seville	WCQ3	Crostobal (5), Bakero (13), Beguiristain (18), Christiansen (86), Aldana (89)
31/03	Denmark	0-1	Copenhagen	WCQ3	
28/04	N. Ireland	3-1	Seville	WCQ3	Salinas (21, 26), Hierro (41)
02/06	Lithuania	2-0	Vilnius	WCQ3	Guerreiro (73, 77)

National Record	P	W	D	L	F	A
EC	70	37	15	18	136	71
WC (Finals)	32	13	7	12	43	37
WC (Qualify)	63	38	9	16	117	58

(Includes Group 3 match v Lithuania 2/6/93)

SWEDEN

Full Name: Svenska Fotbollfoerbrundet   **Founded:** 1904
Address: Bos 1216, S-17123 Solna, Sweden
Phone: (010 46) 8 7350900   **Fax:** (010 46) 8 275147
UEFA Affiliation: 1954   **FIFA Affiliation:** 1904
National Stadium: Rasunda Stadion **Capacity:** 41,000
Colours: Yellow, Blue, Yellow   **Change:** Blue, Blue, Blue

National League Final Table 1992-93

Final Round	P	W	D	L	F	A	Pts
AIK	10	6	2	2	23	11	34
Norrkoping	10	4	2	4	14	18	32
Osters	10	4	2	4	18	17	30
Trelleborg	10	4	0	6	23	29	26
IFK Gothenburg	10	4	1	5	17	17	25
Malmo	10	3	2	5	11	14	24

4-Year One, Two, Three Records

	1st	Pts	2nd		Pts	3rd	Pts
1989-90	Norrkoping	0-2	1-0	0-0	Malmo		4-3pen
1990-91	IFK Gothenburg	3-0	0-0		Norrkoping		
1991-92	IFK Gothenburg	.36	Norrkoping		31	Orebro SK	28
1992-93	AIK	34	Norrkoping		32	Osters	30

5-Year Cup Final Results

1989	Malmo FF	3-0	Djurgardens
1990	Djurgardens IF	2-0	Hacken BK
1991	Norrkoping	4-1	Osters
1992	IFK Gothenburg	3-2	AIK
1993	Degersfors	3-0	Landskrona

International Results 1992-93

Date	Opponents	Result	Venue	Comp.	Scorers
10/06	France	1-1	Stockholm	EC Grp 1	Eriksson (25)
14/06	Denmark	1-0	Stockholm	EC Grp 1	Brolin (59)
17/06	England	2-1	Stockholm	EC Grp 1	Eriksson (51), Brolin (82)
21/06	Germany	2-3	Stockholm	EC SF	Brolin (64 pen), Andersson (89)
26/08	Norway	2-2	Oslo	Frdly	Dahlin (30), Pettersson (63)
09/09	Finland	1-0	Helsinki	WCQ6	Ingesson (79 pen)
07/10	Bulgaria	2-0	Stockholm	WCQ6	Dahlin (56), Pettersson (76)
11/11	Israel	3-1	Tel Aviv	WCQ6	Limpar (37), Dahlin (58), Ingesson (74)
15/04	Hungary	2-0	Budapest	Frdly	Ekstrom (67), Rehn (87)
19/05	Austria	1-0	Stockholm	WCQ6	Eriksson (50)
02/06	Israel	5-0	Stockholm	WCQ6	Brolin (17, 41, 65), Zetterberg (55), Landberg (89)

National Record	P	W	D	L	F	A
EC	50	21	12	17	69	61
WC (Finals)	31	11	6	14	51	52
WC (Qualify)	63	38	9	16	134	65

(Includes Group 6 match v Israel 2/6/93)

SWITZERLAND

Full Name: Schweizerischer Fussballverband   **Founded:** 1895
Address: Maison du Football Suisse, Worbstrasse 48,
                3074 Muri BE, Switzerland
Phone: (010 31) 950 8111   **Fax:** (010 31) 950 8181
UEFA Affiliation: 1954   **FIFA Affiliation:** 1904
National Stadium: Wankdorf, Bern **Capacity:** 58,000
Colours: Red, White, Red   **Change:** White, White, Red

National League Final Table 1992-93

	P	W	D	L	F	A	Pts
FC Aarau	14	9	4	1	21	7	34
Young Boys	14	5	4	5	15	15	28
Lugano	14	7	2	5	21	14	27
Servette	14	5	3	6	16	19	27
Grasshoppers Zurich	14	5	4	5	13	14	26
Neuchatel Xamax	14	4	5	5	16	16	24
Sion	14	4	3	7	17	22	24
Lausanne	14	3	3	8	11	23	21

5-Year One, Two, Three Records

	1st	Pts	2nd	Pts	3rd	Pts
1988-89	FC Lucerne	33	Grasshoppers	30	Sion	29
1989-90	Grasshoppers	31	Lausanne	31	Neuch. Xamax	30
1990-91	Grasshoppers	33	Sion	29	Neuch. Xamax	29
1991-92	Sion	33	Neuch. Xamax	31	Grasshoppers	30
1992-93	FC Aarau	34	Young Boys	28	Lugano	27

5-Year Cup Final Results

1989	Grasshoppers Zurich	2-1	FC Aarau
1990	Grasshoppers Zurich	2-1	Neuchatel Xamax
1991	FC Sion	3-2	Young Boys
1992	FC Lucerne	3-1	Lugano
1993	Lugano	4-1	Grasshoppers Zurich

International Results 1992-93

Date	Opponents	Result	Venue	Comp.	Scorers
16/08	Estonia	6-0	Tallinn	WCQ3	Chapuisat (23, 68), Bregy (29), Knup (46), Ohrel (66), Sforza (84)
09/09	Scotland	3-1	Bern	WCQ1	Krup (2, 71), Bregy (81)
14/10	Italy	2-2	Cagliari	WCQ1	Ohrel (17), Chapuisat (21)
18/11	Malta	3-0	Bern	WCQ1	Bickel (2), Sforza (42), Chapuisat (89)
23/01	Japan	1-1	Hong Kong	CC † SF	B. Sutter (56)
26/01	Hong Kong	3-2	Hong Kong	CC † F	not known
17/03	Tunisia	1-0	Tunis	Frdly	Knup (87)
31/03	Portugal	1-1	Bern	WCQ1	Chapuisat (39)
17/04	Malta	2-0	Valletta	WCQ1	Ohrel (31), Turkyilmaz (89)
01/05	Italy	1-0	Bern	WCQ1	Hottiger (55)

† Carlsberg Challenge

National Record	P	W	D	L	F	A
EC	50	16	13	21	78	75
WC (Finals)	18	5	2	11	28	44
WC (Qualify)	67	27	17	23	90	90

(Includes Group 1 match v Italy 1/5/93)

TURKEY

Full Name: Turkiye Futbol Federasyonu **Founded:** 1923
Address: Konur Sokak #10, Kizilay-Ankara, Turkey
Phone: (010 90) 4 1259182 **Fax:** (010 90) 4 1171090
UEFA Affiliation: 1962 **FIFA Affiliation:** 1923
National Stadium: Inonu Stadi, Ankara **Capacity:** 30,000
Colours: White, White, Red and White **Change:** Red, White, Red and White

National League Final Table 1992-93

	P	W	D	L	F	A	Pts
Galatasaray	30	21	5	4	80	20	68
Besiktas	30	8	10	2	67	20	64
Kocaelispor	30	18	8	4	62	24	62
Trabzonspor	30	15	11	4	54	27	56

Fenerbahce	29	17	5	7	56	37	56
Bursaspor	30	14	7	9	42	35	49
Altay	30	12	5	13	37	38	41
Genclerbirligi	30	9	9	12	39	54	36
Gaziantepspor	30	11	3	16	41	57	36
Sariyer	30	10	5	15	41	44	35
Ankaragucu	30	9	4	17	37	61	31
Karsiyaka	30	7	9	14	39	48	30
Kayserispor	30	7	6	17	27	57	27
Bakirkoyspor	29	5	11	13	30	41	26
Aydinspor	29	6	7	16	19	53	25
Konyaspor	29	2	9	18	27	82	15

5-Year One, Two, Three Records

	1st	Pts	2nd	Pts	3rd	Pts
1988-89	Fenerbahce	90	Besiktas	80	Galatasaray	66
1989-90	Besiktas	75	Fenerbahce	70	Trabzonspor	68
1990-91	Besiktas	69	Galatasaray	64	Trabzonspor	51
1991-92	Besiktas	76	Fenerbahce	71	Galatasaray	60
1992-93	Galatasaray	68	Besiktas	64	Kocaelispor	62

5-Year Cup Final Results

1989	Besiktas	1-0	2-1	Fenerbahce		3-1 on agg
1990	Besiktas	2-0		Trabzonspor		
1991	Galatasaray	3-1		MKE Ankaragucu		
1992	Trabzonspor	0-3	5-1	Bursaspor		5-4 on agg
1993	Galatasaray	1-0	2-2	Besiktas		3-2 on agg

International Results 1992-93

Date	Opponents	Result	Venue	Comp.	Scorers
26/08	Bulgaria	3-2	Trabzon	Frdly	Hami (67), Hakan (71, 72)
23/09	Poland	0-1	Poznan	WCQ2	
28/10	San Marino	4-1	Ankara	WCQ2	Hakan (37, 89), Orhan (87), Hami (90)
18/11	England	0-4	Wembley	WCQ2	
16/12	Holland	1-3	Istanbul	WCQ2	Feyyaz (60)
24/02	Holland	1-3	Utrecht	WCQ2	Feyyaz (36 pen)
10/03	San Marino	0-0	Serravalle	WCQ2	
31/03	England	0-2	Izmir	WCQ2	
28/04	Norway	1-3	Oslo	WCQ2	Feyyaz (57)

National Record	P	W	D	L	F	A
EC	48	12	9	27	31	92
WC (Finals)	3	1	0	2	10	11
WC (Qualify)	62	13	7	42	57	123

(Includes Group 2 match v Norway 28/4/93)

UKRAINE

Full Name: Football Federation of Ukraine
Address: 42 Kuybysheva Street, 252023 Kiev 23, Ukraine
Phone: 044/220 1344   **Fax:** 044/220 1294

National League Final Table 1992-93

	P	W	D	L	F	A	Pts
Dynamo Kiev	30	18	8	4	59	14	44
Dnipro	30	18	8	4	51	20	44
Chernomorets	30	17	4	9	43	31	38
Shakhtyor	30	11	12	7	44	32	34
Metalist	30	12	7	11	37	34	31
Karpaty	30	10	10	10	37	38	30
Metalurg	30	10	9	11	38	35	29
Kryvbas	30	8	11	11	27	40	27
Kremin	30	8	11	11	23	40	27
Bukovina	30	9	8	13	27	32	26
Tavria	30	11	4	15	30	39	26
Volyn	30	10	6	14	37	54	26
Nyva	30	8	9	13	22	25	25
Torpedo	30	9	7	14	32	36	25
Veres	30	9	6	15	29	39	24
Zorya	30	10	4	16	26	46	24

Cup Final Result

1993	Dynamo Kiev	2-1	Karpaty

International Results 1992-93

Date	Opponents	Result	Venue	Comp.	Scorers
27/06	United States	0-0	New Jersey	Frdly	
26/08	Hungary	1-2	Nyiregyhaza	Frdly	Gudimenko (35)
28/10	Byelorussia	1-1	Minsk	Frdly	Maximov (78)
18/05	Lithuania	2-1	Vilnius	Frdly	Leonenko (18), Mikhailichenko (22)

WALES

Full Name: The Football Association of Wales   Founded: 1876
Address: Plymouth Chambers, 3 Westgate Street, Cardiff CF1 1DD
Phone: (010 44) 222 372325   Fax: (010 44) 222 343961
UEFA Affiliation: 1954   FIFA Affiliation: 1910-20, 1924-28, 1946
National Stadium: Cardiff Arms Park   Capacity: 58,000
Colours: Red, Red, Red   Change: Yellow Yellow, Yellow

National League Final Table 1992-93

	P	W	D	L	F	A	Pts
Cwmbran	38	26	9	3	69	22	87
Inter Cardiff	38	26	5	7	79	36	83
Aberystwyth Town	38	25	3	10	85	49	78
Ebbw Vale	38	19	9	10	76	61	66
Bangor City	38	19	7	12	77	58	64
Holywell Town	38	17	8	13	65	48	59
Conwy United	38	16	9	13	51	51	57
Connah's Quay Nomads	38	17	4	17	66	67	55
Porthmadog	38	14	11	13	61	49	53
Haverfordwest County	38	16	5	17	66	66	53
Caersws	38	14	10	14	64	60	52
Afan Lido	38	14	10	14	64	65	52
Mold Alexandra *	38	16	4	18	63	69	49
Llanelli	38	11	8	19	49	64	41
Maesteg Park Athletic	38	9	13	16	52	59	40
Flint Town Utd	38	11	6	21	47	67	39
Briton Ferry Athletic	38	10	9	19	61	87	39
Newtown	38	9	9	20	55	87	36
Llanidloes Town	38	7	9	22	48	93	30
Abergavenny Thursdays	38	7	7	24	36	76	28

* Three points deducted

5-Year Cup Final Results

1989	Swansea City	5-0	Kidderminster Harriers
1990	Hereford United	2-1	Wrexham
1991	Swansea City	2-0	Wrexham
1992	Cardiff City	1-0	Hednesford Town
1993	Cardiff City	5-0	Rhyl

International Results 1992-93

Date	Opponents	Result	Venue	Comp.	Scorers
09/09	Faeroe Islands	6-0	Cardiff	WCQ4	Rush (5, 64, 89), Saunders (28), Bowen (37), Blackmore (71)
14/10	Cyprus	1-0	Nicosia	WCQ4	Hughes (51)
18/11	Belgium	0-2	Brussels	WCQ4	
17/02	Rep. Ireland	1-2	Dublin	Frdly	Hughes (18)
31/03	Belgium	2-0	Cardiff	WCQ4	Giggs (18), Rush (39)
06/06	Faeroe Islands	3-0	Toftir	WCQ4	Saunders (22), Young (31), Rush (69)

National Record	P	W	D	L	F	A
EC	46	19	11	16	61	54
WC (Finals)	5	1	3	1	4	4
WC (Qualify)	59	20	10	29	75	80

(Includes Group 4 match v Faeroe Islands 6/6/93)

European Super Cup
1972-92

The European Super Cup is played annually between the holders of the Champions' Cup and the Cup-Winners' Cup. Games are normally played on a two-leg basis with the aggregate score deciding the winners.

Year	Winners	1st	2nd	Agg	Runners-up
1972	Ajax	3-1	3-2	6-3	Rangers
1973	Ajax	0-1	6-0	6-1	Milan
1974	–				
1975	Dynamo Kiev	1-0	2-0	3-0	Bayern Munich
1976	RSC Anderlecht	1-2	4-1	5-3	Bayern Munich
1977	Liverpool	1-1	6-0	7-1	Hamburg
1978	RSC Anderlecht	3-1	1-2	4-3	Liverpool
1979	Nottingham Forest	1-0	1-1	2-1	Barcelona
1980	Valencia	1-2	1-0	2-2	Nottingham Forest
1981	–				
1982	Aston Villa	0-1	3-0	3-1	Barcelona
1983	Aberdeen	0-0	2-0	2-0	Hamburg
1984	Juventus			2-0	Liverpool
1985	–				
1986	Steaua Bucharest			1-0	Dynamo Kiev
1987	FC Porto	1-0	1-0	2-0	Ajax
1988	KV Mechelen	3-0	0-1	3-1	PSV Eindhoven
1989	Milan	1-1	1-0	2-1	Barcelona
1990	Milan	1-1	2-0	3-1	Sampdoria
1991	Manchester United			1-0	Red Star Belgrade
1992	Barcelona	1-1	2-1	3-2	Werder Bremen

World Club Championship 1960-92

The World Club Championship is played annually between the holders of the European Champions' Cup and the South American Champions' Cup (Libertadores Cup). The event has traditionally been a violent affair and it is not uncommon for the European Champions to decline an invitation to meet their South American counterparts. From 1960 to 1979 the tournament was played on a two-leg home and away basis. Since 1980 the event has been staged as a one-off final in Tokyo and has recently been sponsored by Toyota.

Finals at a Glance

Year	Winners	1st	2nd	Play-off	Runners-up
1960	Real Madrid	0-0	5-1		Penarol
1961	Penarol	0-1	5-0	2-1	Benfica
1962	Santos	3-2	5-2		Benfica
1963	Santos	2-4	4-2	1-0	Milan
1964	Internazionale	0-1	2-0	1-0	Independiente
1965	Internazionale	3-0	0-0		Independiente
1966	Penarol	2-0	2-0		Real Madrid
1967	Racing Club	0-1	2-1	1-0	Celtic
1968	Estudiantes LP	1-0	1-1		Manchester United
1969	Milan	3-0	1-2		Estudiantes LP
1970	Feyenoord	2-2	1-0		Estudiantes LP
1971	Nacional Montevideo	1-1	2-1		Panathinaikos
1972	Ajax	1-1	3-0		Independiente
1973	Independiente	1-0			Juventus
1974	Atletico Madrid	0-1	2-0		Independiente
1975	No Competition				
1976	Bayern Munich	2-0	0-0		Cruzeiro

1977	Boca Juniors	2-2	3-0		B. Monch'bach
1978	*No Competition*				
1979	Olimpia	1-0	2-1		Malmo
1980	Nacional Montevideo	1-0			Nottingham Forest
1981	Flamengo	3-0			Liverpool
1982	Penarol	2-0			Aston Villa
1983	Gremio	2-1			Hamburg
1984	Independiente	1-0			Liverpool
1985	Juventus	2-2 (Won 4-2 on pen)			Argentinos Juniors
1986	River Plate	1-0			Steaua Bucharest
1987	FC Porto	2-1			Penarol
1988	Nacional Montevideo	2-2 (Won 7-6 on pen)			PSV Eindhoven
1989	Milan	1-0			Nacional Medellin
1990	Milan	3-0			Olimpia
1991	Red Star Belgrade	3-0			Colo Colo
1992	Sao Paulo	2-1			Barcelona

1992 Final Details

12th December 1992   *National Stadium, Tokyo*   *80,000*

Sao Paulo   **2**   **Barcelona**   **1**
Rai (26, 79)   Stoichkov (13)

Sao Paulo: Zetti, Victor, Adilson, Ronaldo, Pintado, Ronaldo Luiz, Muller,
Toninho Cerezo (Dinho), Palinha, Rai, Cafu
Barcelona: Zubizarreta, Ferrer, Guardiola, Koeman, Eusebio, Bakero
(Goicoechea), Amor, Stoichkov, Laudrup, Witschge, Berguiristain (Nadal)

The European Championship Final Details 1960-92

Results at a Glance

Year	Winners	Runners-up	Score	
1960	Soviet Union	Yugoslavia	2-1	
1964	Spain	Soviet Union	2-1	
1968	Italy	Yugoslavia	1-1	
	Italy	Yugoslavia	2-0	
1972	West Germany	Soviet Union	3-0	
1976	Czechoslovakia	West Germany	2-2	5-4 on pens
1980	West Germany	Belgium	2-1	
1984	France	Spain	2-0	
1988	Holland	Soviet Union	2-0	
1992	Denmark	Germany	2-0	

Final Line-ups and Scorers

1960

10th July 1960 *Parc des Princes, Paris* *18,000*

Soviet Union 2 **Yugoslavia** 1

Metreveli (49), Ponedelnik (113) Galic (41)

Soviet Union: Yashin, Tchekeli, Maslenkin, Droutikov, Voinov, Netto, Metreveli, Ivanov, Ponedelnik, Bubukin, Meshki

Yugoslavia: Vidinic, Durkovic, Miladinovic, Jusufi, Zanetic, Perusic, Sekularac, Jerkovic, Galic, Matus, Kostic

1964

21st June 1964 *Bernabeu, Madrid* *105,000*

Spain 2 **Soviet Union** 1

Pereda (6), Marcelino (83) Khusainov (8)

Spain: Iribar, Rivilla, Olivella, Calleja, Zoco, Fuste, Amancio, Pereda, Marcelino, Suarez, Lapetra

Soviet Union: Yashin, Chustikov, Shesterniev, Anitchkin, Mudrik,Voronin, Korniev, Chislenko, Ivanov V, Ponedelnik, Khusainov

1968

8th June 1968   *Stadio Olimpico, Rome*   *85,000*

Italy   **1**   **Yugoslavia**   **1**

Domenghini (80)   Dzajic (39)

Italy: Zoff, Burgnich, Guarneri, Facchetti, Ferrini, Castano, Domenghini, Juliano, Anastasi, Lodetti, Prati

Yugoslavia: Pantelic, Fazlagic, Paunovic, Holcer, Damjanovic, Pavlovic, Trivic, Petkovic, Musemic, Acimovic, Dzajic

Replay 10th June 1968   *Stadio Olimpico, Rome*   *50,000*

Italy   **2**   **Yugoslavia**   **0**

Riva (11), Anastasi (32)

Italy: Zoff, Burgnich, Guarneri, Facchetti, Rosato, Salvadore, Domenghini, Mazzola, Anastasi, De Sisti, Riva

Yugoslavia: Pantelic, Fazlagic, Paunovic, Holcer, Damjanovic, Pavlovic, Trivic, Acimovic, Musemic, Hosic, Dzajic

1972

18th June 1972   *Heysel, Brussels*   *65,000*

West Germany   **3**   **Soviet Union**   **0**

Muller (27, 58), Wimmer (52)

West Germany: Maier, Hottges, Schwarzenbeck, Beckenbauer, Breitner, Wimmer, Hoeness, Netzer, Heynckes, Muller, Kremmers

Soviet Union: Rudakov, Dzodzuashvili, Khurtsilava, Kaplichny, Istomin, Kolotov, Troshkin, Konkov (Dolmatov), Baidachni, Banishevski (Kozinkievits), Onishenko

1976

20th June 1976   *Red Star, Belgrade*   *45,000*

Czechoslovakia   **2**   **West Germany**   **2**

Svehlik (8), Dobias (25)   Muller D (28), Holzenbein (89)

Czechoslovakia won 5-4 on penalties

Czechoslovakia: Viktor, Pivarnik, Ondrus, Capkovic, Gogh, Dobias (Vesely F), Moder, Panenka, Masney, Svehlik (Jurkemik), Nehoda

West Germany: Maier, Vogts, Schwarzenbeck, Beckenbauer, Dietz, Wimmer (Flohe), Beer (Bongartz), Bongof, Hoeness, Muller D, Holzenbein

1980

22nd June 1980   *Stadio Olimpico, Rome*   *48,000*

West Germany   **2**   **Belgium**   **1**

Hrubesch (10, 88)   Vandereycken (72)

West Germany: Schumacher, Kaltz, Forster K-H, Stielike, Dietz, Briegel
(Cullmann), Schuster, Muller H, Rummenigge, Hrubesch, Allofs
Belgium: Pfaff, Gerets, Millecamps, Meeuws, Renquin, Cools,
Vandereycken, Van Moer, Mommens, Vander Elst, Ceulemans

1984

27th June 1984   *Parc des Princes, Paris*

France   **2**   **Spain**   **0**

Platini (57), Bellone (90)

France: Bats, Battiston (Amoros), Le Roux, Bossis, Domergue, Giresse,
Tigana, Fernandez, Platini, Lacombe (Genghini), Bellone
Spain: Arconada, Urquiaga, Salva (Roberto), Gallego, Senor, Francisco,
Victor, Camacho, Julio Alberto (Sarabia), Santillana, Carrasco

1988

25th June 1988   *Olympiastadion, Munich*   *72,000*

Holland   **2**   **Soviet Union**   **0**

Gullit (32), Van Basten (53)

Holland: Van Breukelen, Van Aerle, Rijkaard, Koeman R, Van Tiggelen,
Vanenburg, Wouters, Muhren, Koeman E, Gullit, Van Basten
Soviet Union: Dasayev, Demianenko, Aleinikov, Khidiatulin, Rats,
Litovchenko, Zavarov, Mikhailichenko, Gotsmanov (Baltacha), Protasov
(Pasulko), Belanov

1992

26th June 1992   *Nya Ullevi, Gothenburg*   *28,000*

Denmark   **2**   **Germany**   **0**

Jensen J (18), Vilfort (78)

Denmark: Schmeichel, Sivebaek (Christiansen), Nielsen K, Olsen L,
Piechnik, Christofte, Jensen J, Vilfort, Larsen H, Povlsen, Laudrup B
Germany: Illgner, Helmer, Reuter, Kohler, Buchwald, Brehme, Hassler,
Sammer (Doll), Effenberg (Thon), Riedle, Klinsmann

World Cup USA 1994
Qualifying Group Results

Group 1

Date	Team	Team	Score
16/08/92	Estonia	Switzerland	0-6
09/09/92	Switzerland	Scotland	3-1
14/10/92	Italy	Switzerland	2-2
14/10/92	Scotland	Portugal	0-0
25/10/92	Malta	Estonia	0-0
18/11/92	Scotland	Italy	0-0
18/11/92	Switzerland	Malta	3-0
19/12/92	Malta	Italy	1-2
24/01/93	Malta	Portugal	0-1
17/02/93	Scotland	Malta	3-0
24/02/93	Portugal	Italy	1-3
24/03/93	Italy	Malta	6-1
31/03/93	Switzerland	Portugal	1-1
14/04/93	Italy	Estonia	2-0
17/04/93	Malta	Switzerland	0-2
28/04/93	Portugal	Scotland	5-0
01/05/93	Switzerland	Italy	1-0
12/05/93	Estonia	Malta	0-1
19/05/93	Estonia	Scotland	0-3
02/06/93	Scotland	Estonia	3-1
19/06/93	Portugal	Malta	4-0
05/09/93	Estonia	Portugal	
08/09/93	Scotland	Switzerland	
22/09/93	Estonia	Italy	
13/10/93	Portugal	Switzerland	
13/10/93	Italy	Scotland	
10/11/93	Portugal	Estonia	
17/11/93	Italy	Portugal	
17/11/93	Malta	Scotland	
17/11/93	Switzerland	Estonia	

Table at 19 June 1993

		P	W	D	L	F	A	Pts
1.	Switzerland	7	5	2	0	18	4	12
2.	Italy	7	4	2	1	15	6	10
3.	Portugal	6	3	2	1	12	4	8
4.	Scotland	7	3	2	2	10	9	8
5.	Malta	9	1	1	7	3	21	3
6.	Estonia	6	0	1	5	1	15	1

Top two teams in Group qualify for finals.

Group 2

Date	Team	Team	Score
09/09/92	Norway	San Marino	10-0
23/09/92	Norway	Holland	2-1
23/09/92	Poland	Turkey	1-0
07/10/92	San Marino	Norway	0-2
14/10/92	England	Norway	1-1
14/10/92	Holland	Poland	2-2
28/10/92	Turkey	San Marino	4-1
18/11/92	England	Turkey	4-0
16/12/92	Turkey	Holland	1-3
17/02/93	England	San Marino	6-0
24/02/93	Holland	Turkey	3-1
10/03/93	San Marino	Turkey	0-0
24/03/93	Holland	San Marino	6-0
31/03/93	Turkey	England	0-2
28/04/93	England	Holland	2-2
28/04/93	Norway	Turkey	3-1
28/04/93	Poland	San Marino	1-0
19/05/93	San Marino	Poland	0-3
29/05/93	Poland	England	1-1
02/06/93	Norway	England	2-0
09/06/93	Holland	Norway	0-0
08/09/93	England	Poland	
22/09/93	Norway	Poland	
22/09/93	San Marino	Holland	
13/10/93	Holland	England	
13/10/93	Poland	Norway	
27/10/93	Turkey	Poland	
10/11/93	Turkey	Norway	
16/11/93	San Marino	England	
17/11/93	Poland	Holland	

Table at 9 June 1993

		P	W	D	L	F	A	Pts
1.	Norway	7	5	2	0	20	3	12
2.	England	7	3	3	1	16	6	9
3.	Holland	7	3	3	1	17	8	9
4.	Poland	5	3	2	0	8	3	8
5.	Turkey	8	1	1	6	7	17	3
6.	San Marino	8	0	1	7	1	32	1

Top two teams in Group qualify for finals.

Group 3

Date	Team	Team	Score
22/04/92	Spain	Albania	3-0
28/04/92	Northern Ireland	Lithuania	2-2
26/05/92	Rep. Ireland	Albania	2-0
03/06/92	Albania	Lithuania	1-0
12/08/92	Latvia	Lithuania	1-2
26/08/92	Latvia	Denmark	0-0
09/09/92	Northern Ireland	Albania	3-0
09/09/92	Rep. Ireland	Latvia	4-0
23/09/92	Lithuania	Denmark	0-0
23/09/92	Latvia	Spain	0-0
14/10/92	Denmark	Rep. Ireland	0-0
14/10/92	Northern Ireland	Spain	0-0
28/10/92	Lithuania	Latvia	1-1
11/11/92	Albania	Latvia	1-1
18/11/92	Northern Ireland	Denmark	0-1
18/11/92	Spain	Rep. Ireland	0-0
16/12/92	Spain	Latvia	5-0
17/02/93	Albania	Northern Ireland	1-2
24/02/93	Spain	Lithuania	5-0
31/03/93	Denmark	Spain	1-0
31/03/93	Rep. Ireland	Northern Ireland	3-0
14/04/93	Denmark	Latvia	2-0
14/04/93	Lithuania	Albania	3-1
28/04/93	Rep. Ireland	Denmark	1-1
28/04/93	Spain	Northern Ireland	3-1
15/05/93	Latvia	Albania	0-0
25/05/93	Lithuania	Northern Ireland	0-1
26/05/93	Albania	Rep. Ireland	1-2
02/06/93	Denmark	Albania	4-0

02/06/93	Lithuania	Spain	0-2
02/06/93	Latvia	Northern Ireland	1-2
09/06/93	Latvia	Rep. Ireland	0-2
16/06/93	Lithuania	Rep. Ireland	0-1
25/08/93	Denmark	Lithuania	
08/09/93	Albania	Denmark	
08/09/93	Rep. Ireland	Lithuania	
08/09/93	Northern Ireland	Latvia	
22/09/93	Albania	Spain	
13/10/93	Denmark	Northern Ireland	
13/10/93	Rep. Ireland	Spain	
17/11/93	Northern Ireland	Rep. Ireland	
17/11/93	Spain	Denmark	

Table at 16 June 1993

		P	W	D	L	F	A	Pts
1.	Rep. Ireland	9	6	3	0	14	2	15
2.	Spain	9	5	3	1	18	2	13
3.	Denmark	8	4	4	0	9	1	12
4.	Northern Ireland	9	4	2	3	11	10	10
5.	Lithuania	10	2	3	5	8	15	7
6.	Latvia	11	0	5	6	4	19	5
7.	Albania	10	1	2	7	5	20	4

Top two teams in Group qualify for finals.

Group 4

Date	Team	Team	Score
22/04/92	Belgium	Cyprus	1-0
06/05/92	Romania	Faeroe Islands	7-0
20/05/92	Romania	Wales	5-1
03/06/92	Faeroe Islands	Belgium	0-3
16/06/92	Faeroe Islands	Cyprus	0-2
02/09/92	Czechoslovakia	Belgium	1-2
09/09/92	Wales	Faeroe Islands	6-0
23/09/92	Czechoslovakia	Faeroe Islands	4-0
14/10/92	Belgium	Romania	1-0
14/10/92	Cyprus	Wales	0-1
14/11/92	Romania	Czechoslovakia	1-1
18/11/92	Belgium	Wales	2-0
29/11/92	Cyprus	Romania	1-4

14/02/93	Cyprus	Belgium	0-3
24/03/93	Cyprus	Czechoslovakia	1-1
31/03/93	Wales	Belgium	2-0
14/04/93	Romania	Cyprus	2-1
25/04/93	Cyprus	Faeroe Islands	3-1
28/04/93	Czechoslovakia	Wales	1-1
22/05/93	Belgium	Faeroe Islands	3-0
02/06/93	Czechoslovakia	Romania	5-2
06/06/93	Faeroe Islands	Wales	0-3
16/06/93	Faeroe Islands	Czechoslovakia	0-3
08/09/93	Wales	Czechoslovakia	
08/09/93	Faeroe Islands	Romania	
13/10/93	Romania	Belgium	
13/10/93	Wales	Cyprus	
27/10/93	Czechoslovakia	Cyprus	
17/11/93	Wales	Romania	
17/11/93	Belgium	Czechoslovakia	

Table at 16 June 1993

		P	W	D	L	F	A	Pts
1.	Belgium	8	7	0	1	15	3	14
2.	Romania	7	4	1	2	21	10	9
3.	Czechoslovakia	7	3	3	1	16	7	9
4.	Wales	7	4	1	2	14	8	9
5.	Cyprus	8	2	1	5	8	13	5
6.	Faeroe Islands	9	0	0	9	1	34	0

Top two teams in Group qualify for finals.

Group 5

Date	Team	Team	Score
13/05/92	Greece	Iceland	1-0
03/06/92	Hungary	Iceland	1-2
02/09/92	Iceland	Yugoslavia	postponed
09/09/92	Luxembourg	Hungary	0-3
23/09/92	Yugoslavia	Russia	postponed
07/10/92	Iceland	Greece	0-1
14/10/92	Russia	Iceland	1-0
28/10/92	Russia	Luxembourg	2-0
11/11/92	Greece	Hungary	0-0
17/02/93	Greece	Luxembourg	2-0

31/03/93	Hungary	Greece	0-1
14/04/93	Luxembourg	Russia	0-4
28/04/93	Russia	Hungary	3-0
20/05/93	Luxembourg	Iceland	1-1
23/05/93	Russia	Greece	1-1
02/06/93	Iceland	Russia	1-1
16/06/93	Iceland	Hungary	2-0
08/09/93	Hungary	Russia	
08/09/93	Iceland	Luxembourg	
12/10/93	Luxembourg	Greece	
27/10/93	Hungary	Luxembourg	
17/11/93	Greece	Russia	

Table at 16 June 1993

		P	W	D	L	F	A	Pts
1.	RUSSIA	6	4	2	0	12	2	10
2.	GREECE	6	4	2	0	6	1	10
3.	Iceland	7	2	2	3	6	6	6
4.	Hungary	6	1	1	4	4	8	3
5.	Luxembourg	5	0	1	4	1	12	1

Russia and Greece qualify for finals. Yugoslavia excluded due to UN sanctions.

Group 6

Date	Team	Team	Score
14/05/92	Finland	Bulgaria	0-3
09/09/92	Bulgaria	France	2-0
09/09/92	Finland	Sweden	0-1
07/10/92	Sweden	Bulgaria	2-0
14/10/92	France	Austria	2-0
28/10/92	Austria	Israel	5-2
11/11/92	Israel	Sweden	1-3
14/11/92	France	Finland	2-1
02/12/92	Israel	Bulgaria	0-2
17/02/93	Israel	France	0-4
27/03/93	Austria	France	0-1
14/04/93	Austria	Bulgaria	3-1
28/04/93	Bulgaria	Finland	2-0
28/04/93	France	Sweden	2-1
12/05/93	Bulgaria	Israel	2-2
13/05/93	Finland	Austria	3-1

19/05/93	Sweden	Austria	1-0
02/06/93	Sweden	Israel	5-0
16/06/93	Finland	Israel	0-0
22/08/93	Sweden	France	
25/08/93	Austria	Finland	
08/09/93	Finland	France	
08/09/93	Bulgaria	Sweden	
13/10/93	France	Israel	
13/10/93	Bulgaria	Austria	
13/10/93	Sweden	Finland	
27/10/93	Israel	Austria	
10/11/93	Austria	Sweden	
10/11/93	Israel	Finland	
17/11/93	France	Bulgaria	

Table at 16 June 1993

		P	W	D	L	F	A	Pts
1.	Sweden	6	5	0	1	13	3	10
2.	France	6	5	0	1	11	4	10
3.	Bulgaria	7	4	1	2	12	7	9
4.	Austria	6	2	0	4	9	10	4
5.	Finland	6	1	1	4	4	9	3
6.	Israel	7	0	2	5	5	21	2

Top two teams in Group qualify for finals

The World Cup Final Details 1930-1990

1930

30th July 1930　　　　　　*Centenario, Montevideo*　　93,000

Uruguay　　　　　**4**　　　　**Argentina**　　　　**2**

Dorado (12), Cea (58), Iriarte (68), Castro (89)　　Peucelle (20), Stabile (37)

Uruguay: Ballesteros, Nasazzi, Mascheroni, Andrade J, Fernandez, Gestido, Dorado, Scarone, Castro, Cea, Iriarte

Argentina: Botasso, Della Torre, Paternoster, Evaristo J, Monti, Suarez, Peucelle, Varallo, Stabile, Ferreira, Evaristo M

1934

10th June 1934　　　　　　*PNF, Rome*　　　　55,000

Italy　　　　　**2**　　　　**Czechoslovakia**　　　**1**

Orsi (81), Schiavio (95)　　　　　　Puc (71)

Italy: Combi, Monzeglio, Allemandi, Ferraris IV, Monti, Bertoloni, Guaita, Meazza, Schiavio, Ferrari, Orsi

Czechoslovakia: Planicka, Zenisek, Ctyroky, Kostalek, Cambal, Krcil, Junek, Svoboda, Sobotka, Nejedly, Puc

1938

19th June 1938　　　　　　*Colombes, Paris*　　　　55,000

Italy　　　　　**4**　　　　**Hungary**　　　　**2**

Colaussi (5, 35), Piola (16, 82)　　Titkos (7), Sarosi (70)

Italy: Olivieri, Foni, Rava, Serantoni, Andreolo, Locatelli, Biavati, Meazza, Piola, Ferrari, Colaussi

Hungary: Szabo, Polgar, Biro, Szalay, Szucs, Lazar, Sas, Vincze, Sarosi, Szengeller, Titkos

1950

16th July 1950　　　　　　*Maracana, Rio*　　　　199,000

Uruguay　　　　　**2**　　　　**Brazil**　　　　**1**

Schiaffino (66), Ghiggia (79)　　　Friaca (48)

Uruguay: Maspoli, Gonzales, Tejera, Gambetta, Varela O, Andrade V, Ghiggia, Perez, Miguez, Schiaffino, Moran

Brazil: Barbosa, Augusto, Juvenal, Bauer, Danilo, Bigode, Friaca, Zizinho, Ademir, Jair R Pinto, Chico

1954

4th July 1954   *Wankdorf, Berne*   *60,000*
West Germany   **3**   **Hungary**   **2**
Morlock (11), Rahn (16, 83)   Puskas (6), Czibor (8)
West Germany: Turek, Posipal, Liebrich, Kohlmeyer, Eckel, Mai, Rahn,
Morlock, Walter O, Walter F, Schafer
Hungary: Grosics, Buzanszky, Lorant, Lantos, Bozsik, Zakarias, Czibor,
Kocsis, Hidegkuti, Puskas, Toth

1958

29th June 1958   *Rasunda, Stockholm*   *49,000*
Brazil   **5**   **Sweden**   **2**
Vava (10, 32), Pele (56, 89), Zagalo (68)   Liedholm (4), Simonsson (80)
Brazil: Gilmar, Djalma Santos, Bellini, Orlando Pecanha, Nilton Santos, Zito,
Didi, Garrincha, Vava, Pele, Zagalo
Sweden: Svensson, Bergmark, Gustavsson, Axbom, Borjesson, Parling,
Hamrin, Gren G, Simonsson, Liedholm, Skoglund

1962

17th June 1962   *Estadio Nacional, Santiago 68,000*
Brazil   **3**   **Czechoslovakia**   **1**
Amarildo (18), Zito (69), Vava (77)   Masopust (16)
Brazil: Gilmar, Djalma Santos, Mauro R. Oliveira, Zozimo, Nilton Santos,
Zito, Didi, Garrincha, Vava, Amarildo, Zagalo
Czechoslovakia: Schrojf, Tichy, Pluskal, Popluhar, Novak, Kvasnak,
Masopust, Pospichal, Scherer, Kadraba, Jelinek

1966

30th July 1966   *Wembley, London*   *96,000*
England   **4**   **West Germany**   **2**
Hurst (19, 100, 119), Peters (77)   Haller (13), Weber (89)
England: Banks, Cohen, Charlton J, Moore, Wilson, Stiles, Charlton B, Ball,
Hunt, Hurst, Peters
West Germany: Tilkowski, Hottges, Schulz, Weber, Schnellinger, Haller,
Beckenbauer, Seeler, Held, Overath, Emmerich

1970

21st June 1970   *Azteca, Mexico City*   *107,000*
Brazil   **4**   **Italy**   **1**
Pele (18), Gerson (66), Jairzinho (71),   Boninsegna (37)
Carlos Alberto (86)

Brazil: Felix, Carlos Alberto, Brito, Piazza, Everaldo, Clodoaldo, Gerson, Jairzinho, Tostao, Pele, Rivelino
Italy: Albertosi, Burgnich, Cera, Rosato, Facchetti, Bertini (Juliano), Mazzola, De Sisti, Domenghini, Boninsegna (Rivera), Riva

1974

7th July 1974   *Olymiastadion, Munich*   77,000

West Germany   **2**   **Holland**   **1**

Breitner (25), Muller (43)   Neeskens (1)

West Germany: Maier, Vogts, Schwarzenbeck, Beckenbauer, Breitner, Bonhof, Hoeness, Overath, Grabowski, Muller, Holzenbein
Holland: Jongbloed, Suurbier, Rijsbergen (De Jong), Haan, Krol, Jansen, Neeskens, Van Hanegem, Rep, Cruyff, Rensenbrink (Van de Kerkhof)

1978

25th June 1978   *Monumental, Buenos Aires* 77,000

Argentina   **3**   **Holland**   **1**

Kempes (37, 104), Bertoni (114)   Nanninga (81)

Argentina: Fillol, Olguin, Galvan, Passarella, Tarantini, Ardiles (Larrosa), Gallego, Kempes, Bertoni, Luque, Ortiz (Houseman)
Holland: Jongbloed, Krol, Poortvliet, Brandts, Jansen (Suurbier), Van de Kerkhof W, Neeskens, Haan, Rep (Nanninga), Rensenbrink, Van de Kerkhof R

1982

11th July 1982   *Bernabeu, Madrid*   90,000

Italy   **3**   **West Germany**   **1**

Rossi (56), Tardelli (69), Altobelli (80)   Breitner (82)

Italy: Zoff, Cabrini, Scirea, Gentile, Collavati, Oriali, Bergomi, Tardelli, Conti, Rossi, Graziani (Altobelli) (Causio)
West Germany: Schumacher, Kaltz, Stielike, Forster K-H, Forster B, Breitner, Briegel, Dremmler (Hrubesch), Rummenigge (Muller), Littbarski, Fischer

1986

29th July 1986   *Azteca, Mexico City*   114,000

Argentina   **3**   **West Germany**   **2**

Brown (22), Valdano (56), Burruchaga (84)   Rummenigge (73), Voller (82)

Argentina: Pumpido, Cuciuffo, Brown, Ruggeri, Olarticoechea, Batista, Giusti, Enrique, Burruchaga (Trobbiani), Maradona, Valdano
West Germany: Schumacher, Jakobs, Forster K-H, Briegel, Brehme, Eder, Berthold, Matthaus, Magath (Hoeness), Rummenigge, Allofs (Voller)

1990

8th July 1990   *Olimpico, Rome*   *73,000*
West Germany   **1**   **Argentina**   **0**
Brehme (85)

West Germany: Illgner, Berthold, Kohler, Augenthaler, Buchwald, Brehme,
Hassler, Matthaus, Littbarski, Voller, Klinsmann
Argentina: Goycochea, Ruggeri, Simon, Serrizuela, Sensini, Basualdo,
Burruchaga, Trogilo, Lorenzo, Maradona, Dezotti

	Ajax	Cambuur Leeu'	Feyenoord	Go Ahead	FC Groningen	SC Heerenveen	MVV Maastricht	NAC	PSV Eindhoven	RKC	Roda JC
Ajax	•	6/3	24/10	28/11	17/4	30/4	15/1	4/4	5/9	15/8	12/9
Cambuur Leeuwarden	25/9	•	18/12	5/2	28/8	8/9	12/3	21/8	30/10	27/11	20/11
Feyenoord	27/3	15/8	•	26/9	27/2	13/3	31/10	6/2	24/4	30/1	8/5
Go Ahead Eagles	23/4	4/9	5/3	•	23/10	9/4	4/12	2/10	15/1	4/4	29/1
FC Groningen	21/11	30/1	12/9	27/3	•	31/10	24/4	6/3	25/8	20/3	25/8
SC Heerenveen	4/12	19/2	2/10	6/11	4/4	•	7/5	19/3	19/2	16/4	4/9
MVV Maastricht	1/9	2/10	4/4	30/4	27/11	11/12	•	6/11	•	25/8	5/3
NAC	30/10	15/1	4/9	12/3	25/9	16/10	9/4	•	4/12	19/2	14/8
PSV Eindhoven	5/2	4/4	27/11	21/8	18/12	22/1	8/9	30/4	•	2/10	23/10
RKC	19/12	24/4	29/8	31/10	17/10	21/11	23/1	8/9	13/3	•	10/4
Roda JC	27/2	17/4	12/12	28/8	23/1	19/12	26/9	19/12	27/3	7/11	•
Sparta Rotterdam	23/1	20/3	7/11	12/12	1/5	6/2	29/8	17/4	12/9	5/9	3/10
FC Twente	17/10	8/5	23/1	27/2	8/9	19/12	27/3	29/8	21/11	16/1	5/12
FC Urecht	22/8	7/11	1/5	23/1	1/9	26/9	27/2	12/12	17/10	24/10	4/4
Vitesse Arnhem	29/8	24/10	17/4	19/12	12/12	29/8	6/2	28/11	6/3	12/9	20/3
FC Volendam	10/4	25/8	20/2	17/10	13/3	27/3	21/11	12/9	8/5	6/3	16/1
VVV	12/3	4/12	21/8	8/9	5/2	26/2	16/10	22/1	9/4	7/5	23/4
Willem II	7/5	11/9	19/3	16/4	6/11	27/11	14/8	23/10	29/1	4/12	19/2

	Sparta Rot'dam	FC Twente	FC Utrecht	Vitesse Arnhem	FC Volendam	VVV	Willem II
Ajax	25/8	20/3	20/2	30/1	7/11	3/10	12/12
Cambuur Leeuwarden	16/10	11/12	9/4	26/3	22/1	30/4	26/2
Feyenoord	10/4	25/8	5/12	21/11	8/9	16/1	17/10
Go Ahead Eagles	7/5	11/9	25/8	14/8	19/3	19/2	20/11
FC Groningen	5/12	20/2	16/1	8/5	3/10	5/9	10/4
SC Heerenveen	14/8	5/3	29/1	15/1	23/10	11/9	23/4
MVV Maastricht	29/1	23/10	11/9	4/9	16/4	19/3	18/12
NAC	20/11	29/1	7/5	23/4	26/2	25/8	6/3
PSV Eindhoven	26/2	16/4	19/3	25/9	11/12	6/11	28/8
RKC	6/2	22/8	27/3	27/2	26/9	12/12	1/5
Roda JC	13/3	1/5	31/10	17/10	22/8	28/11	8/9
Sparta Rotterdam	•	4/4	6/3	20/2	28/11	24/10	22/8
FC Twente	31/10	•	24/4	10/4	6/2	15/8	13/3
FC Utrecht	26/9	28/11	•	13/3	19/12	17/4	6/2
Vitesse Arnhem	8/9	7/11	3/10	•	1/5	4/4	23/1
FC Volendam	24/4	5/9	15/8	5/12	•	30/1	31/10
VVV	26/3	18/12	20/11	30/10	28/8	•	26/9
Willem II	15/1	2/10	4/9	25/8	4/4	5/3	•

FRENCH LEAGUE

	Angers	Auxerre	Bordeaux	Caen	Cannes	Le Havre	Lens	Lille	Lyon	Marseille	Martigues
Angers	•	15/11	26/3	27/11	29/1	2/10	8/1	9/4	7/8	29/10	14/8
Auxerre	11/8	•	10/11	11/12	29/10	3/3	18/9	27/11	28/8	23/4	29/11
Bordeaux	23/10	16/4	•	11/3	7/8	3/12	3/5	24/9	6/11	5/2	20/11
Caen	3/5	7/8	16/10	•	1/9	29/1	14/8	29/10	3/12	9/4	15/12
Cannes	11/9	2/4	11/12	15/1	•	9/4	11/3	11/8	24/9	31/7	6/10
Le Havre	25/2	6/10	31/7	11/9	6/11	•	23/10	18/12	11/3	11/12	2/4
Lens	28/8	5/2	27/11	18/12	16/10	26/3	•	18/12	11/9	7/5	24/9
Lille	6/11	3/5	18/2	2/4	18/12	14/8	7/8	•	20/11	2/10	24/7
Lyon	11/12	8/1	9/4	31/7	18/2	16/10	29/1	23/4	•	10/11	1/9
Marseille	2/4	20/11	18/9	6/11	3/12	7/8	29/1	23/4	16/4	•	3/5
Martigues	18/12	11/9	23/4	11/8	3/3	29/10	18/2	25/2	15/1	27/11	•
Metz	31/7	14/8	29/1	11/8	2/10	18/9	1/9	10/11	15/12	18/2	8/1
Monaco	24/9	11/3	11/8	25/2	16/4	20/11	2/4	11/9		28/8	23/10
Montpellier	20/11	3/12	3/3	16/4	18/9	1/9	15/12	26/3	6/10	16/10	7/8
Nantes	5/2	28/10	18/12	24/9	20/11	1/9	16/4	31/7	24/7	11/8	6/11
Paris St Germain	15/1	24/9	7/5	28/8	26/5	3/5	6/10	31/7	25/2	18/12	25/2
Saint Etienne	11/3	6/11	28/8	6/10	24/7	15/12	20/11	5/2	5/2	15/1	16/4
Sochaux	24/7	1/9	29/10	23/4	8/1	18/2	2/10	3/3	14/8	26/3	3/12
Strasbourg	16/4	24/7	2/10	23/10	14/8	8/1	3/12	16/10	3/5	3/3	18/9
Toulouse	6/10	25/2	15/1	5/2	3/5	24/7	6/11	28/8	23/10	11/9	11/3

	Metz	Monaco	Montpellier	Nantes	Paris SG	Saint Etienne	Sochaux	Strasbourg	Toulouse
Angers	3/12	18/2	23/4	18/9	1/9	16/10	7/5	10/11	3/3
Auxerre	18/12	16/10	31/7	26/3	18/2	9/4	15/1	7/5	2/10
Bordeaux	11/9	15/12	6/10	14/8	24/7	8/1	2/4	25/2	1/9
Caen	24/7	2/10	10/11	18/2	8/1	3/3	20/11	26/3	18/9
Cannes	25/2	10/11	5/2	23/4	23/10	7/5	28/8	18/12	27/11
Le Havre	5/2	23/4	15/1	27/11	16/4	11/8	24/9	28/8	7/5
Lens	15/1	29/10	11/8	10/11	3/3	23/4	25/2	31/7	9/4
Lille	16/4	29/1	23/10	1/9	3/12	18/9	6/10	11/3	8/1
Lyon	11/8	3/3	7/5	1/9	18/9	29/10	18/12	27/11	26/3
Marseille	24/9	8/1	11/3	2/10	14/8	1/9	23/10	6/10	29/1
Martigues	28/8	26/3	11/12	9/4	2/10	10/11	31/7	5/2	16/10
Metz	•	27/11	9/4	3/3	16/10	26/3	11/12	23/4	29/10
Monaco	3/5	•	18/12	7/5	6/11	11/12	5/2	15/1	31/7
Montpellier	6/11	14/8	•	8/1	29/1	2/10	3/5	29/10	18/2
Nantes	6/10	24/7	28/8	•	2/4	31/7	11/3	11/9	11/12
Paris St Germain	11/3	9/4	11/9	29/10	•	27/11	11/8	11/12	23/4
Saint Etienne	23/10	7/8	25/2	3/12	3/5	•	11/9	24/9	14/8
Sochaux	7/8	18/9	27/11	16/10	15/12	29/1	•	9/4	10/11
Strasbourg	20/11	1/9	2/4	29/1	7/8	18/2	6/11	•	15/12
Toulouse	2/4	3/12	24/9	7/8	20/11	18/12	16/4	11/8	•

	Atalanta	Cagliari	Cremonese	Foggia	Genoa	Internazionale	Juventus	Lazio	Lecce	Milan	Napoli
Atalanta	•	29/8	19/9	24/10	19/12	1/5	27/2	5/12	13/3	30/1	17/4
Cagliari	9/1	•	6/3	6/2	23/1	12/9	27/3	26/9	2/1	24/4	17/10
Cremonese	6/2	24/10	•	13/3	1/5	23/1	9/1	12/9	7/11	26/9	5/9
Foggia	6/3	19/9	31/10	•	17/4	5/9	12/9	9/1	23/1	17/10	1/5
Genoa	24/4	11/9	2/1	12/12	•	21/11	13/3	2/4	27/2	16/1	19/9
Internazionale	2/1	30/1	11/9	16/1	27/3	•	28/11	6/2	10/4	7/11	20/2
Juventus	17/10	21/11	29/8	30/1	31/10	2/4	•	17/4	13/2	6/3	5/12
Lazio	10/4	13/2	30/1	29/8	28/11	19/9	12/12	•	24/4	20/2	20/3
Lecce	31/10	1/5	20/3	11/9	17/10	5/12	26/9	19/12	•	29/8	6/3
Milan	12/9	19/12	13/2	27/2	5/9	20/3	24/10	3/10	9/1	•	21/11
Napoli	12/12	27/2	16/1	2/1	6/2	3/10	10/4	7/11	24/10	27/3	•
Parma	27/3	17/4	27/2	3/10	12/9	13/3	7/11	23/1	5/9	28/11	19/12
Piacenza	20/3	3/10	10/4	28/11	6/3	13/2	24/4	27/2	19/9	11/9	31/10
Reggiana	23/1	5/12	21/11	21/11	20/2	9/1	6/2	5/9	12/12	2/4	2/4
Roma	26/9	2/4	3/10	7/11	9/1	19/12	5/9	24/10	27/3	6/2	12/9
Sampdoria	20/2	7/11	28/11	27/3	10/4	17/4	23/1	1/5	12/9	31/10	9/1
Torino	5/9	13/3	12/12	24/4	26/9	27/2	20/2	27/3	28/11	10/4	23/1
Udinese	28/11	16/1	24/4	10/4	7/11	24/10	2/1	13/3	3/10	12/12	13/2

FIXTURES 1993-94

	Parma	Piacenza	Reggiana	Roma	Sampdoria	Torino	Udinese
Atalanta	21/11	7/11	11/9	13/2	3/10	16/1	2/4
Cagliari	12/12	20/2	10/4	28/11	20/3	31/10	5/9
Cremonese	17/10	5/12	27/3	20/2	2/4	17/4	19/12
Foggia	20/2	2/4	13/2	20/3	21/11	19/12	5/12
Genoa	30/1	24/10	3/10	29/8	5/12	13/2	20/3
Internazionale	31/10	26/9	29/8	24/4	12/12	17/10	6/3
Juventus	20/3	19/12	19/9	16/1	11/9	3/10	1/5
Lazio	11/9	17/10	16/1	6/3	2/1	21/11	31/10
Lecce	16/1	6/2	17/4	21/11	30/1	2/4	20/2
Milan	2/4	23/1	1/5	19/9	13/3	5/12	17/4
Napoli	24/4	13/3	28/11	30/1	29/8	11/9	26/9
Parma	•	1/5	24/10	10/4	13/2	19/9	9/1
Piacenza	2/1	•	30/1	12/12	16/1	29/8	21/11
Reggiana	6/3	12/9	•	31/10	24/4	20/3	17/10
Roma	5/12	17/4	13/3	•	27/2	1/5	23/1
Sampdoria	26/9	5/9	19/12	17/10	•	6/3	6/2
Torino	6/2	9/1	7/11	2/1	24/10	•	12/9
Udinese	29/8	27/3	27/2	11/9	19/9	30/1	•

GERMAN BUNDESLIGA

	B. Leverkusen	Bayern Munich	Bor. Dortmund	Bor. Mon'bach	Cologne	Dynamo Dresden	Ein. Frankfurt	Hamburg SV	Kaiserslautern	Karlsruher SC	MSV Duisburg
Bayer Leverkusen	•	14/8	28/8	5/3	4/9	23/4	18/9	19/2	19/3	2/4	27/11
Bayern Munich	14/2	•	19/3	16/10	2/4	22/8	9/4	2/10	30/10	13/11	26/2
Borussia Dortmund	12/2	25/9	•	29/10	9/4	1/9	23/4	16/10	12/11	6/8	12/3
Bor. Monchengladbach	7/9	6/4	16/4	•	30/4	12/3	6/8	5/11	4/12	12/2	9/10
Cologne	26/2	9/10	23/10	13/11	•	8/9	7/5	16/4	7/8	20/8	26/3
Dynamo Dresden	6/11	11/12	19/2	18/9	5/3	•	19/3	5/9	1/10	15/10	13/8
Eintracht Frankfurt	12/3	23/4	6/11	27/11	19/11	24/9	•	30/4	21/8	31/8	6/4
Hamburg SV	1/9	23/4	6/4	26/3	29/10	26/2	13/11	•	7/5	4/12	24/9
Kaiserslautern	25/9	16/4	30/4	14/8	27/11	26/3	11/12	2/11	•	26/2	22/10
Karlsruher SC	8/10	30/4	27/11	27/8	11/12	6/4	19/2	14/8	3/9	•	6/11
MSV Duisburg	7/8	4/9	18/9	2/4	1/10	4/12	15/10	19/3	9/4	23/4	•
Nuremberg	26/3	6/11	20/11	11/12	13/8	8/10	28/8	27/11	19/2	7/9	19/4
SC Freiburg	23/10	27/11	11/12	4/9	19/2	19/4	5/3	27/8	17/9	2/10	20/11
Schalke 04	6/4	20/11	15/8	19/2	28/8	23/10	4/9	11/12	23/4	19/3	30/4
SG Wattenscheid	20/8	12/3	2/10	2/10	15/10	12/2	30/10	2/4	17/10	30/10	8/9
VfB Leipzig	7/5	19/2	5/3	19/3	19/3	7/8	2/4	17/9	2/4	7/5	27/8
VfB Stuttgart	13/11	29/8	4/9		17/9	7/5	2/10	5/3	12/2	9/4	11/12
Werder Bremen	16/4	8/9	8/10	7/5	23/4	12/11	4/12	23/10		12/3	31/8

	Nuremberg	SC Freiburg	Schalke 04	SG War'cheid	VfB Leipzig	VfB Stuttgart	Werder Bremen
Bayer Leverkusen.........	2/10	9/4	16/10	11/12	20/11	30/4	30/10
Bayern Munich............	23/4	7/8	7/5	18/9	1/9	12/2	5/3
Borussia Dortmund.....	7/5	21/8	4/12	26/3	7/9	26/2	2/4
Bor. Monchengladbach	21/8	26/2	31/8	22/10	26/3	25/9	19/11
Cologne.......................	4/12	1/9	12/2	6/4	25/9	12/3	6/11
Dynamo Dresden.........	2/4	29/10	9/4	28/8	27/11	21/11	30/4
Eintracht Frankfurt.....	12/2	8/9	26/2	16/4	9/10	26/3	14/8
Hamburg SV................	6/8	12/2	21/8	9/10	12/3	8/9	9/4
Kaiserslautern............	31/8	12/3	8/9	5/11	6/4	9/10	28/8
Karlsruher SC..............	5/3	26/3	24/9	19/11	19/4	23/10	18/9
MSV Duisburg.............	30/10	7/5	12/11	5/3	12/2	21/8	19/2
Nuremberg..................	•	25/9	12/3	30/4	22/10	6/4	3/9
SC Freiburg.................	19/3	•	2/4	14/8	30/4	6/11	16/10
Schalke 04...................	18/9	9/10	•	27/11	5/11	16/4	2/10
SG Wattenscheid.........	13/11	4/12	7/8	•	26/2	1/9	19/3
VfB Leipzig.................	9/4	14/11	23/4	4/9	•	4/12	11/12
VfB Stuttgart..............	16/10	23/4	30/10	19/2	14/8	•	27/11
Werder Bremen...........	26/2	6/4	26/3	25/9	17/8	8/8	•

European Club Competition Diary 1993-94

Month	Date	Competition	Round
August	17/18	C1, C2	Preliminary Round, 1st Legs
	31/01	C1, C2	Preliminary Round, 2nd Legs
September	14/15	C1, C2, C3	1st Round, 1st Legs
	28/29	C1, C2, C3	1st Round, 2nd Legs
October	19/20	C1, C2, C3	2nd Round, 1st Legs
November	02/03	C1, C2, C3	2nd Round, 2nd Legs
	24	Champions' League	Series one matches
	23/24	C3	3rd Round, 1st Legs
December	08	Champions' League	Series two matches
	07/08	C3	3rd Round, 2nd Legs
March	02	Champions' League	Series three matches
	01/02	C2, C3	Quarter-Finals, 1st Legs
	16	Champions' League	Series four matches
	15/16	C2, C3	Quarter-Finals, 2nd Legs
	30	Champions' League	Series five matches
	29/30	C2, C3	Semi-Finals, 1st Legs
April	13	Champions' League	Series six matches
	12/13	C2, C3	Semi-Finals, 2nd Legs
	27	C1	Semi-Finals †
	26/28	C3	Final, 1st Leg
May	04	C2	Final
	11	C3	Final, 2nd Leg
	18	C1	Final

† *Champions' Cup Semi-Finals played as single tie on grounds of the clubs finishing top of their respective Champions' League groups.*